How to Organize and Write a Legal Memorandum

ASPEN SELECT SERIES

How to Organize and Write a Legal Memorandum

Paul H. Falon

Wolters Kluwer

Published by Wolters Kluwer in New York.

Wolters Kluwer Legal & Regulatory U.S. serves customers worldwide with CCH, Aspen Publishers, and Kluwer Law International products. (www.WKLegaledu.com)

To contact Customer Service, e-mail customer.service@wolterskluwer.com, call 1-800-234-1660, fax 1-800-901-9075, or mail correspondence to:

Wolters Kluwer
Attn: Order Department
PO Box 990
Frederick, MD 21705

Printed in the United States of America.

1 2 3 4 5 6 7 8 9 0

ISBN 978-1-5438-2115-4

Cover image: iStock/alexi.

Library of Congress Cataloging-in-Publication Data

Names: Falon, Paul H., 1951- author.
Title: How to organize and write a legal memorandum / Paul H. Falon.
Description: New York : Wolters Kluwer, [2020] | Series: Aspen select series | Includes index. | Summary: "This book explains how to organize and write legal memoranda that will communicate information to the reader clearly and effectively. It is written primarily for first-year law students, but upper-class law students and practicing attorneys can also use it, to produce more effective legal memoranda or written legal analyses generally"-- Provided by publisher.
Identifiers: LCCN 2020022301 (print) | LCCN 2020022302 (ebook) | ISBN 9781543821154 (paperback) | ISBN 9781543821161 (ebook)
Subjects: LCSH: Legal composition. | LCGFT: Casebooks (Law)
Classification: LCC KF250 .F365 2020 (print) | LCC KF250 (ebook) | DDC 808.06/634--dc23
LC record available at https://lccn.loc.gov/2020022301
LC ebook record available at https://lccn.loc.gov/2020022302

About Wolters Kluwer Legal & Regulatory U.S.

Wolters Kluwer Legal & Regulatory U.S. delivers expert content and solutions in the areas of law, corporate compliance, health compliance, reimbursement, and legal education. Its practical solutions help customers successfully navigate the demands of a changing environment to drive their daily activities, enhance decision quality and inspire confident outcomes.

Serving customers worldwide, its legal and regulatory portfolio includes products under the Aspen Publishers, CCH Incorporated, Kluwer Law International, ftwilliam.com and MediRegs names. They are regarded as exceptional and trusted resources for general legal and practice-specific knowledge, compliance and risk management, dynamic workflow solutions, and expert commentary.

For my Legal Practice students
at The University of Michigan Law School

Summary of Contents

Table of Contents

Acknowledgments

I would like to thank Grace Tonner, former Director of the Legal Practice Program at The University of Michigan Law School, for allowing me to use two of her memorandum assignments when I first joined the faculty and had yet to develop memorandum assignments of my own. Some of the examples included in the text of this book derive from student submissions on the assignments I borrowed from Grace. In particular, I would like to thank Legal Practice students Christopher Lee and Poul Lundgren for the examples I derived from their submissions.

I would also like to thank the following Legal Practice students, whose submissions on the memorandum assignments I developed form the basis for the amalgamated and edited Sample Legal Memorandum, Sample Informal Memorandum, and Sample E-mail Memorandum included at the end of the book: Madeline Buck, Meredith Collier, Jenna Goldstein, Joshua Heller, Katie Martin-Browne, Daniel Prieve, Christine Quinn, Alexander Reed, Elissa Reidy, and Alexander Terepka.

Finally, I would like to thank the editors with whom I have worked on this book project: Richard Mixter, my original editor at Wolters Kluwer, for the encouragement he gave me at the start of the project; David Herzig and Justin Billing, my subsequent editors at Wolters Kluwer, for the help they gave me in bringing the project to completion; and Sara Nies, Associate Editor, Special Projects, at The Froebe Group, for the help she gave me in formatting the manuscript.

Introduction

i Legal writing and other writing

There is no difference between good legal writing and good expository writing on any other subject. Good writing is clear, well-organized, easy to understand, sufficiently detailed to convey and substantiate the writer's ideas, and appropriate in content, language, and tone for its intended audience and purpose.

Legal writing differs from other kinds of writing in terms of its subject matter, the types of documents attorneys create to address their subject matter, and certain strategies attorneys use to organize their documents effectively.

This book will introduce you to many of those strategies. It is written primarily for first-year law students, but upper-class law students and practicing attorneys can also use it, to produce more effective legal memoranda or written legal analyses generally.

ii Types of legal analysis

Legal writing often includes one or more of the following types of legal analysis.

ii.i Identifying the governing law

The most basic type of legal analysis simply identifies the source or sources of law that govern a specific subject or legal issue. The governing law may derive from a constitution, a statute, a regulation, an executive order, an international treaty, or another form of enacted law. It may derive from judicial decisions construing one or more forms of enacted law, or it may derive from judicial decisions alone, establishing the common law. Frequently, the governing law derives from a combination of enacted law and judge-made law.

Sometimes, there is governing law on a specific subject or legal issue, from one or more sources of law, but the law is not internally consistent, not fully developed, or not finally resolved. In that case, the attorney must identify the state of the law as it then exists. In some contexts, the attorney must decide which version of the existing law is more authoritative, more widely followed, or more persuasive.

Example ii.i.i (identifying the governing statutory and judicial law).

California Civil Code Section 1670.5 governs the unconscionability of contracts.

> (a) If the court as a matter of law finds the contract or any clause of the contract to have been unconscionable at the time it was made the court may refuse to enforce the contract, or it may enforce the remainder of the contract without the unconscionable clause, or it may so limit the application of any unconscionable clause as to avoid any unconscionable result.
> (b) When it is claimed or appears to the court that the contract or any clause thereof may be unconscionable the parties shall be afforded a reasonable opportunity to present evidence as to its commercial setting, purpose, and effect to aid the court in making the determination.

Cal. Civ. Code § 1670.5 (Deering 2006).

California courts have used two approaches to evaluate unconscionability. In the first approach, the courts initially determine if the contract is an adhesion contract. Graham v. Scissor-Tail, Inc., 623 P.2d 165, 171-72 (Cal. 1981). An adhesion contract is a standardized contract drafted by a party with superior bargaining strength; the weaker party can only "adhere to the contract or reject it." Id. at 171. If the contract is adhesive, the courts then determine if it either falls outside the "reasonable expectations" of the weaker party or is "unduly oppressive or 'unconscionable.'" Id. at 172-73.

In the second approach, the courts divide the analysis into procedural and substantive elements. A&M Produce Co. v. FMC Corp., 186 Cal. Rptr. 114, 121-22 (Ct. App. 1982). Procedural unconscionability focuses on how the contract is made and whether that process results in a customer's "oppression" or "surprise." Id. at 122. Substantive unconscionability focuses on the contract itself and whether its terms are overly "harsh" or "one-sided," among other factors. Id. Although both the procedural and substantive elements must be present to make the contract unconscionable, they need not be present in the same degree. Armendariz v. Found. Health Psychcare Serv., Inc., 6 P.3d 669, 690 (Cal. 2000). Thus, the courts invoke a "sliding scale," in which the more substantively unconscionable a contract is, the less evidence of procedural unconscionability is required, and vice versa. Id.

> California courts now generally favor this second approach, developed in A&M Produce. See, e.g., Discover Bank v. Super. Ct., 113 P.3d 1100, 1108 (Cal. 2005); Wayne v. Staples, Inc., 37 Cal. Rptr. 3d 544, 554 (Ct. App. 2006). Nevertheless, the California Supreme Court has acknowledged that either test should lead to the same result. Perdue v. Crocker Nat'l Bank, 702 P.2d 503, 511 n.9 (Cal. 1985).

Occasionally, there is no governing case law for a specific subject or legal issue; it has never been addressed by any court in the relevant jurisdiction. The issue is considered to be one of *first impression*.

ii.ii Explaining what the governing law means

Usually, legal analyses that identify what the law is also explain what the law means. The explanation can take different forms. It can explain the language of a provision of enacted law or a common-law rule, as the courts have interpreted the provision or rule, or, in the absence of any judicial interpretation, as the attorney believes it should be interpreted and why.

The explanation can describe how the courts have applied a provision or rule, in terms of one or more characteristics of the case law, such as the common fact patterns that do or do not satisfy the provision or rule; the types or degrees of evidence that do and do not satisfy the provision or rule; the stringency or leniency with which the courts apply the provision or rule; the consistency, inconsistency, or trends among the judicial interpretations of the provision or rule; or any other important legal principles, definitions, themes, reasoning, policies, patterns, or decision points that characterize the judicial decisions.

> **Example ii.ii.i (explaining the meaning of one factor in a judicial rule).**
>
> In examining claims of surprise—the second factor bearing on procedural unconscionability—courts typically consider the visual appearance of the contract, the seller's silence about its terms, and the relative sophistication of the parties involved. See A&M Produce, 186 Cal. Rptr. at 122, 124. First, the visual appearance of a contract creates surprise where "the supposedly agreed-upon terms of the bargain are hidden in a prolix printed form drafted by the party seeking to enforce the disputed terms." Id. at 122. For example, in Pardee Construction, the court found surprise where dense, single-spaced capital letters made the disputed term difficult to read. 123 Cal. Rptr. 2d at 294-95. Similarly, in Villa Milano, the court found surprise where the disputed term was buried on pages 67 and 68 of a 70-page contract. 102 Cal. Rptr. 2d at 7.

In the case of an issue of first impression, the explanation may need to describe analogous or persuasive authorities from other jurisdictions that address a similar provision or rule, as well any relevant social, legislative, or judicial policies, to predict what the new law governing the issue is likely to be.

ii.iii Applying the governing law to a set of facts

The most comprehensive type of legal analysis identifies the governing law, explains what that law means, and applies it to a set of facts involving the attorney's client or company or certain categories of people, businesses, or activities. The application can proceed by *analogy*: The facts involving the client, the company, or the category resemble the fact patterns that led to a given legal outcome in the prior judicial decisions, so the facts in question should produce the same outcome, too—positive or negative. The analogy can be stated in one or more sentences.

Example ii.iii.i (analogy in two sentences, similar fact patterns; both satisfy rule).

In Childs, the court found that a Super K-Mart provided important benefits to the surrounding community, by reducing local crime, increasing commerce in the area, and supporting residential property values. 2001 WL 1199901, at *4. Here, a court would find that Mr. Hendricks's motorcycle repair business also provides important benefits to the community, by ensuring that the residents have safe motorcycles to ride and, through the supplemental income he earns, by preventing additional home foreclosures in the neighborhood.

Example ii.iii.ii (analogy in single sentence, similar fact patterns; neither satisfies rule).

Just as the court in Rose found no significant harm in the complaining neighbor's respiratory discomfort, where she was extra-sensitive to smoke and fumes, 2009 WL 3276431, at *4, a court would probably find no significant harm in Mr. Lambert's migraines, where he happens to be extra-sensitive to noise.

(Sample Legal Memorandum 8:8-12)[1]

[1] References throughout the book to the Sample Legal Memorandum, the Sample Informal Memorandum, and the Sample E-mail Memorandum are to page numbers:line numbers.

The application of law to fact can proceed by *contrast*: The facts involving the client, the company, or the category differ in important ways from the fact patterns that led to a given legal outcome in the prior judicial decisions, so the facts in question should produce the opposite outcome—positive or negative. Attorneys call this type of legal analysis *distinguishing* the legal significance of one set of facts from that of another. The contrast can be stated in one or more sentences, too.

Example ii.iii.iii (contrast in two sentences, different fact patterns; two satisfy rule but third does not).

In both Mackenzie and Wilke, where the courts found significant harm, noise from the defendants' businesses prevented the plaintiffs from using and enjoying both the outside and the inside of their homes, much if not all of the time—five days a week in Mackenzie, 174 N.W. at 163, and seven days a week in Wilke, 2007 WL 1828788, at *4. Here, the noise from Mr. Hendricks's business only affects Mr. Lambert's backyard entertaining, only on weekends, and only during warm weather—which, in southeastern Michigan, is limited to half the year or less.

(Sample Legal Memorandum 10:28-11:5)

Finally, the application of law to fact can proceed with reference to important social, legislative, or judicial *policies* underlying the governing law and which, in the attorney's opinion, should inform the court's decision making—and produce a positive or negative outcome.

Example ii.iii.iv (reference to judicial policies; facts do not satisfy them).

Michigan's conflict of interest rules were promulgated, in part, to ensure that lawyers "adopt reasonable procedures, appropriate for the size and type of firm and practice, to determine in both litigation and nonlitigation matters . . . whether there are actual or potential conflicts of interest." MRPC 1.7 cmt. The rules also serve to give the public confidence that lawyers have adopted such procedures. Cobb I, 907 F. 1038 at 1050. A Michigan court, therefore, is likely to apply the conflict of interest rules stringently, to effectuate these underlying policies. In the case of the Newman firm's failure to screen Mr. Gillespie for the first three days after he began his employment, a court is likely to find that the firm violated Rule 1.10(b)(1), the extenuating circumstances notwithstanding.

iii The legal memorandum

Attorneys write memoranda to present the results of their legal research and analysis or of other kinds of work in which they are engaged. A legal memorandum is usually an internal document: One attorney in a law office prepares the memorandum for another attorney in the same office or for an attorney in a different office of the same employer. Occasionally, attorneys prepare a memorandum, or a special, edited version of a memorandum, for the client whose legal matters the attorneys are addressing.

iii.i Characteristics

The legal memorandum has three primary characteristics. First, the legal memorandum serves a business purpose. It must present the writer's analysis or information in a way that enables the reader—whether another attorney, a client, or both—to make a decision about one or more aspects of a matter they are addressing, for example, whether to file a lawsuit or how to structure a transaction to achieve a certain tax result.

Second, the legal memorandum requires objectivity. It must be thorough, impartial, and honest, to enable the reader to make an informed decision. It must present the strengths and any weaknesses of the client's legal position or the advantages and any disadvantages of alternate legal arguments or defenses, transactional structures, contract language, or other choices or courses of action.

Third, the legal memorandum frequently educates the reader. It must present the governing law or other background information to a reader who may be unfamiliar with some or all of it—especially if, as is usually the case, the writer did the underlying legal, factual, or document research.

These three characteristics dictate the way that attorneys organize and write legal memoranda. This book will cover the organizational structure of, and the writing conventions for, the legal memorandum in detail.

iii.ii Components

A formal, comprehensive legal research memorandum contains five major components: Heading, Question Presented, Brief Answer, Statement of Facts, and Discussion. Longer memoranda often include a final Conclusion as a separate, sixth major component. Informal and e-mail memoranda, which may address legal research and analysis or other matters arising in a law office, typically have fewer major components.

iii.iii Basic rule of organization

Present your conclusions first. Attorneys are busy people. When a colleague asks you to write a research memorandum, you should create a work product that enables the colleague to find the answers the colleague wants right away, whether to the overall legal issue or to the analysis of one part or sub-part of the applicable rule. The way to do that is to present your conclusions first, within the memorandum as a whole and within each section or subsection in the body of the memorandum. After each conclusion, at each level within the memorandum, add the supporting analysis and details. Even within most individual paragraphs, begin with the main point your reader should learn from the rest of the paragraph—in effect, your conclusion about the content of that paragraph. For memoranda that do not involve legal research, try to present the core content or import of, or the most important information about, the matter you addressed first.

iv Consistent approach to writing legal memoranda

The chapters that follow present a single, consistent approach to preparing the components of a legal memorandum and the various parts within each component. If you are a first-year law student who has never written a legal memorandum before, it will be easier for you to master the basic skills by concentrating on a consistent approach. After you have organized and written—and received feedback on—a number of legal memoranda, both in your legal writing class in law school and in your legal jobs, you will have acquired the experience and confidence to adapt these basic skills to any unique requirements of different assignments. Generally, however, the basic skills will remain appropriate for most of the organization and writing of most of the legal memoranda you will produce in practice. Individual law offices and attorneys may have their own customs, preferences, or requirements for one aspect or another, and you should conform your work product to those expectations. Absent any such reason for varying or departing from the basic approach set forth in this book, follow it.

v How to use this book

This book divides the legal memorandum into its component parts and in eleven chapters provides concise but specific instruction about the purpose, format, organization, and effective presentation of each part. The instruction is supplemented by examples taken from three complete memoranda, included at the end of the book, and from other sources—including examples of how *not* to organize or present different parts of a memorandum. In addition, several chapters addressing the main Discussion component of a memorandum end with short *Templates*—succinct, annotated outlines of the structure and content of the different parts of the Discussion—intended to assist the book's readers in moving from instruction to work product. Finally, the book contains two chapters on formatting a memorandum and writing clearly.

For ease of reference, the first ten chapters follow the order in which the component parts appear in a formal, comprehensive legal research memorandum; the eleventh chapter covers the component parts of informal and e-mail memoranda. You may consult the chapters in any order you find useful when planning, writing, or revising a memorandum, or in the order that your legal writing course covers these topics. If you are a first-year law student just learning about legal writing and analysis, you may wish to begin with Chapter 5, *How to Organize the Discussion*. Chapter 5 emphasizes the importance, during the research process, of identifying the judicial rule that applies to your legal issue and of using the structure of that rule to organize your substantive analysis in the Discussion. Identifying the rule and its structure will help you understand, and plan, your legal analysis before committing it to writing in the memorandum.

vi A note about nomenclature

Different attorneys and legal writing teachers refer to the components and parts within a legal memorandum by different names. Some of the names have acquired reasonably widespread currency, whereas others have not and just reflect individual preferences. For example, this book refers to the opening few paragraphs of the Discussion component as the *Overview* because they state the overall legal conclusion, the governing law and its important parts, and the key reasons supporting the conclusion—a high-level precis of the full analysis to follow. Other attorneys and teachers may refer to these opening paragraphs as the *roadmap* or by another name. The names do not matter: Use the names the assigning attorney or your legal writing teacher prefers. What matters is that you learn the underlying strategies and skills this book presents for organizing and writing effective legal memoranda.

Chapter 1
How to Write the Heading to a Memorandum

1.1 Purpose

The Heading is the first component of a legal memorandum. It identifies the person for whom it is written, the person who wrote it, the date of the memorandum, and the subject addressed by the memorandum.

1.2 Format

Print the Heading at the top of the first page of the document, below a label that identifies the type of document it is: *MEMORANDUM.* Line up the four categories in the Heading—*TO, FROM, DATE,* and *RE*—at the left margin. Line up the items that correspond to the four categories so they form a neat, vertical column; use tabs, not the space bar. Use capitalized, bold (but not italicized) fonts for the document label and the four categories. Use initial caps and regular fonts for the names, date, and subject. Follow the Heading by a single line across the page. Note, however, that many employers require attorneys to use a uniform visual format for their legal memoranda, contained in a macro on the office computers, with the company's name, logo, and perhaps its office address or other information printed at the top or the bottom of the page, or both. Obviously, you should use the memorandum format your employer requires, even if it differs from the format described in this book.

<u>**Example 1.2.1**</u> **(typical memorandum Heading).**

Employer's Name
Employer's Address

MEMORANDUM

TO:	Assigning Attorney's Name
FROM:	Writer's Name
DATE:	Date
RE:	Client: Matter

1.3 Names

Use the assigning attorney's first and last name and your first and last name. Include middle names or initials and *Jr.*, *III*, or similar suffixes if they are part of the name that a person uses professionally, but omit professional titles, such as *Esq.*, *Partner*, and *Associate.* If a more experienced person in the office advises you of a different practice or of a specific attorney's preference as to names in the Heading, follow that advice, whether the names are more formal (*Ms. Williams*) or more informal (*Mary Lou*).

1.4 Date

Use the date on which you complete the memorandum. The date is important to indicate when you conducted the legal research and analysis contained in the memorandum. Your employer may confront a similar legal issue in the future, and an attorney who refers back to your memorandum will need to know how current the research and analysis are.

1.5 Subject line

Use the subject line to identify the client and the specific matter the memorandum addresses—in that order. (If your assignment does not involve a client, just identify the specific matter.) The subject line in the Heading is usually denoted by *RE* or *SUBJECT.* Either one is acceptable, but be consistent. If your employer has a memorandum macro, it will specify one or the other. At some employers, a client-matter or file number is included in the subject line of the heading, too. Legal memoranda and other documents generated electronically will be stored within word processing folders on one or more computers throughout the office or in multiple offices. If an employer also maintains paper files, the subject line of a memorandum will help direct the hard copy to the correct client and matter file.

Chapter 2
How to Write the Question Presented

2.1 Purpose

The Question Presented is the second component of a legal memorandum. It identifies each legal issue you were asked to research. If you were asked to research multiple issues, use separate, numbered questions within the Question Presented component.

2.2 When to draft it

Draft the Question Presented early in your research process, to ensure that you understand what the issue is. Use it to help develop a research strategy aimed at answering the issue and to help keep your research focused on that issue. If necessary, revise your draft Question Presented as you learn more during the research process.

2.3 Format

There are two common formats for the Question Presented: (i) a single-sentence question, combining a potential legal result and a few key facts that may determine the result, and (ii) a few short sentences describing the key determinative facts, followed by a single-sentence question about the legal result from those facts. The single-sentence format is more common. If the number of key facts makes the sentence too long, however, use the multiple-sentence format. If your issue is a pure question of law, independent of a specific set of facts, use the single-sentence format. Indent the first line of the Question Presented.

2.3.1 The single-sentence Question Presented

Use a complete sentence. Although some attorneys prefer to begin the Question Presented with *Whether*, that results in a stilted-sounding sentence fragment. Organize the Question Presented by asking whether the potential legal result will follow from the key facts—in that order. Introduce the facts with a word such as *where*, *when*, or *if*.

Example 2.3.1.1 (single-sentence Question Presented, based on set of facts).

Does a home motorcycle repair business create a private nuisance under Michigan law where it operates on evenings and weekends and the intermittent noise it produces aggravates one neighbor's migraines, wakes the neighbor's young children, and interferes with the neighbor's backyard entertaining?

(Sample Legal Memorandum 1:10-14)

> **Comment.** In Example 2.3.1.1, the opening clause—*Does a home motorcycle repair business create a private nuisance under Michigan law*—states the potential legal result; it is phrased as a question. The rest of the sentence adds the key facts, introduced by *where*. The single-sentence format can accommodate the number of facts in this example, but any more facts would make it too long. It would be acceptable to rewrite this Question Presented using the multiple-sentence format. (See Example 2.3.2.1.)

Example 2.3.1.2 (single-sentence Question Presented, independent of set of facts).

Does Florida law recognize a cause of action for intentional infliction of emotional distress?

> **Comment.** The single-sentence format in Example 2.3.1.2 is appropriate for a pure question of law.

2.3.2 The multiple-sentence Question Presented

Begin with a few short sentences that state the key facts. End with a single, complete sentence that asks whether a potential legal result will follow. Do not include any facts in the final question.

<u>Example 2.3.2.1</u> (multiple-sentence Question Presented, based on set of facts).

A home motorcycle repair business operates on evenings and weekends. The intermittent noise it produces aggravates one neighbor's migraines, wakes the neighbor's young children, and interferes with the neighbor's backyard entertaining. Does the business create a private nuisance under Michigan law?

> **Comment.** Example 2.3.2.1 keeps the key facts in the opening sentences of the multiple-sentence format separate from the question about the legal result from those facts, stated in the final sentence.

<u>Example 2.3.2.2</u> (bad example: multiple-sentence Question Presented with facts included in final sentence).

A home motorcycle repair business operates on evenings and weekends and produces intermittent noise. Does the business create a private nuisance under Michigan law where the noise aggravates one neighbor's migraines, wakes the neighbor's young children, and interferes with the neighbor's backyard entertaining?

> **Comment.** Example 2.3.2.2 also uses the multiple-sentence format, but it states the key facts both before and within the final sentence. The final sentence should just ask about the legal result from the preceding facts.

2.4 The form of question

2.4.1 Yes-or-no question

Where possible, phrase the question about the legal result—whether in the single-sentence or the multiple-sentence Question Presented format—so you can answer it *yes* or *no*. Remember that your job in writing the memorandum is to provide a preliminary answer to the legal issue you were asked to research. Phrase the question in a way that you can answer it succinctly. Even if a particular legal issue does not lend itself to a yes-or-no question, phrase the question so you can answer it succinctly.

Example 2.4.1.1 (yes-or-no question, single-sentence format).

Is a credit union's ATM fee unconscionable under California law where the credit union incurs a $0.20 direct cost for each transaction but imposes a $4.00 surcharge on non-members, the surcharge applies only at ATMs in rural locations where no alternatives exist for obtaining cash, and the surcharge is more than double that for ATM transactions in populated areas in the State?

Example 2.4.1.2 (yes-or-no question, multiple-sentence format).

A credit union incurs a $0.20 direct cost for each of its ATM transactions but imposes a $4.00 surcharge on non-members. The surcharge applies only at ATMs in rural locations where no alternatives exist for obtaining cash. The surcharge is more than double that for ATM transactions in populated areas in the State. Is the credit union's ATM fee unconscionable under California law?

Comment. In Example 2.4.1.2, the final sentence in the multiple-sentence format is phrased as a yes-or-no question. (See also Example 2.3.2.1: *Does the business create a private nuisance under Michigan law?*)

Example 2.4.1.3 (legal issue not suitable to yes-or-no question).

How stringently do the Eastern District courts apply the screening and notification requirements of Michigan Rule of Professional Conduct 1.10(b) to law firms subject to a motion to disqualify counsel?

Comment. The legal issue in Example 2.4.1.3 requires a qualified answer, rather than a simple *yes* or *no*. The Question Presented is phrased so that the answer can be stated succinctly: *very stringently*.

2.4.2 Governing law

If there is no doubt about which jurisdiction's law applies to the legal issue, identify that law in the Question Presented. You may identify it by the jurisdiction's name (*under Wisconsin law*), by identifying the jurisdictional source of law that governs the issue (*under the Wisconsin Family and Medical Leave Act*), or even by identifying a specific legal provision if your issue is framed that narrowly (*under* [or *within the meaning of*] *Wis. Stat. Ann. § 103.10(1)(g)*). If the choice of applicable law requires separate legal analysis in the memorandum to follow, do not refer to the governing law in the Question Presented.

2.4.3 Conclusory question

Do not phrase the Question Presented to incorporate one or more conclusions about the legal analysis to follow in the memorandum. A Question Presented is conclusory, for example, if it incorporates a legal or factual assumption that leads to only one possible legal result.

Example 2.4.3.1 (bad example: facts incorporate legal assumptions).

Is a credit union's ATM fee unconscionable under California law where the transaction presents an adhesion contract and the $4.00 surcharge on non-members is shockingly high?

> **Comment.** In Example 2.4.3.1, the second half of the sentence incorporates legal assumptions relevant to the two-part rule in California for unconscionable contracts—which requires both procedural unconscionability and substantive unconscionability—rather than just presenting the key facts a court would first have to assess. Those assumptions do not belong in the Question Presented: They make it conclusory.

2.4.4 Client's perspective

A legal memorandum must present your honest, objective conclusion about the issue you were asked to research, even if it is not the conclusion that your senior colleague or your client wants. Nevertheless, when you write the Question Presented, try to phrase it from your client's perspective, to indicate which side of the issue you are on. Regardless of the conclusion you present, your colleague and your client may be displeased if the first thing they read in your memorandum is a Question Presented phrased from the other side's perspective. Whether you use the single-sentence or the multiple-sentence format, you can incorporate the client's perspective by your word choice and your selection of the key facts to include. Do not incorporate the client's perspective, however, if it results in awkward language or a conclusory question.

Example 2.4.4.1 (Question Presented, plaintiff's perspective, single-sentence format).

Is a waiver of liability for negligence unenforceable under California law where required by a medical service provider as a condition of receiving treatment?

Comment. Example 2.4.4.1 incorporates the plaintiff's perspective by asking whether the waiver will be *unenforceable*—the legal result the plaintiff patient wants—and by emphasizing the unavoidability of signing the waiver to get any kind of treatment.

Example 2.4.4.2 (Question Presented, defendant's perspective, multiple-sentence format).

A patient schedules elective, experimental medical therapy at a nonprofit hospital. The patient must execute a waiver of liability before the hospital will admit him. Is the waiver enforceable under California law?

Comment. Example 2.4.4.2 incorporates the defendant's perspective by asking whether the waiver will be *enforceable*—the legal result the defendant hospital wants—and by emphasizing the optional nature of the procedure.

Example 2.4.4.3 (Bad example: awkward language to achieve client's perspective).

Does a home motorcycle repair business not create a private nuisance under Michigan law where it operates on evenings and weekends and the intermittent noise it produces aggravates one neighbor's migraines, wakes the neighbor's young children, and interferes with the neighbor's backyard entertaining?

Comment. Not all legal issues readily lend themselves to phrasing from the client's perspective. Example 2.4.4.3 attempts to incorporate the defendant's perspective by asking whether the business will not create a private nuisance—the legal result the defendant wants. The addition of *not* to the question makes the language slightly awkward, by asking whether the disfavored legal result will not occur. Other formulations to achieve the same perspective would be even more awkward, as in *Is there no private nuisance under Michigan law where . . . .* • By comparison, a legal issue lends itself to phrasing from the client's perspective if you can ask whether the favored result will occur, whether the client is the plaintiff or the defendant. (See Example 2.4.4.2: *Is the waiver enforceable under California law?*) • Thus, for legal issues similar to the one in this Example 2.4.4.3, it is better just to state the question without the negative formulation, especially if you can still incorporate the client's perspective by your choice of key facts. Example 2.4.4.3 still incorporates the defendant's perspective by emphasizing the occasional nature of the noise and the fact that only one neighbor has complained of it.

2.5 The key facts

2.5.1 Legal relevance

For either the single-sentence or the multiple-sentence Question Presented format, include a few key facts that may determine the legal result—that is, facts important for the outcome under the rule or part of the rule you are analyzing. If the applicable rule has two or more parts, as most rules do, try to include key facts for each part. If the number of key facts would make the Question Presented too long, however, just select facts relevant to the most important part or parts of the rule. Select facts that convey the actors' relationship to each other and the legal significance of their actions, too.

Example 2.5.1.1 (key facts relevant to parts of applicable rule).

Is a credit union's ATM fee unconscionable under California law where the credit union incurs a $0.20 direct cost for each transaction but imposes a $4.00 surcharge on non-members, the surcharge applies only at ATMs in rural locations where no alternatives exist for obtaining cash, and the surcharge is more than double that for ATM transactions in populated areas in the State?

Comment. Example 2.5.1.1 includes facts important for both parts of the California rule on unconscionable contracts, which requires procedural unconscionability and substantive unconscionability: There are no alternatives for obtaining cash at the ATM locations and the surcharge is discriminatory and unjustifiably high. • The facts also convey the actors' relationship to each other and the legal significance of their actions: The credit union is imposing the ATM surcharge only on users who do not belong to the credit union. If the facts said *truck drivers* instead of *non-members*, the significance of credit-union membership to the issue of substantive unconscionability would be missing.

<u>Example 2.5.1.2</u> (key facts relevant to most important part of multi-part rule).

Is a private driving school's waiver of liability for negligence enforceable under California law where the school teaches students how to drive sports cars quickly?

> **Comment.** California law governing contractual waivers of liability turns on a six-factor judicial test for whether the contract affects the public interest. A Question Presented that included key facts for each factor would be too long, even in the multiple-sentence format. Example 2.5.1.2 just includes facts relevant to the most important factor, whether the underlying transaction is a matter of public importance, which may often be a practical necessity for some members of the public. • The facts establish the business-customer relationship between the actors, and they attempt to convey the legal significance of the action—that teaching people to drive sports cars quickly is not a matter of public importance or practical necessity. • Note, too, that by these means—and by the choice of *enforceable* in the opening clause—this Question Presented also incorporates the defendant driving school's perspective, suggesting that the waiver is enforceable because the school's services do not affect the public interest.

2.5.2 Generic or specific references

The Question Presented, and the corresponding Brief Answer, can be written using generic references for the actors involved in the legal issue—*home motorcycle repair business* or *neighbor*—or they can be written using the specific names—*Popity Pop Motorcycle Repair* or *Dave Lambert*. You should prefer generic references, for several reasons.

2.5.2.1 Reader's familiarity

Your reader may not recognize one or more specific names when just starting to read your memorandum. The Statement of Facts, containing all the specific names and descriptions, appears after the Question Presented and the Brief Answer. The busy senior attorney who asked you to write the memorandum, but who is juggling multiple projects, may not have read the complete document file before giving it to you, may not participate in additional factual development before you write the memorandum, and may not know or remember the specific names when you deliver the memorandum.

2.5.2.2 Actors' relationship

If you use the actors' specific names, you may need to lengthen the Question Presented to explain who they are and suggest the nature of their relationship and the significance of their actions.

Example 2.5.2.2.1 (bad example: specific references do not convey actors' relationship).

Does Popity Pop Motorcycle Repair create a private nuisance under Michigan law where it operates on evenings and weekends and the intermittent noise it produces aggravates Dave Lambert's migraines, wakes his young children, and interferes with his backyard entertaining?

> **Comment.** In Example 2.5.2.2.1, the use of formal names rather than generic descriptions omits important, legally significant information about the actors: Popity Pop is a home business, and Mr. Lambert occupies a neighboring house.

Example 2.5.2.2.2 (bad example: specific and generic references create wordy Question Presented).

Does Popity Pop Motorcycle Repair, a home motorcycle repair business, create a private nuisance under Michigan law where it operates on evenings and weekends and the intermittent noise it produces aggravates the migraine headaches that the next-door neighbor, Dave Lambert, experiences, wakes Mr. Lambert's young children, and interferes with his backyard entertaining?

> **Comment.** In Example 2.5.2.2.2, the use of both formal names and generic descriptions, to convey legally significant information about the actors, makes the Question Presented too long. It would be too long even if restated in the multiple-sentence format.

2.5.2.3 Research focus

In your research to answer the issue, you will be looking for the law applicable to generic categories of actors, which will encompass not only your specific facts but also other analogous or distinguishable fact patterns. (If you only look for the law applicable to your specific facts, you may not find any.) When you are first developing your research strategy, draft the Question Presented in terms of the generic question, to ensure that your research is sufficiently broad. In your completed memorandum, phrase the

Question Presented in the same generic terms, to indicate the scope of the legal issue you researched.

Chapter 3
How to Write the Brief Answer

3.1 Purpose

The Brief Answer is the third component of a legal memorandum. It states a succinct conclusion for each legal issue you identified in the Question Presented. If you were asked to research multiple issues, use separate, numbered conclusions that correspond to the separate, numbered questions you included in the Question Presented.

3.2 When to draft it

Try to draft a preliminary Brief Answer at the end of your research. If you cannot, you may need to do more research or just continue to analyze the results of your research. Many attorneys continue to refine their preliminary conclusion about the issue as they proceed to analyze the law and the facts in detail, within the Discussion component of the memorandum. If you refine your conclusion as you write the Discussion, be sure to revise your preliminary Brief Answer to reflect your final conclusion.

3.3 Format

The Brief Answer consists of a single paragraph with three parts: (i) an answer to the question (see §3.4); (ii) a short statement of the applicable rule (see §3.5); and (iii) one or more reasons supporting the answer (see §3.6)—in that order. Indent the first line of the paragraph, to match the Question Presented. (See §2.3.)

3.3.1 Length

The length of the Brief Answer will vary depending on the complexity of the legal issue, but, in general, it should not exceed about two-thirds of a double-spaced page.

3.3.2 Multiple issues

If you researched multiple issues, use a separate, numbered paragraph—with the corresponding answer, rule, and supporting reasons—for each one. That will lengthen the Brief Answer, of course.

3.4 The form of answer

3.4.1 Yes-or-no answer

Begin the Brief Answer by answering the yes-or-no question in the Question Presented: Say *Yes* or *No*.

3.4.2 Substantive answer

After saying *Yes* or *No*, restate the question about the potential legal result as a declarative sentence, containing the substantive answer. This sentence should be the mirror image of the Question Presented; use substantially similar language. You may omit the key facts from your substantive answer, to keep it concise. You may even omit the entire sentence if the Question Presented is succinct and your reader will not be confused about what the substantive answer entails. When in doubt, however, include the substantive answer.

Example 3.4.1.1 (substantive answer restates question about legal result).

QUESTION PRESENTED

Does a home motorcycle repair business create a private nuisance under Michigan law where it operates on evenings and weekends and the intermittent noise it produces aggravates one neighbor's migraines, wakes the neighbor's young children, and interferes with the neighbor's backyard entertaining?

BRIEF ANSWER

No. A Michigan court would probably conclude that the home motorcycle repair business does not create a private nuisance.

(Sample Legal Memorandum 1:9-17)

Comment. In Example 3.4.1.1, the Question Presented includes both a question about the potential legal result and a number of facts that may determine the result. The Brief Answer begins with a yes-or-no answer, followed by a declarative sentence that restates the question as a substantive answer, but without the key facts. (The supporting reasons that follow will refer to the key facts.) The Brief Answer also uses substantially similar language about the legal result: *the home motorcycle business does not create a private nuisance*.

Example 3.4.1.2 (substantive answer does not restate question about legal result).

QUESTION PRESENTED

Does Florida state law recognize a cause of action for intentional infliction of emotional distress?

BRIEF ANSWER

Yes.

Comment. In Example 3.4.1.2, the Question Presented is succinct, and it states a pure question of law. The Brief Answer begins with just the yes-or-no answer, without restating the question as a declarative sentence. A reader would not be confused about the substantive answer.

3.4.3 Answer to question not suitable to yes-or-no formulation

For a Question Presented that does not lend itself to a yes-or-no question, begin the Brief Answer with a short phrase that answers the question or with a declarative sentence containing the substantive answer, but not with both.

Example 3.4.1.3 (answer to question not suitable to yes-or-no formulation).

QUESTION PRESENTED

How stringently do the Eastern District courts apply the screening and notification requirements of Michigan Rule of Professional Conduct 1.10(b) to law firms subject to a motion to disqualify counsel?

BRIEF ANSWER

Very stringently.

> **Comment.** In Example 3.4.1.3, the Question Presented does not lend itself to a yes-or-no question. The Brief Answer begins with just a short phrase that answers the question. Alternatively, the Brief Answer could begin with a declarative sentence containing the answer: *The Eastern District courts apply the screening and notification requirements of Michigan Rule of Professional Conduct 1.10(b) very stringently to law firms subject to a motion to disqualify counsel.* If the Question Presented is succinct, the short-phrase answer should be sufficient.

3.4.4 Degree of certainty

The attorney who asked you to write the memorandum will expect you to reach a conclusion about the legal issue you had to research. Try to state your conclusion with as much certainty as you can. Begin your Brief Answer with *Yes* or *No*. That is your conclusion. You may include a reasonable amount of qualification in the substantive answer—*A Michigan court would probably conclude*—but not so much that it undermines your conclusion. Conversely, do not overstate your conclusion—*A Michigan court will unquestionably conclude*—because courts are always unpredictable, even as to issues where you think only one result is possible. It would be better to convey your confidence by writing, *A Michigan court should conclude*. Finally, do not equivocate: *It is not completely clear whether a Michigan court would conclude that . . . .* The assigning attorney will conclude that you have not completed your analysis.

3.5 The applicable rule

After you answer the question, briefly identify the applicable judicial rule. If it derives from some form of enacted law, such as a constitutional or statutory provision, you may note that at the outset, but do not describe the provision in detail. (You will be able to describe it in detail in the Overview to the Discussion. See Chapter 6.) Focus on the rule that the courts apply to the issue. If you can succinctly identify the major parts of the rule, do that. Otherwise, just state the basic rule alone. (You will be able to identify the major parts of the rule, explicitly or implicitly, when you present your supporting reasons; you may be able to identify secondary parts of the rule or legal analysis, too. See §3.6.) Use no more than two or three sentences to identify the applicable rule, its source, if any, and its major parts.

<u>**Example 3.5.1**</u> **(statement identifies major parts of applicable rule).**

Under Michigan law, private nuisance requires proof of significant harm resulting from unreasonable interference with the use or enjoyment of property.

(Sample Legal Memorandum 1:17-19)

> **Comment.** In Example 3.5.1, the Brief Answer identifies the applicable rule on private nuisance in Michigan, including the rule's two major parts: significant harm and unreasonable interference.

<u>**Example 3.5.2**</u> **(statement identifies statutory source and major parts of applicable rule).**

Section 1670.5 of the California Civil Code authorizes courts to find contracts unconscionable. The courts apply a two-part test for unconscionability. The first part, evaluating procedural unconscionability, focuses on the context in which the contract is made. The second part, evaluating substantive unconscionability, focuses on the terms of the contract itself.

> **Comment.** In Example 3.5.2, the Brief Answer uses one sentence to identify the statute governing contractual unconscionability and two sentences to identify the applicable judicial rule and its major parts. This part of the Brief Answer should not be any longer. The Brief Answer must still accommodate the most important reasons supporting your conclusion, without becoming unmanageably long.

3.6 The supporting reasons

After you identify the applicable rule, briefly state one or more reasons supporting your substantive conclusion about the legal issue. Introduce the reasons with a word or phrase, such as *Here*, *In this case*, or *As applied to . . .*, or with a short transitional sentence.

3.6.1 The parts of the rule

If, in the preceding sentences of the Brief Answer, you identified the major parts of the applicable rule, state a conclusion and supporting reason for each one. If that would make the Brief Answer too long, just focus on the most important parts, conclusions, and reasons. State your conclusions in the same order in which you introduced the parts of the rule. If you did not identify the major parts of the rule, state reasons supporting the overall, substantive conclusion that imply what the major parts, or the most important parts, are. If there is room, you may also state reasons that imply what the next level of the rule or legal analysis entails.

3.6.2 The corresponding key facts

State the supporting reasons to refer to key facts you included in your Question Presented, to suggest why or how those facts should determine the legal result. You may introduce additional facts within the supporting reasons, as long as they do not expand the Brief Answer beyond a manageable length.

3.6.3 Generic or specific references

If you phrased the Question Presented using generic references, use the same generic references in the Brief Answer. Avoid the temptation to state the Brief Answer using the specific names of the people, places, or entities involved. If you used the specific names in the Question Presented, however, use them in the Brief Answer.

Example 3.6.3.1 (supporting reasons introduced by transitional sentence, correspond to parts of applicable rule, refer to key facts included in Question Presented, imply next level of legal analysis, introduce additional key facts, and maintain generic references).

QUESTION PRESENTED

Does a home motorcycle repair business create a private nuisance under Michigan law where it operates on evenings and weekends and the intermittent noise it produces aggravates one neighbor's migraines, wakes the neighbor's young children, and interferes with the neighbor's backyard entertaining?

BRIEF ANSWER

No. A Michigan court would probably conclude that the home motorcycle repair business does not create a private nuisance. Under Michigan law, private nuisance requires proof of significant harm resulting from unreasonable interference with the use or enjoyment of property. The neighbor would not be able to establish either requirement. A court would likely find no significant harm because the noise would not cause physical discomfort to persons of ordinary sensibilities and it causes only minimal disruption to the neighbor's use of his backyard. A court would also likely find that any interference is not unreasonable. Although the neighborhood is residential, the noise is sporadic and ends by 11:00 p.m., the noise is a necessary part of the repair business, and the business contributes to the social and economic well-being of the neighborhood.

(Sample Legal Memorandum 1:9-27)

Comments. • In Example 3.6.3.1, a transitional sentence in the Brief Answer leads from the statement of the applicable, two-part rule to the supporting reasons: *The neighbor would not be able to establish either requirement.* • The supporting reasons state conclusions for the two parts of the rule, in the same order as the parts appear in the rule: *A court would likely find no significant harm . . . . A court would also likely find that any interference is not unreasonable.* • Each conclusion is supported by concise reasons that refer to key facts included in the Question Presented: *A court would likely find no significant harm because the noise would not cause physical discomfort to persons of ordinary sensibilities and it causes only minimal disruption to the neighbor's use of his backyard.* • The statement of the applicable rule in the Brief Answer does not attempt to introduce the secondary level of analysis governing unreasonable interference caused by noise. The supporting reasons for that part of the rule, however, imply some of the relevant considerations: the residential nature of the neighborhood; the frequency and timing of the noise; and the necessity and social utility of the conduct that causes the noise. • These reasons also introduce a few new, determinative facts, but without making the Brief Answer too long. • The Brief Answer uses the generic references from the Question Presented—*home motorcycle repair business* and *neighbor*—rather than switching prematurely to the specific names.

3.7 Legal citations

In general, do not include legal citations in the Brief Answer. (You will include all the necessary legal citations in the Discussion component, starting with the Overview to the Discussion. See Chapter 6.) When stating the applicable rule, however, you may abbreviate the name of a statute or rule—*Wis. Stat. Ann. § 103.10(1)(g)* or *Fed. R. Civ. P. 12(b)(6)*—but do not begin a sentence with such an abbreviation. (See Example 3.5.2: *Section 1670.5 of the California Civil Code authorizes courts to find contracts unconscionable.*) If, but only if, a single, dispositive authority dictates the answer to the legal issue in your memorandum, you may include a citation to it in the Brief Answer.

Chapter 4
How to Write the Statement of Facts

4.1 Purpose

The Statement of Facts is the fourth component of a legal memorandum. It presents, in one place, the facts upon which you base your analysis of the legal issue you were asked to research. Not only will the attorney who gave you the assignment read your memorandum, other attorneys working on the same client matter may read it at some point during the representation. The Statement of Facts should enable any of these readers to review the specific factual context giving rise to your research issue. An experienced attorney, even one unfamiliar with the facts you present, will be able to see in them certain legal relationships and implications and, for that reason, will be better prepared to read and assess your legal analysis to follow.

4.2 When to draft it

Draft the Statement of Facts in several stages.

4.2.1 Preliminary draft

Try to draft a complete, preliminary Statement of Facts at the end of your research, at the same time that you draft a preliminary Brief Answer. (See §3.2.) That way, you can assure yourself that your legal conclusions take account of the important facts.

4.2.2 Interim revision

Be prepared to revise your draft Statement of Facts as you write the main Discussion component of the memorandum. You may refine or even revise your preliminary conclusions as you analyze the law and the facts in detail. As part of that process, you may realize that certain facts are more important than you previously thought or that other facts are not as important or not important at all. If that happens, revise the Statement of Facts by adding or deleting facts, increasing or decreasing the level of detail about certain facts, reorganizing the way you present the facts, or some combination of all three.

4.2.3 Final review

After you have written the Discussion, review your Statement of Facts to make sure it contains all of the facts you included in your legal analysis. Do not include any facts in the Discussion that do not first appear in the Statement of Facts.

4.3 Format

The Statement of Facts should briefly explain why you are writing the memorandum (see §4.4) and then present the important facts (see §4.5).

4.3.1 Chronology

Present the facts in chronological order, unless there is a good reason to use a different sequence. For example, in a memorandum analyzing a client's defenses to a hit-and-run prosecution, it may be preferable to describe the accident first before describing your client's actions and whereabouts at the time.

4.3.2 Length

The Statement of Facts can be quite short or very long, depending on the complexity of the legal issue and the relevant circumstances. Use multiple paragraphs, unless the facts are very brief.

4.3.3 Sections

If your Statement of Facts is longer than two or three pages, divide it into sections with short headings identifying the subject matter of each section.

4.4 Statement of context

Begin the Statement of Facts by summarizing the business or legal context in which you are writing the memorandum. Identify the client and briefly include some combination of the client's current legal situation, what the client wants to know or do, and what your office has been asked or agreed to do. A single sentence may suffice. If it is necessary to use two or three sentences, start a new paragraph when you begin to present the facts. If the relevant facts are lengthy or complex, end the Statement of Facts by returning to the context for the memorandum, in a short transitional paragraph before the legal analysis you present in the Discussion.

Example 4.4.1 (opening statement of context).

Jon Hendricks has asked our firm to defend him in a lawsuit filed in Washtenaw County Circuit Court. Mr. Hendricks's next-door neighbor, Dave Lambert, is suing him for private nuisance in connection with a motorcycle repair business that Mr. Hendricks operates at his home.

(Sample Legal Memorandum 1:29-32)

Comment. Example 4.4.1 is the first paragraph of a one-and-one-half-page Statement of Facts in the Sample Legal Memorandum. It contains an opening sentence identifying the client and his request for a legal defense, followed by a second sentence succinctly describing the lawsuit in question.

Example 4.4.2 (closing statement of context).

In his lawsuit, Mr. Lambert is seeking an injunction and damages.

(Sample Legal Memorandum 3:7)

Comment. Example 4.4.2 is the final paragraph of the same Statement of Facts. It returns to the context for the memorandum by briefly identifying the plaintiff's legal demands.

4.5 Facts to include

The Statement of Facts should include all of the facts that are important to your legal analysis (*material facts*) and any background, explanatory, or other facts necessary to make the material facts meaningful to your reader. Use specific references; the generic references you may have used in the Question Presented and Brief Answer are no longer appropriate. Omit unnecessary details, names, and dates. Omit any statements about the applicable law, too; you will introduce the law in the Overview to the Discussion. (See Chapter 6.)

4.5.1 Material facts

A fact is material if its presence, absence, or nature affects one or more parts of your legal analysis. Include material facts that affect your analysis unfavorably as well as favorably: A memorandum is the place to identify the weaknesses in your client's legal position, not only the strengths. Note that the same fact can be material to the analysis of one legal issue but not material to the analysis of another. The fact that a client drives a titanium-silver car is not material to whether a document she signed to participate in a high-speed-driving-skills course, releasing the school from liability for negligence, is enforceable. You would not include it in the Statement of Facts for a memorandum analyzing the enforceability of the exculpatory clause. The color of the car would be material to a hit-and-run prosecution, where a witness identified the vehicle as gray. You would include the color of the car in the Statement of Facts for a memorandum analyzing the client's defenses.

Example 4.5.1.1 (material and background facts).

Our client, Mercury Trucking, wishes to file a class action lawsuit against the Triathlon Credit Union. Triathlon Oil Company ("Triathlon") operates this credit union for its employees' benefit. During the past two years, Triathlon has established ATMs in fifty of its rural California truck stop and gas station locations. There are no other ATMs within a twenty-five-mile radius of each one.

(Opening paragraph for Statement of Facts in memorandum analyzing contractual unconscionability of ATM fee under California law)

> **Comment.** In Example 4.5.1.1, the fact that Triathlon Oil Company operates a credit union for its employees' benefit is not material to the issue of contractual unconscionability. Instead, it helps establish the background for a fact that is material, that the credit union treats non-members differently than members by imposing a surcharge on non-members for ATM transactions. • In contrast, the fact that there are no other ATMs within a twenty-five-mile radius of each Triathlon ATM is material, because it helps substantiate one part of the analysis for contractual unconscionability, that the Mercury truckers have no choice but to obtain cash from the Triathlon ATMs. • Facts about other benefits provided to credit union members are neither material nor necessary to the reader's understanding of the material facts. The specific dates when Triathlon established its network of rural ATMs are not material or necessary, either. The writer does not include any of those facts.

4.5.2 Names

If your client is an individual, use the client's full name the first time you mention the client in the Statement of Facts. In subsequent references, refer to adult clients formally, using their last name and an appropriate prefix, such as *Mr.*, *Mrs.*, *Ms.*, *Dr.*, etc., but refer to children by their first names. Do the same for other individuals you include in the Statement of Facts. For businesses with long names, you may use a shorter version of their names when you introduce them. You may also introduce an even shorter defined term to refer to the business throughout the rest of the memorandum: *Triathlon Oil Company ("Triathlon") operates this credit union for its employees' benefit.*

4.5.3 Dates

Include the specific dates for key material facts. Do not write, for example, that an important event happened *a week ago*. Legal analyses, requirements, and results often turn on when events happened or were supposed to happen. A reader who reviews your memorandum days, weeks, or months after you delivered it may not remember when the key events occurred—if the reader even knew that in the first place. Always include the specific dates for the important facts—for instance, that an accident occurred *on Saturday, October 6, 2012, at 8:40 a.m.*

4.5.4 Quotations and citations

Quote key portions of important documents or key statements by people involved in the underlying events. If a legal issue turns on the language of a contractual provision, quote the key language in that provision. Paraphrase the rest of the provision, if it is material or helpful as background. Identify the document by name and the number of the provision. Identify the source of any key statements you quote, if they appear in a transcript, court document, or other record. In general, however, you do not need to include citations for the contents of the Statement of Facts.

4.5.5 Missing facts

If you are missing a fact that could be material to your analysis, one way or the other, just note that it is missing in the Statement of Facts. You can explain why it might be material when you apply the law to your facts in the Rule Application. (See §9.9.)

<u>Example 4.5.5.1</u> (identifying unknown material facts).

To diagnose and repair motorcycles with engine problems, Mr. Hendricks needs to start, run, and stop them. The engines are loud, so Mr. Hendricks tries to limit the number of startups each day. We do not know exactly how loud the engines are, however, or for how long Mr. Hendricks runs them.

(Sample Legal Memorandum 2:22-26)

> **Comment.** Example 4.5.5.1, part of the Statement of Facts in the Sample Legal Memorandum, identifies two material facts that are missing. The Discussion component of the memorandum explains their potential legal significance.

4.6 Presentation of the facts

Once you select the facts to include, let those facts speak for themselves. Do not gloss over, generalize from, or editorialize about the facts. Do not substitute vague or subjective descriptions for objective facts. Do not give the reader a false or incomplete sense of the facts, only to surprise the reader by augmenting the facts in a piecemeal fashion in the Discussion—or, worse, by omitting a material fact altogether. In addition, do not include any form of legal analysis, characterization, or conclusion in the Statement of Facts.

<u>Example 4.6.1</u> (bad example: subjective description).

The police report indicated that our client was driving slowly as she approached the intersection.

> **Comment.** In Example 4.6.1, the word *slowly* displaces a more objective fact, the actual speed at which the client was driving (assuming the report stated the actual speed). It also introduces a subjective judgment about that speed. *Slowly* could mean *5 m.p.h.* or *35 m.p.h.* The actual speed could have different legal consequences, depending on the other facts, such as a 20-m.p.h. posted speed limit on the street. Your reader needs to know the specific, objective fact—and you will have to analyze that fact, anyway, in the Discussion. Include it in the Statement of Facts, without gloss or adornment.

<u>Example 4.6.2</u> (bad example: legal conclusion; vague description).

Mr. Hendricks lives in North Ypsilanti. It is a residential neighborhood made up of small and medium-sized houses occupied by families, working-class people, and local college students. The closest stores are some distance away, on Cross Street and Michigan Avenue.

> **Comment.** In Example 4.6.2, the residential character of the location where the alleged nuisance occurs is part of the applicable legal

analysis that the writer must address within the Discussion component of the memorandum. Thus, the word *residential*, when added to a sentence describing the houses and occupants in the North Ypsilanti neighborhood, conveys a legal conclusion that does not belong in the Statement of Facts. • Similarly, the distance from the houses to the nearest stores is legally relevant to the nuisance analysis. The vague description, *some distance*, would make that part of the analysis impossible. If there is a specific distance, include it in the Statement of Facts: *a half-mile*. Do not save it to introduce in the Discussion.

Example 4.6.3 (specific description without legal conclusion).

Mr. Hendricks lives in North Ypsilanti. The surrounding neighborhood consists of small and medium-sized houses occupied by families, working-class people, and local college students. The closest stores are a half-mile away, on Cross Street and Michigan Avenue.

(Sample Legal Memorandum 2:1-4)

Comment. Example 4.6.3 represents a better version of the facts stated in Example 4.6.2. It omits the legal conclusion about the character of the neighborhood, and it includes the specific distance to the nearest stores.

Chapter 5
How to Organize the Discussion

5.1 Purpose

The Discussion is the fifth and largest component of a legal memorandum. It presents your detailed analysis of the legal issue stated in the Question Presented. If you were asked to research multiple issues, use separate sections within the Discussion to analyze each one.

5.2 Format

The Discussion consists of an Overview at the beginning, which summarizes the substantive analysis to follow (see Chapter 6), and one or more sections presenting that analysis in detail. The sequence in which you arrange those sections (and any subsections) throughout the Discussion is called *large-scale organization*. (See §5.3.) The sequence in which you present your substantive analysis within each section (and each subsection) is called *small-scale organization*. (See §5.4.)

5.3 Large-scale organization

Generally, for each issue you were asked to research, there is an applicable judicial rule, which the courts apply to the facts presented to determine the legal consequences. Organize your substantive analysis in the Discussion by dividing it into sections and subsections that correspond to the structure of the applicable rule.

5.3.1 Research focus

Early in your research process, try to identify the judicial rule that applies to your legal issue. If the issue is ultimately governed by some form of enacted law, such as a constitutional, statutory, or regulatory provision, note that, but continue to look for the rule by which the courts interpret the provision and apply it to different fact patterns. (For some issues, the courts may apply a statutory or regulatory provision directly, without an interpretative rule.) In essence, your substantive analysis will consist of trying to predict how a new court will apply the applicable rule (or provision) to your client's fact pattern.

5.3.2 Rule structures

Once you have found the applicable judicial rule, identify its structure.

5.3.2.1 Levels of analysis

Each judicial rule may have one or more levels of analysis. The levels derive from the text of the rule itself, judicial interpretations of the rule, or well-accepted practices among the courts. The primary level of analysis contains the major parts of the rule that the courts apply to a given legal issue. Frequently, there is a secondary level, containing sub-parts for some or all of the major parts of the rule; the courts analyze the sub-parts to determine if the major parts are satisfied. Sometimes, there is a third or even a fourth level, containing further subdivisions for some or all of the parts at the preceding level. For example, in California, a leading judicial rule on unconscionable contracts contains two major parts, addressing procedural unconscionability and substantive unconscionability. Each major part has its own sub-parts; for procedural unconscionability, the sub-parts address the presence of oppression and surprise during contract formation. Oppression—but not surprise—has further subdivisions; they address the opportunity for contract negotiation and meaningful choice. Thus, the rule extends to three levels of analysis. Be sure to identify the levels of analysis in the judicial rule that applies to your legal issue.

5.3.2.2 Number of parts at each level

Each level of analysis in a judicial rule will have one or more parts. For the California rule on unconscionable contracts, the primary level of analysis has two parts. At the secondary level, procedural unconscionability has two parts—and substantive unconscionability has another four. Conversely, for the judicial rule in California on exculpatory clauses, the primary level of analysis has a single part: Exculpatory clauses are invalid if they affect the public interest. At the secondary level, the courts have developed a six-part test for whether exculpatory clauses affect the public interest. Be sure to identify the number of parts at each level of analysis in the applicable judicial rule.

5.3.2.3 Relationship among the parts

At each level of analysis, the parts of the rule may bear a different relationship to each other. Be sure to identify whether the parts are all required (as for both major parts of the rule on unconscionable contracts) or only some combination or aggregate of them is required (as for the six-part test for exculpatory contracts affecting the public interest—and for other judicial balancing tests).

5.3.2.4 Generic references

Use consistent terminology to describe the parts at each level of analysis in the rule structure. Use *element* to refer to the parts of the rule at the primary level of analysis, *factor* to refer to the parts at the secondary level of analysis, and *consideration* to refer to the parts at the tertiary level of analysis, if any. These terms are not arbitrary; many courts use them. If the courts in your jurisdiction use different terms when describing the rule structure, use those terms, instead. The main thing is to avoid confusing your reader about which level of analysis you are referring to at any point in your memorandum. Always refer to the parts at the same level in the rule structure by the same term—*element*, *factor*, or *consideration*. In addition, if the rule lists the parts at a given level of analysis in a certain order, refer to that order when you introduce each part, for example, the *first* element, the *second* factor, the *third* consideration. (See §7.4.1.)

5.3.2.5 Specific references

Use a succinct, substantive word or phrase to refer to a specific part at a given level of analysis in the rule: *control* or *the control factor* (in the six-part test for exculpatory contracts affecting the public interest). Do not refer to a specific part of the rule by an ordinal number alone: *A court would probably find that the Skip Barber Driving School satisfies the sixth factor*. Your reader may not remember what the number refers to, especially if a lot of text separates the numerical reference from the nearest, prior specific reference.

Example 5.3.2.5.1 (introduction to rule and rule structure in Overview to Discussion).

"A private nuisance is a nontrespassory invasion of another's interest in the private use and enjoyment of land." Restatement (Second) of Torts § 821D (1979). Following the Restatement's analysis, most Michigan courts find one person liable to another for private nuisance if

(a) the other has property rights and privileges in respect to the use or enjoyment interfered with,
(b) the invasion results in significant harm,
(c) the actor's conduct is the legal cause of the invasion, and
(d) the invasion is either (i) intentional and unreasonable, or (ii) unintentional and otherwise actionable under the rules governing liability for negligent, reckless, or ultrahazardous conduct.

Adkins v. Thomas Solvent Co., 487 N.W.2d 715, 720 (Mich. 1992) (citing Restatement (Second) of Torts §§ 821D-F); Capitol Props. Grp. v. 1247 Ctr. St., LLC, 770 N.W.2d 105, 112 (Mich. Ct. App. 2009). Although all four elements are required, see Capitol Props. Grp., 770 N.W.2d at 112, the courts tend to concentrate on just two, significant harm and unreasonable interference, because the other elements, property rights and causation, are usually not in dispute. See, e.g., id.; Adams v. Cleveland-Cliffs Iron Co., 602 N.W.2d 215, 222 (Mich. Ct. App. 1999).

Where an alleged nuisance involves noise, the courts evaluate significant harm by considering two factors: whether the noise causes the plaintiff "actual physical discomfort" and whether it prevents the plaintiff from using and enjoying the property. Smith v. W. Wayne Cty. Conservation Ass'n, 158 N.W.2d 463, 468, 470 (Mich. 1968) (per curiam) (citing Borsvold v. United Dairies, 81 N.W.2d 378, 382 (Mich. 1957)); Adams, 602 N.W.2d at 222. The courts evaluate unreasonable interference by considering a number of factors, including the character of the neighborhood in which the noise occurs, the character of the noise itself, and the nature and value of the conduct that produces the noise. Smith, 158 N.W.2d at 468.

(Sample Legal Memorandum 3:11-4:11)

Comment. Example 5.3.2.5.1, part of the Overview to the Discussion in the Sample Legal Memorandum, introduces the governing law in Michigan on private nuisance. • It identifies the ultimate source of that law, in the Restatement (Second) of Torts, followed by the structure of the applicable judicial rule: (i) the four elements of the rule most Michigan courts use to decide if conduct creates a private nuisance; (ii) the two elements courts emphasize most; (iii) the two factors courts consider for substantial harm, which is the secondary level of analysis for the first key element of the rule; and (iv) three factors courts consider for unreasonable interference, which is the secondary level of analysis for the second key element of the rule. • In addition, the text identifies the relationship among the parts of the rule at two different levels of analysis: All four elements are required, but just two are central to the courts' analysis, whereas only some aggregate of the three factors is required for the unreasonable interference element. • The text also refers back to the substantial harm and unreasonable interference elements of the rule by their specific names—*the courts evaluate significant harm*—not *the courts evaluate the first key element.* • Thus, at the start of the Discussion, the Overview identifies the relevant rule structure—and the rest of the Discussion is divided into sections and subsections that correspond to that structure.

5.3.3 Sequence of analysis

Where a leading judicial decision in your jurisdiction establishes a rule for a given legal issue, subsequent courts usually analyze how the rule applies to new fact patterns by covering the levels in the rule structure and the parts at each level in the same sequence in which they appear in the rule. Organize the substantive analysis in your Discussion using the same sequence, too.

5.3.4 Sections and subsections

Divide your substantive analysis into sections, subsections, and, where appropriate, further subdivisions that follow the structure of the applicable rule. Use as many organizational divisions as necessary to ensure that your analysis is accurate and easy for your reader to assimilate—but do not use more organization than necessary.

5.3.4.1 Separate analyses

In general, use a separate section to cover each element of the applicable judicial rule, a separate subsection to cover each factor for a given element, and a separate subdivision to cover each consideration for a given factor.

5.3.4.2 Combined analyses

Especially at the secondary and lower levels of analysis in the rule structure, there may be occasions when it is preferable to cover two or more parts of the rule at the same level within a single section, subsection, or subdivision. You may combine your analysis if the courts cover those parts of the rule together, rather than separately, in the case law. You may combine your analysis if those parts of the rule are so interrelated, conceptually or factually, that it would be more efficient to analyze them together. You may combine your analysis if one level of the rule contains so many parts that it would be more efficient to group similar parts together than to cover each one separately. You may combine your analysis at one level in the rule structure if the analysis of each part of the rule at the next lowest level would be very short.

Example 5.3.4.2.1 (subsection covering one factor presents combined analysis of parts of rule at next lowest level in rule structure).

B. Character of the Noise

A second factor courts evaluate when deciding if noise creates an unreasonable interference is the character of the noise itself. Smith, 158 N.W.2d at 468 (citing Borsvold, 81 N.W.2d at 382). The courts balance several considerations: the nature and volume of the noise, its frequency and duration, and the time of day when it occurs. Id. Here, a court would likely find that the motorcycle noise from Mr. Hendricks's business, although loud, is produced only intermittently, does not last long, and occurs when adult neighbors are awake and can hear other suburban noise.

Courts find greater evidence of unreasonable interference the higher the volume of a noise and the more abrasive its sound. . . .

On the other hand, courts find less evidence of unreasonable interference as the frequency and duration of the noise decrease, and they tend to give frequency and duration greater weight than the sheer volume and abrasiveness of the noise. . . .

In addition, courts find less evidence of unreasonable interference the more the noise is confined to adults' waking hours and times when other, ordinary noise occurs. . . .

Here, a court would almost certainly find some evidence of unreasonable interference because the motorcycle noise from Mr. Hendricks's business is loud and potentially disruptive. . . .

Conversely, a court would probably find no evidence of unreasonable interference in the infrequency and short duration of the motorcycle noise, and those characteristics would tend to outweigh the volume and abrasiveness of the noise. . . .

Nor would a court be likely to find evidence of unreasonable interference in Mr. Hendricks's evening and weekend hours of operation.

(Sample Legal Memorandum 15:26-19:16)

Comment. The text in Example 5.3.4.2.1 comes from a subsection in the Sample Legal Memorandum that analyzes one factor for the unreasonable interference element of the private nuisance rule. Courts analyze that factor, the character of the noise, by weighing five different considerations—which constitute the next level of analysis in the rule structure. The subsection presents a combined analysis of the parts of the rule at that next level of analysis. ● Two groups of two considerations are closely related—nature and volume; frequency and duration—so the subsection analyzes those groups together. To analyze each consideration separately would require five subdivisions, and the analysis in each one would be very short. It is more efficient, therefore, to cover all five considerations in a single, undivided subsection.

5.3.5 Headings

Use the following guidelines for the headings within the Discussion component. (See Chapter 12 for more detailed format conventions.) Note that the headings for the memorandum components themselves—Question Presented, Brief Answer, Statement of Facts, Discussion, and Conclusion—are typically printed in bold, capital letters and centered on the page. Note, too, that the Overview to the Discussion does not require a heading. (See §6.3.) If your employer or the assigning attorney has different preferences for the headings, use those.

5.3.5.1 Content

Use subject headings for each section, subsection, and subdivision within the Discussion. A subject heading is a brief term or phrase that identifies a specific element, factor, and consideration within the rule structure: *Unreasonable Interference*; *Character of the Noise*. You may include the number of a statutory or regulatory source for the part of the rule you identify in the subject heading, as in *The Screening Requirement: Rule 1.10(b)(1)*, but do not use the number alone.

5.3.5.2 Numbering and alignment

Number the first level of headings within the Discussion, for the sections analyzing the elements of the applicable rule, with Roman numerals, aligned at the left margin. For the second and third levels of headings, corresponding to the subsections and subdivisions analyzing the factors and considerations within the rule structure, use capital letters and Arabic numbers. (See §12.6.2.) Indent each new level of heading one half-inch from the left margin. Keep the text of each section, subsection, or subdivision aligned at the left margin of the page, regardless of where the heading is located. Some word processing programs automatically indent the paragraph tabs for each new level of headings. Either change the automatic settings on your computer or undo the indentations manually, to preserve a uniform appearance for the text in the memorandum. (See §12.9.)

5.3.5.3 Fonts and spacing

Use bold fonts for the main section headings in the Discussion; use either bold or underlined fonts for the headings of any subsections or further subdivisions. (See §12.3.4.) If you underline the headings for subsections or subdivisions, just underline the text of each heading, not the letter or number to the left of the text. Use initial capital letters for the major words in the subject headings: *Character of the Neighborhood.* Double-space before and after each heading. Use the same format for all the headings at a given level within your Discussion.

5.3.6 Outline

Try to use an outline when you are planning the large-scale organization of your Discussion, to identify the topics you plan to cover and the sequence in which you plan to cover them. You can even begin the outline during your research, to map out the structure of the applicable judicial rule. Follow the guidelines for headings in §5.3.5; when you are finished, the outline will resemble a table of contents. After you have created the outline, you can begin to fill it in with notes about the authorities, the facts, and the conclusions you plan to include in the text of each section, subsection, or subdivision. Then you can convert your notes to the actual text. Should it be necessary, it is much easier to reorganize your Discussion at the outline stage than after you have started to write it, when you would have to cut and paste entire sections, subsections, or subdivisions from one place to another.

Example 5.3.6.1 (outline of Discussion in Sample Legal Memorandum, showing applicable rule structure).

DISCUSSION

I. Significant Harm
   A. Actual Physical Discomfort
   B. Inability to Use and Enjoy Property
II. Unreasonable Interference
   A. Character of the Neighborhood
   B. Character of the Noise
   C. Necessity and Value of the Conduct

Comment. The outline in Example 5.3.6.1 identifies the structure of the Michigan rule on private nuisance. Creating the outline in advance would make it easy to determine the appropriate large-scale organization for the Discussion component of the Sample Legal Memorandum. In the finished Memorandum, the Discussion incorporates the rule structure in its headings and subheadings.

5.4 Small-scale organization

Large-scale organization creates sections, subsections, and further subdivisions in the Discussion to track the structure of the rule that applies to your legal issue. Small-scale organization provides the sequence for presenting your substantive analysis within each one. In general, state your conclusion and identify the specific part of the rule first, explain the law, and then show how and why a court would apply that law to your facts. Use the following series of five components:

5.4.1 Conclusion

Begin with an opening paragraph that presents your conclusion for the particular part of the rule you are analyzing. State how a court would apply it to your facts. (See Chapter 7.)

5.4.2 Rule Statement

Identify the specific part of the rule you are analyzing. You may choose to include the Rule Statement with the Conclusion in the opening paragraph. (See Chapter 7.)

5.4.3 Rule Explanation

Explain what that part of the rule means. Use examples from the case law describing how the courts interpret it and apply it to different fact patterns. (See Chapter 8.)

5.4.4 Rule Application

Apply that part of the rule to your own facts. Compare your facts to the facts and findings in the case law and predict what a court would find as to your facts. (See Chapter 9.)

5.4.5 Restated Conclusion

For lengthy or complex sections or subsections, end with a final paragraph that briefly restates your conclusion. (See Chapter 9.)

5.5 Intentional repetition

As you follow the guidelines in this book for organizing the Discussion—and for organizing the other components of a memorandum—you will be repeating a conclusion, describing a rule, or presenting an analysis in several places, but with different levels of detail. That repetition is intentional, to assist the range of different readers who may consult your memorandum: the attorney who assigned it to you; other attorneys working on the same matter with you; other attorneys at your employer who address the same issue in the future; and, occasionally, the client or in-house counsel to the client. Some of those readers may be satisfied with an overall conclusion. Some may read your analysis of just one part of the rule. Some may read the whole thing. By repeating essential information in multiple places, you will be making the different parts of the memorandum reasonably self-sufficient, so your readers will always have ready access to what they need to know.

Chapter 6
How to Write the Overview to the Discussion

6.1 Purpose

The Overview provides a high-level summary of your legal analysis at the start of the Discussion. It serves as a transition between the concise summary of your conclusion in the Brief Answer and your detailed analysis in support of that conclusion in the Discussion sections to follow. It contains the same three categories of information as the Brief Answer—answer; rule; supporting reasons—but includes more detail about the last two. A reader should come away from the Overview with a good idea of the substance of the rest of the Discussion.

6.2 Format

The Overview states your overall conclusion about the issue you were asked to research (see §6.3), introduces the applicable law (see §6.4), and summarizes the important reasons supporting your conclusion (see §6.5)—in that order. Its length will vary in proportion to the length and complexity of your analysis in the Discussion. For memoranda containing long, complex analyses, the Overview generally should not exceed about two pages; for memoranda with shorter or simpler analyses, the Overview should be shorter, too. Remember that the Overview is still a summary, although a more detailed one than the Brief Answer.

6.3 The overall conclusion

Begin the Overview right after the main heading for the Discussion, without another heading. State your overall conclusion about the legal issue you were asked to research, using a single sentence, in a separate paragraph. You may use a conclusion similar to that in the Brief Answer or a variation of it. Use specific, not generic, references to the persons and entities involved in the legal issue—

both in the Overview and throughout the rest of the Discussion. Your reader will be familiar with the specific names from the preceding Statement of Facts.

Example 6.3.1 (conclusions at start of Brief Answer and Overview).

BRIEF ANSWER

No. A Michigan court would probably conclude that the home motorcycle repair business does not create a private nuisance. . . .

DISCUSSION

A Michigan court would probably conclude that Mr. Hendricks's home motorcycle repair business does not create a private nuisance.

(Sample Legal Memorandum 1:15-17, 3:8-10)

Comment. In Example 6.3.1, the conclusion in the Overview varies the conclusion in the Brief Answer by adding the specific name of the owner of the business. • Note that there is no separate heading for the Overview—just the main heading for the Discussion.

6.4 The applicable law

The Overview is especially important to introduce the sources and basic features of the legal analysis that applies to your issue. Begin a new paragraph after the overall conclusion. If possible, use a single paragraph to introduce the applicable law; if necessary, use no more than two or three. You can introduce more detailed information about the law in the Discussion sections to follow. Do not turn this part of the Overview into a treatise.

6.4.1 Descending levels of authority

Begin with the highest level of authority and work downward, explaining how each level relates to the preceding one. If the legal issue is governed by a constitutional, statutory, or regulatory provision, say so, quote the most relevant language, and briefly paraphrase any other important language or provisions. Then identify the rule that the courts use to apply the governing provision to the facts presented in different cases. If the legal issue is not governed by enacted law, begin directly with the common-law rule.

6.4.2 Descending levels of analysis within rule

Identify the primary and secondary levels of analysis the courts use—the elements of the judicial rule and the factors within each element. Occasionally, for complex analyses, you may also identify the tertiary level of analysis—the considerations for each factor—if you can do so succinctly. In most memoranda, save the tertiary and any lower levels of analysis to introduce later in the Discussion.

6.4.3 Information about operation of rule

Briefly identify the most important information about the actual operation of the primary and secondary levels of analysis in the judicial decisions. For example, are all of the elements of the rule, or all of the factors for one element, required or just weighed against each other? Do the courts give greater weight to some elements or factors in arriving at the legal outcome at each level? Do not describe specific examples from the decisions, however. You will do that in the individual Discussion sections.

6.4.4 Historical or other background information

Just explain what the law is as of the time of the material facts in your case. Do not present the applicable law chronologically or describe how the current law evolved, unless that information is relevant to the analysis the courts currently apply.

6.4.5 Legal citations and leading decisions

Starting with the Overview and throughout the rest of the Discussion, include appropriate legal citations for all your statements about the law. Cite the governing enacted law, if any. Cite the leading decision in your jurisdiction that established the applicable judicial rule and analysis. Prefer decisions from the highest court. If the leading decision is an older one, you may add a second citation to a more recent decision that applies the same rule and analysis, even if it is from an intermediate appellate court. If the leading decisions are from a higher court level than the court in which your matter may be heard, you may also include a citation to a recent decision in that lower court. Cite leading decisions for the levels of analysis you identify in the Overview, as well as for important information about the operation of the rule. Just cite the leading decisions, however; avoid long string citations. Do not describe the relevant facts about the decisions, either in the text or in parentheticals following the citations. You will do that in the Discussion sections to follow.

6.4.6 Unpublished decisions

Do not rely on or cite unpublished decisions as authority for any judicial rule and analysis, in the Overview or the rest of the Discussion. If there are not enough published decisions to use in the Discussion, you may use unpublished decisions only to illustrate how the courts apply the rules established in the published decisions to different fact patterns. Check with the assigning attorney before you begin to include unpublished decisions. Some jurisdictions do not permit citation to unpublished decisions in documents filed with the courts. Attorneys in those jurisdictions may prefer that you do not include them in your written work product—even memoranda prepared prior to filing documents with the court.

6.4.7 Quotations and visual aids

6.4.7.1 Enacted law

Quote the most relevant language of any governing enacted law. Paraphrase the rest of the language and any other important provisions. Use a single-spaced block format for all quotations of fifty words or more and for quotations of fewer than fifty words, if it is important to emphasize the language. Use a short textual sentence to identify the subject of the quotation before you include the language. Avoid excessively long quotations or an excessive number of quotations. If necessary, divide very long quotations into shorter parts, preceded by textual sentences that identify the subject of each part.

<u>Example 6.4.7.1.1</u> (Overview identifies governing enacted law).

California Civil Code section 1670.5 governs the unconscionability of contracts.

> (a) If the court as a matter of law finds the contract or any clause of the contract to have been unconscionable at the time it was made the court may refuse to enforce the contract, or it may enforce the remainder of the contract without the unconscionable clause, or it may so limit the application of any unconscionable clause as to avoid any unconscionable result.
>
> (b) When it is claimed or appears to the court that the contract or any clause thereof may be unconscionable the parties shall be afforded a reasonable opportunity to present evidence as to its commercial setting, purpose,

and effect to aid the court in making the determination.

Cal. Civ. Code § 1670.5 (Deering 2006).

Comment. This Overview, in a memorandum analyzing the unconscionability of a contract under California law, begins, after the overall conclusion (omitted in the example), by quoting the governing statutory provision, which is the highest legal authority on the subject. • The sentence preceding the quotation identifies the subject of the language to follow. It does not introduce the quotation with language that could refer to any subject, such as *California Civil Code section 1670.5 states:* • The two paragraphs of quoted statutory language are about as long as any single quotation should be in the Overview.

6.4.7.2 Judicial rule

In general, paraphrase the applicable judicial rule. If the rule contains important key phrases, quote them. Do not quote the rule in full, unless it is short and essential for the reader to know the exact language.

6.4.7.3 Lists

As an alternative to quoting a statute, regulation, or judicial rule, you may use a list to identify the key provisions. Lists help the reader visualize and remember those provisions and their relationship to each other. They are also easy for the reader to consult later on, for quick reference. Denote the items in a formal list with letters, numbers, or bullets. Incorporate short lists within a sentence in the text. Set off longer lists from the text using the single-spaced block quotation format. (See Example 6.4.7.3.1.) In either type of list, you may combine paraphrased language with short quotations for key terms or phrases; occasionally, you may use a list to present a complete quotation, for greater visual clarity. As with quotations, do not overuse lists in the Overview—or elsewhere in the Discussion.

Example 6.4.7.3.1 (Overview identifies applicable judicial rule and analysis, uses list to present rule).

"A private nuisance is a nontrespassory invasion of another's interest in the private use and enjoyment of land." Restatement (Second) of Torts § 821D (1979). Following the Restatement's analysis, most Michigan courts find one person liable to another for private nuisance if

(a) the other has property rights and privileges in respect to the use or enjoyment interfered with,
(b) the invasion results in significant harm,
(c) the actor's conduct is the legal cause of the invasion, and
(d) the invasion is either (i) intentional and unreasonable, or (ii) unintentional and otherwise actionable under the rules governing liability for negligent, reckless, or ultrahazardous conduct.

Adkins v. Thomas Solvent Co., 487 N.W.2d 715, 720 (Mich. 1992) (citing Restatement (Second) of Torts §§ 821D-F); Capitol Props. Grp. v. 1247 Ctr. St., LLC, 770 N.W.2d 105, 112 (Mich. Ct. App. 2009). Although all four elements are required, see Capitol Props. Grp., 770 N.W.2d at 112, the courts tend to concentrate on just two, significant harm and unreasonable interference, because the other elements, property rights and causation, are usually not in dispute. See, e.g., id.; Adams v. Cleveland-Cliffs Iron Co., 602 N.W.2d 215, 222 (Mich. Ct. App. 1999).

Where an alleged nuisance involves noise, the courts evaluate significant harm by considering two factors: whether the noise causes the plaintiff "actual physical discomfort" and whether it prevents the plaintiff from using and enjoying the property. Smith v. W. Wayne Cty. Conservation Ass'n, 158 N.W.2d 463, 468, 470 (Mich. 1968) (per curiam) (citing Borsvold v. United Dairies, 81 N.W.2d 378, 382 (Mich. 1957) (en banc)); Adams, 602 N.W.2d at 222. The courts evaluate unreasonable interference by considering a number of factors, including the character of the neighborhood in which the noise occurs, the character of the noise itself, and the nature and value of the conduct that produces the noise. Smith, 158 N.W.2d at 468. . . .

There is no dispute as to the two other elements of the private nuisance rule, property rights or causation. This memorandum will not address them.

(Sample Legal Memorandum 3:11-4:11, 27-29)

Comment. When introducing the governing law, the Overview from the Sample Legal Memorandum begins by quoting the definition of private nuisance from the Restatement (Second) of Torts. Although not enacted law, the Restatement is a highly authoritative secondary source. Many state courts adopt its rules; in that sense, it is the source of the Michigan judicial rule on private nuisance. • The Overview then quotes the key language of the four-element rule Michigan courts developed for private nuisance. It uses a list format, for ease of reference. • The text that follows the quotation presents

> important information about how the rule operates. All four elements are required, but two are rarely in dispute, so courts give greater weight to the other two. • In the next paragraph, the Overview introduces the secondary level of analysis within the rule, the factors the courts evaluate for each element. The text does not include details about how the courts evaluate the factors; they would make this part of the Overview too long. Instead, those details are included in the corresponding part of the Discussion sections that follow.

6.4.8 Limiting the scope of the memorandum

It may be appropriate to use the Overview to limit the scope of the substantive analysis in your memorandum—for example, if you have been instructed to address only part of the applicable rule for your legal issue or if the analysis for your issue requires that you address only part of the rule. Introduce the entire rule in the Overview, identify which parts of the rule your memorandum will and will not address, and say why: *There is no dispute as to the two other elements of the private nuisance rule, property rights or causation. This memorandum will not address them.* (Sample Legal Memorandum 4:27-29.) You may limit the scope of the memorandum in the middle of the Overview, when you present the applicable law, or at the very end, after the supporting reasons. It may also be appropriate to focus the Question Presented and especially the Brief Answer on just the part of the rule your memorandum will address: *Under Michigan law, private nuisance requires proof of significant harm resulting from unreasonable interference with the use or enjoyment of property.* (Sample Legal Memorandum 1:17-19.)

6.5 The supporting reasons

After describing the applicable law in one or more paragraphs, start a new paragraph and summarize the main legal and factual reasons supporting your overall conclusion. If possible, use a single paragraph to present the supporting reasons; if necessary, use no more than two or three paragraphs, corresponding to the main parts of the judicial rule structure. Remember to keep the entire Overview to a manageable length. (See §6.2.)

6.5.1 Transitional sentence

If your Overview is lengthy or complex, you may begin the supporting reasons with a transitional sentence that restates the overall conclusion or some variation of it: *A Michigan court would probably conclude that Mr. Hendricks's motorcycle repair business does not satisfy either key element for a private nuisance claim.* (Sample Legal Memorandum 4:12-14.) If your

Overview is shorter and simpler, you may omit a transitional sentence and just present your supporting reasons directly.

6.5.2 Reasons at the different levels of the rule

Provide a supporting reason for your conclusion as to each part of the rule you identified. Refer to the key facts that determine the legal result. If providing supporting reasons at the primary and secondary levels of the rule would take up too much space, just provide a reason for the most important parts of the analysis—especially those parts you may have identified as most likely to determine the legal outcome. If you did not identify the secondary or tertiary levels of the rule structure when introducing the applicable law, you can imply what they are by the content of your supporting reasons for the levels you did identify.

6.5.3 Sequence for presenting the reasons

Present your supporting reasons in the same order in which you introduced the parts of the rule. If you plan to cover the parts of the rule in the Discussion sections in a different order, explain why, as part of the Overview, and present your supporting reasons in that order, instead.

6.5.4 Legal citations

Although you must provide legal citations in the Overview when you introduce the applicable law, you can generally omit them when you present the supporting reasons for your legal conclusions.

Example 6.5.4.1 (supporting reasons in the Overview).

A Michigan court would probably conclude that Mr. Hendricks's motorcycle repair business does not satisfy either key element for a private nuisance claim. A court would probably find no significant harm because Mr. Lambert's aggravated migraines and his children's interrupted sleep would not cause actual physical discomfort to ordinary persons. In addition, a court would probably find that interference with Mr. Lambert's backyard entertaining represents just a minimal harm.

Similarly, a Michigan court would probably find no unreasonable interference because the motorcycle noise is sporadic, brief, and confined during the week to evening hours when most adults are awake. A court would find that Mr. Hendricks's neighborhood is residential and subject to stricter limits on noise; however, a court would also find that the production of noise is unavoidable for a motorcycle repair business and that the value this successful business confers on its customers and the community at large outweighs the harms of which Mr. Lambert complains.

There is no dispute as to the two other elements of the private nuisance rule, property rights or causation. This memorandum will not address them.

(Sample Legal Memorandum 4:12-29)

Comment. A transitional sentence, restating the overall conclusion, introduces the supporting reasons. • The Overview provides supporting reasons for the conclusions as to each part of the judicial rule identified in the preceding introduction to the applicable law—to the two factors courts evaluate for significant harm involving noise and to the three factors courts evaluate for unreasonable interference. The reasons appear in separate paragraphs for each element. • The supporting reasons for the three factors courts evaluate for unreasonable interference imply the several considerations courts evaluate for each factor, that is, the next level of analysis within the rule structure. It would have taken up too much space in the Overview to identify those considerations explicitly. • The supporting reasons do not include legal citations. • The complete Overview covers one-and-three-quarter pages, an appropriate length for a memorandum of twenty-four pages. • The Overview ends by limiting the scope of the memorandum to just the two determinative elements in the four-element judicial rule.

6.6 Optional repeated conclusion

If your Overview is lengthy or complex, you may include a final paragraph after the supporting reasons to repeat your overall conclusion, in a single sentence. Use the same or similar language as that in the conclusion at the start of the Overview; begin with a word or phrase such as *Thus*, *Accordingly*, or *For these reasons*. If you used the overall conclusion as a transition between the applicable law and the supporting reasons (see §6.5.1), you may either omit a restated conclusion at the end of the Overview or include one, using different language. If your Overview is shorter and simpler, you may omit both the transitional sentence and the repeated conclusion.

Example 6.6.1 (supporting reasons introduced by transitional sentence and followed by repeated conclusion).

A California court would likely conclude that the Triathlon ATM fee presents both elements of unconscionability. A court would probably find the surcharge procedurally unconscionable based on its oppressive effect on

Mercury's truckers. The truckers cannot negotiate the amount of the fee because Triathlon presents them with a standardized contract at an automated machine. Further, they have no meaningful choice as to whether or not to accept the contract because they have no realistic market alternative. Although a court might find that the truckers are not surprised by the surcharge because the ATM screen notifies them of it, surprise is not required for procedural unconscionability if the degree of oppression is high.

A California court would probably find the ATM surcharge substantively unconscionable, as well, based on a number of facts courts examine for this element of the test. Triathlon's considerable profit margin on each of its ATM transactions falls outside the fair range of profitability and results in excessively large cumulative profits for the company. These profits are the product of a fee significantly higher than the prevailing market price for ATM surcharges. Yet Triathlon suffers little risk or inconvenience in providing the ATM service. Although the ATMs supply the truckers with a much-needed source of cash, a court would probably reject Triathlon's argument that this benefit justifies its overly one-sided fee.

For these reasons, a California court would probably find that Triathlon's $4.00 ATM surcharge is unconscionable.

(Emphasis added.)

Comment. A transitional sentence introduces the supporting reasons in the Overview to this memorandum analyzing the unconscionability of an ATM surcharge under California law. • A restated conclusion, in a separate paragraph, follows the supporting reasons. • The transition and the restated conclusion use different language: the transition focuses on the elements of the rule on unconscionability—which the preceding presentation of the applicable law just established—whereas the restated conclusion focuses on the overall legal issue of unconscionability. • Including a transition and a restated conclusion is not unnecessarily repetitive in this Overview, given the length and detailed content of the supporting reasons. Where the supporting reasons are even slightly shorter, as in the Sample Legal Memorandum, it would be acceptable to use only one or the other. (See Example 6.5.4.1.)

6.7 Overviews in individual Discussion sections

Always use a short overview to begin any section that you divide into subsections or any subsection that you divide into further subdivisions. You may also use a short overview to begin an undivided section or subsection if it would be helpful to the reader to introduce the topics you will cover in successive paragraphs within that section or subsection. Just as the Overview at the start of the Discussion summarizes the substantive analysis to follow in the rest of the Discussion, an overview at the start of an individual section or subsection summarizes the substantive analysis to follow in that section or subsection. Use a single paragraph for each short overview, containing no more than three or four sentences. Begin the overview right after the section or subsection heading, without another heading.

6.7.1 Divided sections

Begin the short overview by identifying the part of the rule you are addressing. Then introduce its relevant subparts within the rule structure. End by briefly stating what a court would conclude about that part of the rule and why; provide supporting reasons that refer to the subparts of the rule. After the overview, begin the first subsection or subdivision. Use a series of overviews if you divide a section into subsections and then divide one or more subsections into further subdivisions.

Example 6.7.1.1 (successive short overviews for divided section and subsection).

I. Procedural Unconscionability

The first element of the judicial test, procedural unconscionability, focuses on the formation of the contract. A & M Produce, 186 Cal. Rptr. at 122. For this element, the courts consider two factors: oppression and surprise. Id. In the case of the Triathlon ATM fee, a court would likely conclude that the contracting process between Triathlon and the Mercury truckers is characterized by oppression but not surprise. Mercury's legal position is still strong, however, because the courts have found a fee procedurally unconscionable even in the absence of any surprise during contract formation.

A. Oppression

The first factor bearing on procedural unconscionability is oppression. A & M Produce, 186 Cal. Rptr. at 122. In examining this factor, courts consider whether there was a lack of "real negotiation" and the complaining party had a "meaningful choice." Id. A court would likely find the Triathlon ATM transactions oppressive because the Mercury truckers have neither an opportunity to negotiate the ATM fee nor a meaningful choice about whether or not to use the ATMs.

1. Negotiation

Comment. Section I of this memorandum analyzing contract unconscionability in California covers the first element in the judicial rule, procedural unconscionability. The element has two factors, oppression and surprise. The section is divided into two subsections, which analyze each factor. • Section I begins with a short overview that identifies the element that is the subject of the section, introduces the next level of analysis in the rule, the two factors, and ends with a conclusion about that element and supporting reasons as to the two factors. • Subsection I.A. of the memorandum covers the first factor for procedural unconscionability, oppression. The oppression factor has two relevant considerations, negotiation and meaningful choice. The subsection is divided into two further subdivisions, which analyze each consideration. • Subsection I.A begins with a short overview that identifies the factor that is the subject of the subsection, introduces the next level of analysis in the rule, the two considerations, and ends with a conclusion about that factor and supporting reasons as to the two considerations.

6.7.2 Undivided sections

Begin the short overview by identifying the part of the rule you are addressing. Then introduce its relevant subparts within the rule structure, if the rule contains formal subparts, or the parts at the next level of analysis that the courts apply in the case law, if it would be helpful to the reader to identify them together at the start of the section. (If there is no further level of analysis, however, do not use a short overview to begin the section. Just use the standard conclusion and rule statement for an individual section. See Chapter 7.) End the short overview by briefly stating what a court would conclude about the part of the rule you are addressing and why. Provide supporting reasons that refer to the subparts of the rule or the parts at the next level of analysis.

Example 6.7.2.1 (short overview for undivided section).

B. Character of the Noise

A second factor courts evaluate when deciding if noise creates an unreasonable interference is the character of the noise itself. Smith, 158 N.W.2d at 468 (citing Borsvold, 81 N.W.2d at 382). The courts balance several considerations: the nature and volume of the noise, its frequency and duration, and the time of day when it occurs. Id. Here, a court would likely find that the motorcycle noise from Mr. Hendricks's business, although loud, is produced only intermittently, does not last long, and occurs when adult neighbors are awake and can hear other suburban noise.

(Sample Legal Memorandum 15:26-16:4)

Comment. Subsection II.B in the Sample Legal Memorandum covers one factor, the character of the noise, bearing on the second element of the Michigan rule on private nuisance, unreasonable interference. This factor does not contain formal subparts, but the Michigan courts tend to consider several categories of fact patterns, informally. Although it is not necessary to divide Subsection II.B into further subdivisions to cover those considerations, it is helpful to the reader to list them together at the start of the subsection. Thus, the subsection begins with a short overview that identifies the factor that is the subject of the subsection, introduces the next level of analysis, and ends with a conclusion about that factor and supporting reasons as to the several considerations.

6.8 Templates

Template 6A: Overview to Discussion.

DISCUSSION[1]

¶1: Overall conclusion

¶2: Introduction to applicable law:
- Enacted law, if any
- Judicial rule and analysis
- Important information about how judicial rule operates[2]

¶3: Summary of reasons supporting conclusion:
- Transitional sentence stating conclusion or variation of conclusion[3]
- Fact-specific reason supporting conclusion for each major part of judicial analysis—or just for the most important parts[4]

¶4: Optional repeated conclusion[5]

[1] No separate heading needed for Overview. Just begin text after heading for *DISCUSSION.*

[2] If necessary, use no more than two or three paragraphs to introduce applicable law.

[3] You may omit if you include repeated conclusion at the end; for most Overviews, you do not need to use both. For short Overviews, you do not need to use either one.

[4] If necessary, use no more than two or three paragraphs to present the key fact-specific supporting reasons. Keep length of Overview proportionate to length of Discussion component overall.

[5] You may include if Overview is lengthy or complex. You may use final paragraph to narrow scope of Discussion to only some parts of rule; you may also do that at end of introduction to applicable law, instead.

Template 6B: Overview to Individual Section.[1]

[X.] Subject heading for section[2 3 4]

Sentence 1: State the part of the rule the section addresses

Sentence 2: Introduce the subparts for that part of the rule or the next level of analysis from the case law

Sentence 3: State the conclusion for the part of the rule the section addresses; included succinct supporting reasons[5]

[1] Always use short overview at start of section divided into subsections; optional for undivided section.

[2] No separate heading needed for overview; just begin text after heading for individual section.

[3] Use a single paragraph for overview.

[4] Adjust font style for level of heading. (See §5.3.5.3.)

[5] If necessary, you may use another sentence or two. Keep length of overview proportionate to length of section.

Chapter 7
How to Write the Conclusion and Rule Statement for an Individual Section or Subsection

7.1 Purpose

The Conclusion and Rule Statement are the first two components in the small-scale organizational structure for presenting your substantive analysis within a single section or subsection in the Discussion. They inform your reader of the specific part of the legal analysis you are addressing, your conclusion about that part of the analysis, and, usually, a brief reason for your conclusion. They perform the same function that the Overview performs at the beginning of the Discussion—but with a narrower focus and less detail.

7.2 Format

You may present the Conclusion and Rule Statement at the start of a section or subsection in one of two sequences: (i) with the Conclusion in the first paragraph and the Rule Statement at the start of the second paragraph (see §7.2.1), or (ii) with the Conclusion and the Rule Statement combined in the first paragraph (see §7.2.2). Whichever sequence you use, use it consistently to start each section or subsection within the same organizational part of your Discussion—for example, all the subsections within a single section.

7.2.1 Separate paragraphs

State your substantive conclusion and a brief supporting reason in the first paragraph after the section heading. State the part of the rule you are addressing at the start of the second paragraph. The Rule Explanation component in the small-scale organizational structure begins with the second sentence of the second paragraph. (See §8.2.)

Example 7.2.1.1 (Conclusion and Rule Statement in separate paragraphs).

A. Physical Discomfort

A court would likely find that Mr. Lambert's aggravated migraines and his children's problems sleeping are too unique to them to satisfy an objective standard of harm.

One factor courts consider in evaluating significant harm is whether the conduct causes actual physical discomfort. . . .

B. Inability to Use and Enjoy Property

A court would likely find that the disruptions to Mr. Lambert's backyard entertaining on warm weekends represent only minimal harm.

The other factor courts consider in evaluating significant harm is whether the conduct interferes with the use and enjoyment of property.

(Sample Legal Memorandum 5:15-20, 9:19-23)

Comment. Example 7.2.1.1 contains the opening text of the two subsections in Section I of the Sample Legal Memorandum. Each subsection uses the same format to present the Conclusion and the Rule Statement. • In each one, the first paragraph states a conclusion about the subject of the subsection and includes a brief supporting reason. The first sentence in the second paragraph states the part of the rule the subsection addresses. The Rule Explanation component begins with the second sentence of the second paragraph. (See Sample Legal Memorandum 5:21-23, 9:24-25.)

7.2.2 Combined paragraph

Use a single paragraph after the section heading to state the part of the rule you are addressing, your conclusion about that part of the rule, and a brief supporting reason—in that order. In general, use no more than two or three sentences. If it would be helpful to your reader to identify the next level of the rule structure or judicial analysis at the start of the section, add a sentence after the opening statement of the rule to do so, before your conclusion and supporting reason. You will be converting the combined opening paragraph into a short overview to an undivided section. (See §6.7.2.) The Rule Explanation component in the small-scale organizational structure begins with the paragraph after the combined opening paragraph. (See §8.2.)

Example 7.2.2.1 (Rule Statement and Conclusion in combined paragraph).

A. Character of the Neighborhood

One factor courts evaluate when deciding if noise creates an unreasonable interference is the character of the neighborhood in which the noise occurs. Smith, 158 N.W.2d at 468 (citing Borsvold, 81 N.W.2d at 382). Here, a court would likely find that Mr. Hendricks's neighborhood is residential and that Mr. Hendricks is therefore subject to stricter standards regarding the production of noise. Nevertheless, a court would probably conclude that the noise from Mr. Hendricks's business does not create an unreasonable interference within the neighborhood because the noise itself is not unreasonable. . . .

B. Character of the Noise

A second factor courts evaluate when deciding if noise creates an unreasonable interference is the character of the noise itself. Smith, 158 N.W.2d at 468 (citing Borsvold, 81 N.W.2d at 382). The courts balance several considerations: the nature and volume of the noise, its frequency and duration, and the time of day when it occurs. Id. Here, a court would likely find that the motorcycle noise from Mr. Hendricks's business, although loud, is produced only intermittently, does not last long, and occurs when adult neighbors are awake and can hear other suburban noise. . . .

C. Necessity and Value of the Conduct

A third factor courts evaluate when deciding if noise creates an unreasonable interference is the necessity and value of the conduct responsible for the noise, compared to the harms of which the plaintiff complains. Waier, 251 N.W. at 553; Adams, 602 N.W.2d at 219, 222-23. A court would probably find that noise is necessary to a motorcycle repair business and that the social and economic value of Mr. Hendricks's business outweighs Mr. Lambert's complaints about the noise it produces.

(Sample Legal Memorandum 12:8-17, 15:26-16:4, 20:18-25)

Comment. Example 7.2.2.1 contains the opening text of the three subsections in Section II of the Sample Legal Memorandum. Each subsection uses the same format to present the Conclusion and the Rule Statement. The Sample Legal Memorandum contains both types of format—separate paragraphs and a single, combined paragraph—but uses one type consistently within each main organizational part of the Discussion. • Each combined paragraph in Example 7.2.2.1 begins by identifying the part of the rule that the subsection addresses. Each one ends with a conclusion about that part of the rule and a brief supporting reason. The Rule Explanation component begins with the second paragraph of each subsection. (See Sample Legal Memorandum 12:18-13:2; 16:5-21, 20:26-21:19.) • The opening paragraph in Section II.B, on the character of the noise, uses the second sentence to introduce the next level of judicial analysis, before presenting the conclusion and supporting reasons. In so doing, it converts the combined opening paragraph into a short overview to begin the subsection.

7.3 The Conclusion

State your substantive conclusion about the part of the rule that is the subject of the section or subsection, followed by a brief supporting reason. Typically, the substantive conclusion predicts how a court would apply the part of the rule you address to the facts in your research assignment, and the supporting reason refers to one or more key, determinative facts.

7.3.1 Substantive focus

Keep your substantive conclusion focused on the specific part of the rule you address in the section or subsection. If you address an element of the judicial rule in one section, state your conclusion for that element. If you address a factor for one element of the rule in a subsection, state your conclusion for that factor. Do not state a broader conclusion than the one that corresponds to the part of the rule you address. In particular, do not state a substantive conclusion about the overall legal issue, based on your analysis of any single part of the rule. Save your conclusion about the overall legal issue for the Brief Answer, the Overview, and the final Conclusion in the memorandum.

Example 7.3.1.1 (substantive conclusion focused on specific part of rule).

B. Character of the Noise

A second factor courts evaluate when deciding if noise creates an unreasonable interference is the character of the noise itself. Smith, 158 N.W.2d at 468 (citing Borsvold, 81 N.W.2d at 382). The courts balance several considerations: the nature and volume of the noise, its frequency and duration, and the time of day when it occurs. Id. Here, a court would likely find that the motorcycle noise from Mr. Hendricks's business, although loud, is produced only intermittently, does not last long, and occurs when adult neighbors are awake and can hear other suburban noise.

(Sample Legal Memorandum 15:26-16:4)

> **Comment.** The substantive conclusion in the final sentence of this combined opening paragraph predicts what a court would find as to the specific part of the rule that the subsection addresses—the character of the noise, as measured by several considerations. The conclusion is properly focused on the subject of the subsection.

Example 7.3.1.2 (bad example: substantive conclusion focused on overall legal issue).

B. Character of the Noise

A second factor courts evaluate when deciding if noise creates an unreasonable interference is the character of the noise itself. Smith, 158 N.W.2d at 468 (citing Borsvold, 81 N.W.2d at 382). The courts balance several considerations: the nature and volume of the noise, its frequency and duration, and the time of day when it occurs. Id. Here, a court would find that motorcycle noise does not create a private nuisance because it occurs sporadically, briefly, and only when adults are awake and can hear other suburban noise.

> **Comment.** In this revised example of the combined opening paragraph from Example 7.3.1.1, the substantive conclusion predicts how a court would rule on the overall legal issue, rather than what the court would find as to the specific part of the rule that the subsection addresses. That overall conclusion is premature—and it may be inaccurate if the court would have to evaluate other parts of the rule before reaching a conclusion about the overall legal issue.

7.3.2 Length

Keep the Conclusion to a manageable length, whether you present it in the first paragraph alone or with the Rule Statement in a combined opening paragraph. Where possible, use a single sentence to state your substantive conclusion and a brief supporting reason. If stating the substantive conclusion and supporting reason together would make a single sentence too long, use two sentences. Occasionally, you may use a third sentence, if the Conclusion is sufficiently complex, legally or factually, to require it.

Example 7.3.2.1 (Conclusion in single sentence).

Here, a court would likely find that the motorcycle noise from Mr. Hendricks's business, although loud, is produced only intermittently, does not last long, and occurs when adult neighbors are awake and can hear other suburban noise.

(Sample Legal Memorandum 16:1-4)

> **Comment.** In Example 7.3.2.1, the Conclusion is stated in a single sentence, at the end of the combined opening paragraph in Section II.B of the Sample Legal Memorandum. It predicts what a court would find as to the several considerations relevant to the character of the noise, based on a few key facts. Although it covers several discrete findings, the sentence is not too long. A single-sentence Conclusion should not be any longer.

Example 7.3.2.2 (Conclusion in two sentences).

Here, a court would likely find that Mr. Hendricks's neighborhood is residential and that Mr. Hendricks is therefore subject to stricter standards regarding the production of noise. Nevertheless, a court would probably conclude that the noise from Mr. Hendricks's business does not create an unreasonable interference within the neighborhood because the noise itself is not unreasonable.

(Sample Legal Memorandum 12:12-17)

> **Comment.** In Example 7.3.2.2, the Conclusion is stated in two sentences, at the end of the combined opening paragraph in Section II.A of the Sample Legal Memorandum. The first sentence predicts what a court would find as to the character of the neighborhood and the corresponding legal standard. The second sentence conveys the weight courts give to the character of the neighborhood, relative to the second factor bearing on unreasonable interference, the character of the noise. A single sentence that tried to express both ideas would be too long.

7.4 The Rule Statement

State the specific part of the rule that is the subject of the section or subsection. Identify its place within the rule structure, to remind your reader—who may not have been familiar with the rule before receiving your memorandum—of the big legal picture. Quote any key language with which the courts articulate the specific part of the rule, too.

7.4.1 Context within rule structure

Introduce the specific part of the rule by identifying it as an *element* of the rule, a *factor* for a particular element, or—if the Discussion component includes subdivisions covering a tertiary level of analysis—a *consideration* for a particular factor. If the rule lists the parts at the same level of analysis in a certain order, refer to that order when you introduce each part: *the first element*, *the second factor*, or *the third consideration*. If the rule does not list the parts in a certain order, if you cover the parts out of order, or if you cover some but not all of the parts—for example, only the relevant the parts in a multiple-part balancing test—do not refer to a definitive order when you introduce each part in the Rule Statement. If the courts apply fewer than all the parts of the rule at a certain level of analysis, but they apply those parts in the same order, you may refer to that order in the Rule Statement.

Example 7.4.1.1 (Rule Statement at primary level of analysis).

The first key element of the test for private nuisance is whether the plaintiff suffers significant harm. Adkins, 487 N.W.2d at 720.

(Sample Legal Memorandum 5:2-3) (emphasis added)

Example 7.4.1.2 (Rule Statement at secondary level of analysis).

The second factor for determining whether an exculpatory clause affects the public interest is whether the "party seeking exculpation is engaged in performing a service of great importance to the public, which is often a matter of practical necessity for some members of the public." Tunkl, 383 P.2d at 445.

(Emphasis added)

Example 7.4.1.3 (Rule Statement at secondary level of analysis).

A second factor courts evaluate when deciding if noise creates an unreasonable interference is the character of the noise itself. Smith, 158 N.W.2d at 468 (citing Borsvold, 81 N.W.2d at 382).

(Sample Legal Memorandum 15:27-29) (emphasis added)

Example 7.4.1.4 (Rule Statement at tertiary level of analysis).

The *first consideration* courts assess in evaluating oppression is whether there was a lack of "real negotiation" between the contracting parties. Id. at 121-22.

(Emphasis added)

Comment. In Example 7.4.1.1, the Rule Statement introduces one part of the rule at the primary level of analysis and identifies it as an *element*. Michigan courts do not typically apply all four elements of the rule to the facts presented in different cases—two of the elements are rarely in dispute—so the Rule Statement refers to the order in which the courts apply the other two elements: the *first key element*. • In Example 7.4.1.2, the Rule Statement—in a memorandum analyzing the validity of an exculpatory clause under California law—introduces one part of the rule at the secondary level of analysis. It identifies the part of the rule as a *factor* and refers to the order in which the rule lists the factors: the *second factor*. • In Example 7.4.1.3, the Rule Statement also introduces one part of the rule at the secondary level of analysis and identifies it as a *factor*. The Michigan rule on private nuisance does not list the factors for unreasonable interference in a definitive order, so the Rule Statement just refers to the specific part of the rule as *A second factor*, not *The second factor*. • In Example 7.4.1.4, the Rule Statement introduces a specific part of the California rule governing unconscionable contacts at the tertiary level of analysis. It identifies that part as a *consideration*, relevant to the judicial analysis of the oppression factor, and it introduces the part by referring to the order in which the rule lists it: the *first consideration*. There is an established rule structure at the tertiary level of analysis in the California rule.

7.4.2 Quotations

Quote any key terms or phrases with which the courts articulate the specific part of the rule. If necessary, quote the entire language. Quote a key term or phrase, even if it has an ordinary meaning, the first time you state that part of the rule, whether in the Overview to the Discussion, an overview to a section, or an individual Rule Statement. Use the term or phrase without quotation marks afterwards, if the context makes clear that the term or phrase is part of the rule. Quote any language that is, or should be, critical to the courts' interpretation and application of the rule in the case law, whether or not you quoted it in a prior overview. Do not paraphrase, condense, or omit that critical language in the Rule Statement: It serves as the reference point for your substantive analysis to follow.

Example 7.4.2.1 (rule containing ordinary term).

Where an alleged nuisance involves noise, the courts evaluate significant harm by considering two factors: whether the noise causes the plaintiff "actual physical discomfort" and whether it prevents the plaintiff from using and enjoying the property. Smith v. W. Wayne Cty. Conservation Ass'n, 158 N.W.2d 463, 468, 470 (Mich. 1968) (per curiam) (citing Borsvold v. United Dairies, 81 N.W.2d 378, 382 (Mich. 1957) (en banc)); Adams, 602 N.W.2d at 222. . . .

I. **Significant Harm**

The first key element of the test for private nuisance is whether the plaintiff suffers significant harm. Adkins, 487 N.W.2d at 720. For this element, the courts use an objective standard to evaluate whether a plaintiff experiences actual physical discomfort or is unable to use and enjoy the property. . . .

A. Actual Physical Discomfort

A court would likely find that Mr. Lambert's aggravated migraines and his children's problems sleeping are too unique to them to satisfy an objective standard of harm.

One factor courts consider in evaluating significant harm is whether the conduct causes actual physical discomfort. Smith, 158 N.W.2d at 468 (citing Borsvold, 81 N.W.2d at 378).

(Sample Legal Memorandum 4:1-7, 5:1-6, 15-21)

Comment. Example 7.4.2.1 contains three Rule Statements covering the first factor for the significant harm element of the private nuisance rule. That factor requires proof of actual physical discomfort. Although the term has an ordinary meaning, the Overview to the Discussion quotes it when introducing both factors for the first time. Subsequent references, in the overview to the section on significant harm and in the Rule Statement to the subsection on actual physical discomfort, omit the quotation marks. The context makes clear that the term is part of the rule.

<u>Example 7.4.2.2</u> (rule containing critical judicial language).

The second factor for determining whether an exculpatory clause affects the public interest is whether the "party seeking exculpation is engaged in performing a service of great importance to the public, which is often a matter of practical necessity for some members of the public." <u>Tunkl</u>, 383 P.2d at 445.

<u>Example 7.4.2.3.</u> (bad example: paraphrase omits critical language).

The second factor for determining whether an exculpatory clause affects the public interest is whether the service is a matter of public importance and practical necessity. <u>Tunkl</u>, 383 P.2d at 445.

> **Comment.** Example 7.4.2.2 states the second factor in the California rule on the validity of exculpatory clauses. The language with which the leading decision articulates the factor establishes two considerations and a specific relationship between them: The service may be a practical necessity for some people, but it must be a matter of public importance. The language was intended to exclude matters that are not of public importance, even if they are a practical necessity to some people. The California decisions analyzing the second factor mostly adhere to that intent. • The Rule Statement in Example 7.4.2.3, however, distorts the meaning of the factor by omitting the *which is often* language that subordinates the second consideration to the first. That distortion would create an inaccurate basis for analyzing the courts' interpretation and application of the second factor in the case law.

7.4.3 Legal citations

Include a legal citation after the Rule Statement. Cite the leading decision in your jurisdiction that established the specific part of the rule and the other parts at the same level of analysis—especially if you cited the same decision when you introduced the applicable law in the Overview to the Discussion or an overview to a divided section. Cite that leading decision after the Rule Statement for each part of the rule—for example, in successive subsections that cover the factors for a single element of the rule. If different decisions established different parts of the rule, just cite the relevant decisions after the different Rule Statements. You may cite a second, more recent or lower-court decision to support the Rule Statement (see §6.4.5), but avoid long string citations; you will be able to cover other important decisions in the Rule Explanation component. Do not cite an unpublished decision as authority for any Rule Statement. (See §6.4.6.) If you use a short overview paragraph to begin any section or section, include a legal citation after introducing the parts at the next level within the rule structure or the next level of judicial analysis. (See §6.7.)

Example 7.4.3.1 (Citations after successive Rule Statements).

A. Character of the Neighborhood

One factor courts evaluate when deciding if noise creates an unreasonable interference is the character of the neighborhood in which the noise occurs. Smith, 158 N.W.2d at 468 (citing Borsvold, 81 N.W.2d at 382). . . .

B. Character of the Noise

A second factor courts evaluate when deciding if noise creates an unreasonable interference is the character of the noise itself. Smith, 158 N.W.2d at 468 (citing Borsvold, 81 N.W.2d at 382). The courts balance several considerations: the nature and volume of the noise, its frequency and duration, and the time of day when it occurs. Id. . . .

C. Necessity and Value of the Conduct

A third factor courts evaluate when evaluating if noise creates an unreasonable interference is the necessity and value of the conduct responsible for the noise, compared to the harms of which the plaintiff complains. Waier, 251 N.W. at 553; Adams, 602 N.W.2d at 219, 222-23.

(Sample Legal Memorandum 12:8-12, 15:26-16:1, 20:18-22)

Comment. Example 7.4.3.1 contains the Rule Statement for the three subsections in Section II of the Sample Legal Memorandum, which cover three factors for the second element of the private nuisance rule. The first two factors derive from the same leading decision, *Smith*, and the first two Rule Statements are followed by a citation to *Smith*. The third factor derives from a different decision, *Waier*, and the third Rule Statement is followed by a citation to *Waier* and a citation to a more recent, appellate-court decision, *Adams*, which also identifies the third factor. • The Rule Statement for the second factor, the character of the noise, is followed by a sentence introducing the next level in the judicial analysis of that factor. That sentence, like the preceding Rule Statement, is followed by a legal citation—which happens to be to the same leading decision, *Smith*, from which the first two factors derive.

7.5 Templates

Template 7A: Conclusion and Rule Statement in Separate Paragraphs.

[X.] Subject heading for section[1]

¶1: State substantive conclusion for subject of section, followed by brief supporting reason[2]

¶2: In first sentence, state specific part of the rule the section addresses.[3] [4]

- Add legal citation to leading decision
- Begin Rule Explanation component in second sentence

---

[1] Adjust font style for level of heading. (See §5.3.5.3.)

[2] Use one or two sentences of moderate length. If necessary, use a third sentence for especially complex conclusions.

[3] Identify the rule's place in the rule structure.

[4] Quote key terms and phrases, or more extended, critical language, courts use to articulate rule.

Template 7B: Conclusion and Rule Statement in Combined Paragraph.

[X.] Subject heading for section[1]

¶1: Combined opening paragraph

- State specific part of the rule the section addresses[2] [3]
- Add legal citation to leading decision[4]
- State substantive conclusion for subject of section
- State brief supporting reason[5]

¶2: Begin Rule Explanation component

---

[1] Adjust font style for level of heading. (See §5.3.5.3.)

[2] Identify the rule's place in the rule structure.

[3] Quote key terms and phrases, or more extended, critical language, courts use to articulate rule.

[4] If helpful to reader, add second sentence after citation to introduce next level of rule structure or judicial analysis. Add legal citation.

[5] Use one or two sentences of moderate length for substantive conclusion and supporting reason. If necessary, use a third sentence for especially complex conclusions.

Chapter 8
How to Write the Rule Explanation for an Individual Section or Subsection

8.1 Purpose

The Rule Explanation is the third component in the small-scale organizational structure for presenting your substantive analysis within a single section or subsection in the Discussion. It tells your reader how the courts have interpreted the specific part of the rule you are addressing and how they have applied it to different fact patterns. In essence, the Rule Explanation provides the legal foundation for your conclusion about how a new court would apply the same part of the rule to your facts.

8.2 Format

The Rule Explanation begins after the opening Conclusion and Rule Statement end. If your section begins with the Conclusion in the first paragraph and the Rule Statement in the first sentence of the second paragraph, the Rule Explanation begins with the second sentence of the second paragraph. If your section begins with a paragraph combining the Rule Statement and the Conclusion, the Rule Explanation begins at the start of the second paragraph. Each Rule Explanation contains one or more paragraphs, presented successively. The Rule Application component in the small-scale organizational structure begins after the final Rule Explanation paragraph ends. (See §9.2.)

8.2.1 Deductive presentation

Organize the Rule Explanation deductively, moving from the general to the particular. The goal is to tell your reader what is important about the case law on the part of the rule you are addressing. Your reader often will be unfamiliar with the case law—you are the one who did the legal research—so you need to educate the reader about it. Your reader probably will be busy with other matters in the office, too, so you need to make it as easy as possible for the reader to learn the important information. The best way to do that is to state one or more insights, or main points, about the relevant case law, which you have distilled from your research. (See §8.3.) Use a separate paragraph to state each point, and illustrate that point by describing specific case law examples. (See §8.2.2.) Do not just describe a series of cases, without more, and force your reader to figure out their significance. Similarly, begin each case description with the holding or finding that illustrates the main point: That is the most important information about each case. Do not just begin with the facts. Organizing the Rule Explanation deductively is hard work, but your substantive analysis will be sharper for forcing yourself to articulate what is important about the case law and each case law example. Your reader will recognize and appreciate your hard work, too.

8.2.2 Paragraphs

Organize each Rule Explanation paragraph around a single main point about the relevant case law. State that point in the first sentence or, if the paragraph begins with the Rule Statement, in the second sentence. Complete the paragraph by illustrating the main point with specific case law examples. (See §8.5.) Do not begin any Rule Explanation paragraph by describing an individual case, without first stating the main point about the case law to which it relates. Do not introduce a different main point about the case law in the middle of any Rule Explanation paragraph; use a separate paragraph to state and illustrate the different point.

8.2.3 Length

The Rule Explanation component in any section or subsection is *elastic*: it can be shorter or longer, as necessary to tell your reader what is important about the case law on the part of the rule you are addressing. For some parts of your substantive analysis, it may be sufficient to state and illustrate a single main point about the case law, in a single Rule Explanation paragraph. For others, it may be necessary to state and illustrate several points, in successive Rule Explanation paragraphs, because of the importance or complexity of that part of the analysis. If, however, it is necessary to state and illustrate a lot of main points about one part of the analysis—generally, four or more points—cover them in shorter, more manageable subdivisions within the section or subsection. Individual Rule Explanation paragraphs should not exceed about one double-spaced page, although the occasional paragraph can be a little longer, if necessary.

Example 8.2.3.1 (Rule Explanation paragraph stating single main point).

The other factor courts consider in evaluating significant harm is whether the conduct interferes with the use and enjoyment of property. Adams, 602 N.W.2d at 222. Where noise is concerned, the courts find significant harm if the interference is pervasive, inside and outside the home. See Restatement (Second) of Torts § 821F cmt. c ("[T]here must be a real and appreciable invasion of the plaintiff's interests before he can have an action.") For example, in Mackenzie, the court found significant harm where machinery noise from a lumberyard and interior trim factory caused pervasive interference with the neighbors' use and enjoyment of their property. 174 N.W. at 163. The noise lasted all day, it went through the neighbors' homes, whether the windows were closed or not, and people could not escape from it. Id. One neighbor even had to leave his home. Id. Similarly, in Wilke, the court found significant harm where rock-crushing noise from a concrete plant caused pervasive interference with the neighbors' "[ability] to function inside their homes." 2007 WL 1828788, at *4. The noise began early in the morning, ended late at night, and continued unabated on the weekends. Id. at *3-4. Several neighbors were unable to sit in their backyards, use portions of their houses, or hear the television or radio inside their homes. Id.; cf. Smith, 158 N.W.2d at 468-69 (finding no harm where evidence showed noise from gun shooting range prevented only some homeowners but not others from concentrating, engaging in conversation, watching television, or remaining at home). Conversely, in Childs, the court found no significant harm where vehicle and pedestrian noise from a Super K-Mart store caused only minimal interference with a neighboring family's use of its property. 2001 WL 1199901, at *4. The family complained that the honking horns, squealing brakes, loud radios, and noise from freight delivery vehicles caused them significant harm. Id. at *3. The court disagreed: "By describing their alleged injuries merely as 'problems' and 'diminution' of the use [and] enjoyment . . . of their property, plaintiffs failed to set their claims apart from minimal damages insufficient to support a claim of nuisance." Id. at *4; see also id. (rejecting as minimal harm plaintiffs' claims that excessive light made it difficult to sleep, read, work, or concentrate inside their home and that exhaust fumes made it difficult to plant flowers and socialize outside).

(Sample Legal Memorandum 9:22-10:25)

Comment. Example 8.2.3.1 contains the single Rule Explanation paragraph in Section I.B of the Sample Legal Memorandum. • The first sentence is the Rule Statement. It identifies the inability to use and enjoy property as a second factor the courts consider in evaluating significant harm, the first key element of the rule for private nuisance. • The Rule Explanation begins with the main point stated in the second sentence, about the degree to which noise must interfere with the use and enjoyment of property to constitute significant harm. It is the only point about this part of the analysis that the writer includes, so there is just the one Rule Explanation paragraph. • Every case description in the paragraph illustrates that same main point, either by positive example—as in *Mackenzie* and *Wilke*—or by negative example—as in *Childs*. (See §8.4.1.) • The paragraph, slightly longer than one double-spaced page, is as long as any Rule Explanation paragraph should be.

Example 8.2.3.2 (successive Rule Explanation paragraphs stating different main points).

One factor courts consider in evaluating significant harm is whether the conduct causes actual physical discomfort. Smith, 158 N.W.2d at 468 (citing Borsvold, 81 N.W.2d at 378). The courts do not find significant harm, however, if the conduct would not cause actual physical discomfort to an ordinary person. Id. at 470. . . .

The courts tend to find significant harm only if the conduct in question causes actual physical discomfort to multiple people. . . .

The courts are especially likely to find significant harm if noise causes actual physical discomfort to multiple adults by depriving them of sleep. . . .

(Sample Legal Memorandum 5:19-23, 6:27-28, 7:11-13)

Comment. Example 8.2.3.2 contains the beginning of the three successive Rule Explanation paragraphs in Section I.A of the Sample Legal Memorandum. • The first sentence in the first paragraph is the Rule Statement. It identifies actual physical discomfort as one factor courts consider in evaluating significant harm, the first key element of the rule for private nuisance. • The Rule Explanation begins with the main point stated in the second sentence of the first paragraph, about the necessary effect of the conduct upon an ordinary person. In this part of the analysis, the writer states three different points about how the courts interpret and apply the rule, in three successive Rule Explanation paragraphs. (The example includes only the beginning of each paragraph.) • Although the three points are different, the three paragraphs are similar in that the rest of each paragraph illustrates the main point with specific examples from the case law.

8.3 Main points about the case law

State one or more main points in the Rule Explanation to identify what seems important to the courts when they interpret and apply the part of the rule you are addressing—and what seems important to you about the way the courts do so. In this regard, think of the Rule Explanation as the written equivalent of your half of an office conference with the assigning attorney, who asks you, *What do I need to know about the law on this part of the rule?* To provide the most helpful response, start with the big picture, the main point or points you have distilled from your research. Include only those points that will be relevant when you apply the law to your facts. Omit any other points about the case law if you do not incorporate them in the Rule Application.

8.3.1 Categories of main points

Main points about the case law identify the common themes, patterns, requirements, reasoning, and other decision points that characterize the courts' analysis of the part of the rule you are addressing—why and how the courts decide if that part of the rule is satisfied. Helpful main points might cover the following: (i) the legal *standards* the courts establish for satisfying the part of the rule; (ii) the courts' *interpretation* of key terms or phrases in, or the general language of, the part of the rule; (iii) the type or amount of *evidence* that satisfies or tends to satisfy the part of the rule; (iv) the *facts* or categories of facts that do and do not satisfy the part of the rule; (v) the *relative weight* the courts give to different legal and factual criteria in their analysis of the part of the rule; (vi) the *trend* of judicial interpretations or applications of the part of the rule or important *exceptions* to a trend; (vii) any important *unresolved issues* with respect to the part of the rule; and (viii) important legal, judicial, or public *policies* underlying the courts' analysis of the part of the rule. The different categories of main points are not mutually exclusive: a single insight about the case law could span more than one. Do not worry about pigeonholing your insights into discrete categories. Do not feel obligated to include different categories, either. Just decide what is most important to tell your reader about how the courts analyze the particular part of the rule, and state your main point or points accordingly.

<u>Example 8.3.1.1</u> (main point identifying legal standard for satisfying rule).

The courts do not find significant harm, however, if the conduct would not cause actual physical discomfort to an ordinary person.

(Sample Legal Memorandum 5:21-23)

Example 8.3.1.2 (main point identifying courts' interpretation of general language of rule).

Although the language of Rule 1.10(b)(1) is silent as to timing, the Eastern District courts construe it to require "timely" screening, consistent with the Rule's objective of protecting client confidences.

(Sample Informal Memorandum 2:24-27)

> **Comment.** The insight about the case law in Example 8.3.1.2 spans two categories of main points, judicial interpretations of general language and important policies underlying a rule.

Example 8.3.1.3 (main point identifying evidence tending to satisfy rule).

Courts find greater evidence of unreasonable interference the higher the volume of a noise and the more abrasive its sound.

(Sample Legal Memorandum 16:5-6)

Example 8.3.1.4 (main point identifying fact pattern that satisfies rule).

The courts are especially likely to find significant harm if noise causes actual physical discomfort to multiple adults by depriving them of sleep.

(Sample Legal Memorandum 7:11-13)

> **Comment.** Examples 8.3.1.3 and 8.3.1.4 focus primarily on different categories of main points—evidence sufficient to satisfy a rule and fact patterns that satisfy a rule, respectively. Note, however, that the insight about the case law presented in each one also spans the other category.

Example 8.3.1.5 (main point identifying important exception to trend of decisions).

Nevertheless, the Eastern District courts may construe the prompt written notice requirement more leniently in an exceptional case, where the hiring firm fully complied with the screening requirement and its delay in providing written notice was only slight.

(Sample Informal Memorandum 5:11-14)

Example 8.3.1.6 (bad example: main point not relevant to legal analysis).

Conduct that causes or threatens loss of property value, however, does not constitute significant harm.

Comment. Example 8.3.1.6 contains an accurate insight about the case law on the part of the rule covered in Section I of the Sample Legal Memorandum, the element of significant harm. That insight, however, is irrelevant to the analysis in the Memorandum. The plaintiff, Mr. Lambert, has not alleged loss of property value due to noise from the motorcycle repair business next door. There would be nothing to say in the Rule Application about how a court would apply this aspect of the case law to the facts. Thus, Section I does not include a main point about property value or a full Rule Explanation paragraph illustrating it.

8.3.2 Stating the main point

State each main point in a single, succinct sentence.

8.3.2.1 Relation to the rule

State each main point so it clearly relates to the part of the rule you are addressing in the section or subsection—the specific element, factor, or consideration in the overall rule structure. You may refer to that part of the rule directly: *The courts tend to find significant harm only if the conduct in question causes actual physical discomfort to multiple people.* (Sample Legal Memorandum 6:27-28) (emphasis added). You may refer to the part of the rule indirectly, as long as you include sufficient terminology to identify it: *The courts are likely to find that a neighborhood is residential even if some businesses are interspersed among the dwellings.* (Sample Legal Memorandum 12:18-19) (emphasis added). You may also refer to the next-highest level in the rule structure, if that context is relevant to the insight you are presenting in the main point: *The courts tend to find significant harm only if the conduct in question causes actual physical discomfort to multiple people.* (Sample Legal Memorandum 6:27-28) (emphasis added).

8.3.2.2 Key judicial terms

State each main point in your own words, for the most part. If the courts use a key term or phrase for one aspect of the legal analysis in the case law, use the same or similar language if you include a main point about that aspect: *The courts do not find significant harm, however, if the conduct would not cause actual physical discomfort* to an ordinary person. (Sample Legal Memorandum 5:21-23) (emphasis added). In limited instances, you may include a longer quotation from a case if it articulates a specific point you want to make—but introduce it or frame it in your own words: *To ensure that screening measures are timely, the Eastern District courts require a hiring firm to implement them no later than the time when the "potentially disqualifying event occur[s], either when the attorney first join[s] the firm or when the firm accept[s] a case presenting an ethical problem."* (Sample Informal Memorandum 2:43-3:2) (citation omitted). (See §8.6.) Do not repeat language from the rule itself as a main point; add something new, based on your reading of the case law.

8.3.2.3 Judicial findings and conclusions

Where possible, state a main point that identifies what the courts find or conclude when they pursue an inquiry: *The courts tend to find significant harm only if the conduct in question causes actual physical discomfort to multiple people.* (Sample Legal Memorandum 6:27-28.) Do not settle for a main point that just identifies the inquiry in the abstract: *When assessing significant harm, the courts consider how many people experience actual physical discomfort from the conduct in question.* Tell your reader the *result* when the courts assess, consider, evaluate, analyze, examine, balance, weigh, measure, or undertake similar inquiries. You may present the result by focusing your main point on the courts: *The courts tend to find significant harm only if the conduct in question causes actual physical discomfort to multiple people.* (Sample Legal Memorandum 6:27-28.) Alternatively, you may present the result by focusing directly on its substance: *The necessity or unavoidability of creating noise during an activity tends to lessen the unreasonableness of any disturbance the noise causes.* (Sample Legal Memorandum 20:26-27.) Try to use the same focus, however—on the courts or on the substance—for every main point within the same Rule Explanation.

Example 8.3.2.3.1 (main points in Rule Explanation focus directly on result of courts' inquiries).

The necessity or unavoidability of creating noise during an activity tends to lessen the unreasonableness of any disturbance the noise causes. . . .

Similarly, the social benefits of noise-producing activity tend to lessen the overall unreasonableness of any disturbance the noise causes. . . .

(Sample Legal Memorandum 20:26-27, 21:20-21) (citations omitted)

Comment. The two main points in the Rule Explanation in Example

8.3.2.3.1, from section II.C of the Sample Legal Memorandum, could have been written to focus on the courts, instead—for example, *The courts find that the necessity or unavoidability of creating noise during an activity tends to lessen the unreasonableness of any disturbance the noise causes.* Focusing on the courts, however, can make the main points wordier, as in this revision. (More concise revisions are possible, however.) • Legal memoranda commonly predict how a new court will apply a rule to a set of facts, so it is often most helpful to explain the case law to your reader in terms of what courts in the past have found or concluded. Most of the main points in the Sample Legal Memorandum focus on the courts. See, for instance, Example 8.2.3.2.

<u>Example 8.3.2.3.2</u> (bad example: main points in Rule Explanation change focus from courts conducting inquiry to result of courts' inquiry).

The courts find that the necessity or unavoidability of creating noise during an activity tends to lessen the unreasonableness of any disturbance the noise causes. . . .

Similarly, the social benefits of noise-producing activity tend to lessen the overall unreasonableness of any disturbance the noise causes. . . .

Comment. In Example 8.3.2.3.2, the first main point focuses on the courts conducting one inquiry, whereas the second main point focuses on the result of another inquiry. A reader might be surprised, and disoriented, by the change in the way the writer is explaining the law.

8.3.2.4 Positive points

State positive main points, about what courts do: *Although the language of Rule 1.10(b)(1) is silent as to timing, the Eastern District courts construe it to require "timely" screening, consistent with the Rule's objective of protecting client confidences.* (Sample Informal Memorandum 2:24-27.) Avoid negative main points, about what courts do not do. Negative points are ambiguous: *The Eastern District courts do not interpret the language of Rule 1.10(b)(1) to mean there are no timing constraints as to when hiring firms must implement screening measures.* Note, however, that a main point can be positive even if it identifies a judicial action that is substantively negative: *Eastern District courts reject oral notice as a substitute for the written notice required by Rule 1.10(b)(2).*

8.3.2.5 Specific points

State specific, substantive main points: *In addition, courts find less evidence of unreasonable interference the more the noise is confined to adults' waking hours and times when other, ordinary noise occurs.* (Sample Legal Memorandum 17:15-17.) Avoid main points devoid of useful information: *In addition, courts find less evidence of unreasonable interference when the noise is confined to certain times of the day.* Force yourself to identify and articulate exactly what the case law is telling you—and your reader—about the subject matter; do not stop halfway, with an empty generalization. State specific main points whether you focus on what the courts do, find, or conclude (as in the first example in this §8.3.2.5) or on the substance of what they do, find, or conclude: *There is less evidence of unreasonable interference the more the noise is confined to adults' waking hours and times when other, ordinary noise occurs.*

8.3.2.6 Accurate points

State your main points accurately. Do not overstate your points or make other assertions that the case law will not support. Do not state that *the courts* do something when only one court did it in one decision. On the other hand, do not state your main points so narrowly that they do not help your reader understand how the courts interpret or apply the rule to a spectrum of different fact patterns. For example, do not write, *courts often find that condominium purchasers have no real bargaining power when presented with a pre-printed contract cast in standardized, generic language*, if the case law on this point extends to other types of consumers and your client signed a form contract to participate in a driving-skills course. Finally, because your legal analysis in a memorandum must be objective, do not fail to include important, relevant aspects of the case law that may disfavor your client's legal position: *The more residential the neighborhood, the more strictly will the courts evaluate the noise that may be permissible in it.* (Sample Legal Memorandum 13:3-4.)

8.3.2.7 Single insight

In general, state main points that present a single insight about the case law: *The more residential the neighborhood, the more strictly will the courts evaluate the noise that may be permissible in it.* (Sample Legal Memorandum 13:3-4.) Occasionally, you may state a main point that presents two insights—but only if they are closely related and you can illustrate both insights in one manageable Rule Explanation paragraph. Be sure to include both insights in the main point. Do not include one insight in the main point at the start of the paragraph and introduce the second insight in another main point later in the same paragraph. Use two different main points and two different Rule Explanation paragraphs if the two insights are not closely related or if you cannot illustrate the two insights adequately in the same paragraph.

Example 8.3.2.7.1 (Rule Explanation paragraph with single main point presenting two related insights).

On the other hand, courts find less evidence of unreasonable interference as the frequency and duration of the noise decrease, and they tend to give frequency and duration greater weight than the sheer volume and abrasiveness of the noise. Smith, 158 N.W.2d at 471. For example, in Smith, the court found that noise from a gun shooting range was not unreasonable, "especially considering" that the noise happened very infrequently, during approximately ten competitive meets each year. Id. Similarly, in Cunningham, the court found that spectator noise at high-school football games fell "short of constituting an unreasonable burden," with only three or four home games each season and between eleven and twenty-four loud bursts of noise during each game. 2001 WL 716882, at *4. In Radziewicz, the court found that noise from a paddlewheel boat's whistle was not unreasonable where the boat made seven or fewer tours a day, the whistle sounded only several times each tour, and the whistle blasts lasted no more than six seconds. 2009 WL 297433, at *2-3. Notably, in both Smith and Cunningham, the courts found the infrequency of the interference more important than its volume: both noises exceeded 80 decibels, Smith, 158 N.W.2d at 469-70; Cunningham, 2001 WL 716882, at *4, and the court in Cunningham characterized the loudest noises as "extreme eruptions of sound," which would "disturb[] . . . a reasonable person," 2001 WL 716882, at *4. The courts in both cases found the interference was not unreasonable because the loud noises did not occur often enough. Smith, 158 N.W.2d at 471; Cunningham, 2001 WL 716882, at *4.

(Sample Legal Memorandum 16:22-17:14) (emphasis added)

Comment. Example 8.3.2.7.1 contains the second of three Rule Explanation paragraphs from Section II.B of the Sample Legal Memorandum. The section covers the second factor in the courts' analysis of unreasonable interference, the character of the noise. The second paragraph presents a combined analysis of two of the relevant considerations for that factor, the frequency and duration of the noise. (See §5.3.4.2.) • The main point, in the first sentence, presents two closely related insights about the case law. The first identifies a fact pattern involving frequency and duration that tends not to satisfy the unreasonable interference factor. The second identifies the greater weight courts give to frequency and duration than to the volume and nature of the noise, two other considerations in the courts' analysis. • Following the main point, the paragraph first illustrates how infrequency and short duration lessen potential unreasonable interference. Then it illustrates how infrequency and short duration outweigh volume and abrasiveness of noise. • The paragraph illustrates both insights in less than one page, a manageable length.

Example 8.3.2.7.2 (bad example: Rule Explanation paragraph with two main points, presenting related insights in different places).

On the other hand, courts find less evidence of unreasonable interference as the frequency and duration of the noise decrease. Smith, 158 N.W.2d at 471. For example, in Smith, the court found that noise from a gun shooting range was not unreasonable, "especially considering" that the noise happened very infrequently, during approximately ten competitive meets each year. Id. Similarly, in Cunningham, the court found that spectator noise at high-school football games fell "short of constituting an unreasonable burden," with only three or four home games each season and between eleven and twenty-four loud bursts of noise during each game. 2001 WL 716882, at *4. In Radziewicz, the court found that noise from a paddlewheel boat's whistle was not unreasonable where the boat made seven or fewer tours a day, the whistle sounded only several times each tour, and the whistle blasts lasted no more than six seconds. 2009 WL 297433, at *2-3. *Further, the courts tend to give frequency and duration greater weight than the sheer volume and abrasiveness of the noise.* In both Smith and Cunningham, the courts found the infrequency of the interference more important than its volume: both noises exceeded 80 decibels, Smith, 158 N.W.2d at 469-70; Cunningham, 2001 WL 716882, at *4, and the court in Cunningham characterized the loudest noises as "extreme eruptions of sound," which would "disturb[] . . . a reasonable person," 2001 WL 716882, at *4. The courts in both cases found the interference was not unreasonable because the loud noises did not occur often enough. Smith, 158 N.W.2d at 471; Cunningham, 2001 WL 716882, at *4.

(Emphasis added)

Comment. In Example 8.3.2.7.2, the main point in the first sentence fails to inform the reader of the two, related insights the Rule Explanation paragraph actually covers. The second insight, in a separate main point, is buried in the middle of the paragraph, where a busy reader easily could overlook it. At a minimum, a reader might be momentarily disoriented, if not irked, by the unexpected change of subject. • To avoid the problem, the paragraph could be either written with both insights in the opening main point, as in Example

8.3.2.7.1, or divided into two separate Rule Explanation paragraphs, with the second paragraph starting with the second main point.

8.3.3 Covering multiple main points

Generally, state the most important main point or points first. State points that relate to the basic subject of the part of the rule you are addressing before you cover any exceptions or ancillary issues. You may use a different sequence, however, if there is an important threshold issue, such as an applicable legal standard or interpretation of a key term in the rule, or a logical or chronological relationship among the points you want to make—even if the most important point comes last. If the courts follow a standard sequence of steps in analyzing the part of the rule, you may follow that sequence, too.

Example 8.3.3.1 (main point identifying legal standard precedes main points identifying fact patterns that satisfy rule).

The courts do not find significant harm, however, if the conduct would not cause actual physical discomfort to an ordinary person. . . .

The courts tend to find significant harm only if the conduct in question causes actual physical discomfort to multiple people. . . .

The courts are especially likely to find significant harm if noise causes actual physical discomfort to multiple adults by depriving them of sleep. . . .

(Sample Legal Memorandum 5:21-23, 6:27-28, 7:11-13)

Comment. Example 8.3.3.1 contains the three main points from the Rule Explanation in Section I.A of the Sample Legal Memorandum, addressing the actual physical discomfort factor for the significant harm element of the rule on private nuisance. • The first point identifies the applicable legal standard for assessing actual physical discomfort. It is necessary to cover this point before the two following points, which then present insights about how the courts apply the legal standard.

8.3.4 Legal citations

If you derive a main point from a specific judicial decision, cite that decision after stating the point. If you derive a main point from a number of judicial decisions, do not interrupt the flow of your Rule Explanation paragraph by including a long string citation after the main point. Just include the key decisions in the rest of the paragraph, and cite each one when you describe it; your reader will understand that you derived the main point from those decisions. Do not cite an unpublished decision as authority for a main point.

Example 8.3.4.1 (main point, derived from specific decision, followed by citation).

One factor courts consider in evaluating significant harm is whether the conduct causes actual physical discomfort. Smith, 158 N.W.2d at 468 (citing Borsvold, 81 N.W.2d at 378). The courts do not find significant harm, however, if the conduct would not cause actual physical discomfort to an ordinary person. Id. at 470.

(Sample Legal Memorandum 5:19-23)

> **Comment.** In Example 8.3.4.1, the first sentence states the part of the private nuisance rule addressed in Section I.A of the Sample Legal Memorandum. The second sentence states the first of three main points in the Rule Explanation about that part of the rule. This first point derives from the *Smith* decision, as the following citation acknowledges. • *Smith* is one of the leading Michigan decisions on private nuisance law, and many other main points in the Sample Legal Memorandum also derive from it. Each one cites *Smith* for direct or indirect support.

Example 8.3.4.2 (main point, derived from multiple decisions, not followed by citation).

The courts tend to find significant harm only if the conduct in question causes actual physical discomfort to multiple people.

(Sample Legal Memorandum 6:27-28)

> **Comment.** The sentence in Example 8.3.4.2 states the second main point in Section I.A of the Sample Legal Memorandum. It derives from multiple decisions. It is not followed by a citation, but the remainder of the Rule Explanation paragraph describes, and cites, the key decisions that illustrate the point.

8.4 Cases that illustrate the main points

For each Rule Explanation paragraph, include the key cases that best illustrate the substance of your main point.

8.4.1 Supporting cases

Include cases that support your main point first and any important contrary cases second. A case supports your main point either because the facts in the case lead to the result your point identifies (a *positive example*) or because different facts lead to the opposite result (a *negative example*). Depending on the available case law, you may include both types of supporting cases to show the range of results—but include the positive examples before the negative ones. A case is contrary to your main point if facts similar to those in the positive supporting examples lead to the opposite result. You may need to rephrase your main point to account for any contrary cases or, if there are a lot of them, reconsider whether your point is accurate. (See §9.5.)

Example 8.4.1.1 (positive case law examples in Rule Explanation paragraph precede negative examples).

The courts tend to find significant harm only if the conduct in question causes actual physical discomfort to multiple people. In O'Connor v. Jersey Creamery Co. of Detroit, 248 N.W. 557, 558 (Mich. 1933), *the court found significant harm* where smoke, odors, and noise from a creamery plant adversely affected the health of twenty-two neighbors. In Mackenzie v. Frank M. Pauli Co., 174 N.W. 161, 161, 163-64 (Mich. 1919), *the court found significant harm* where machinery noise from a lumberyard and interior trim factory adversely affected the health of twelve neighbors. In Smith, however, *the court found no significant harm*, in part because there was conflicting testimony from the plaintiff residents and other neighbors as to whether noise from the gun shooting range caused them actual physical discomfort. 158 N.W.2d at 469. Similarly, in Radziewicz v. Frankenmuth Paddlewheel Tours, No. 282648, 2009 WL 2974733, at *1, *3 (Mich. Ct. App. Sept. 17, 2009) (per curiam), *the court found no significant harm* to the single complaining property owner, who experienced only "minor annoyance"—not actual physical discomfort—from a paddlewheel boat's whistle soundings.

(Sample Legal Memorandum 6:27-7:10) (emphasis added)

Comment. In Example 8.4.1.1., the main point in the Rule Explanation paragraph, stated in the first sentence, identifies a certain fact pattern that tends to lead the courts to find significant harm. • The first two cases the writer includes, *O'Connor* and *Mackenzie*, provide positive examples of the main point. In each one, the court found significant harm when the same fact pattern was present. • The second two cases, *Smith* and *Radziewicz*, provide negative examples. The court did not find significant harm when the same fact pattern was not present. Nevertheless, as negative examples, *Smith* and *Radziewicz* also support the main point.

Example 8.4.1.2 (positive case law examples of substantively negative main point).

One factor courts consider in evaluating significant harm is whether the conduct causes actual physical discomfort. Smith, 158 N.W.2d at 468 (citing Borsvold, 81 N.W.2d at 378). *The courts do not find significant harm*, however, if the conduct would not cause actual physical discomfort to an ordinary person. Id. at 470. In Smith, *the Michigan Supreme Court found no significant harm* where noise from a gun shooting range would not cause actual physical discomfort to an ordinary person. Id. at 471. . . . Similarly, in Rose v. Braciszewski, No. 285316, 2009 WL 3276431, at *4 (Mich. Ct. App. Oct. 13, 2009) (per curiam), *the court found no significant harm* where smoke from burning yard waste on a neighboring property and exhaust fumes from the neighbor's automobiles would not cause actual physical discomfort to an ordinary person. . . .

(Sample Legal Memorandum 5:19-6:18) (emphasis added)

Comment. In the Rule Explanation paragraph in Example 8.4.1.2, the first sentence is the Rule Statement. The main point, stated in the second sentence, identifies a legal standard that prevents a finding of substantial harm when the facts do not satisfy the standard. • The two cases the writer includes, *Smith* and *Rose*, provide positive examples of the main point. In each one, there was no significant harm because the facts did not satisfy the legal standard. • Although the main point identifies the negative operation of the legal standard, *Smith* and *Rose* provide positive examples of the point because, on their facts, they present the negative operation of the standard, too. • A negative example of this main point would be a case where different facts *satisfied* the legal standard, that is, where the conduct caused actual physical harm to an ordinary person.

8.4.2 Similar and dissimilar cases

Where possible, include supporting cases with fact patterns similar to your own. Including similar cases to illustrate your main points will make it easier for you to analogize your facts to those in the case law examples, in the Rule Application. You may even be able to phrase main points that identify important fact patterns in the case law to emphasize the similarity to your facts: *In addition, courts find less evidence of unreasonable interference the more the noise is confined to adults' waking hours and times when other, ordinary noise occurs*. (Sample Legal Memorandum 17:15-17.) If, however, the only—or the most important—supporting cases available to illustrate a given main point contain facts dissimilar to your own, include them, and distinguish your facts from theirs in the Rule Application. Try to phrase the main point to emphasize the dissimilarity, too: *The courts find that customers do have a meaningful choice when a business offers one or more options for obtaining the same basic service*. (Memorandum analyzing unconscionability, under California law, of ATM fee at rural locations, where ATM users lack alternatives for obtaining cash.)

8.4.3 Number of cases

Include more than a single case to illustrate each main point, unless there is only a single case for that point.

8.4.4 Level and date of authority

Try to include cases from the highest court in your jurisdiction. Recognize, however, that there will be many more cases from the lower courts. Include cases from the appellate court and the trial court that would have jurisdiction over your matter; occasionally, you may include cases from other courts, as persuasive authority. Among equally supporting cases, prefer the more recent ones. If more recent cases expressly rely on an older one, you may include that older case, too. Include unpublished decisions, if at all, only to illustrate how the courts apply a main point to additional fact patterns. (See §6.4.6.)

8.5 Descriptions of individual cases

Within each Rule Explanation paragraph, use one or more sentences to describe the key cases you select to illustrate the main point. Begin each description by stating why or how the case illustrates the main point, and then add the necessary explanatory details. Keep the description focused on how the case relates to that main point, not to a different point or the overall legal issue.

8.5.1 Length

Use several sentences to describe the most important or complicated cases, especially the first time you describe them. Three sentences are generally sufficient (see §8.5.4), but sometimes you may need to use more than three to cover the relevant facts or reasoning or to include an important quotation. At other times, you may be able to use only one or two sentences to say everything you need to say about a case. You will often use the same case to illustrate more than one main point in your memorandum; the length of your descriptions of that case will vary according to how much you need to say about it to illustrate each point. For every case description, include only the information that is relevant to the main point of the paragraph in which the description appears.

8.5.2 Factual context

Provide sufficient factual context about the cases you describe, so a reader unfamiliar with them can appreciate how the legally significant aspects of the cases arose. Include the particular businesses, occupations, actions, and other material facts to establish reference points to apply to your own facts in the Rule Application. A really good Rule Explanation will enable your reader to anticipate the analogies to, or distinctions from, the client's facts that are the subject of the memorandum. Do not, however, discuss the client's facts in the Rule Explanation; you will do that in the Rule Application.

8.5.3 Language

Use the past tense to describe each case, but use the present tense to state any rules to which the courts refer. Use words carefully when you describe the different parts of a judicial opinion. Use *held, ruled*, or *found* to describe a legal holding or finding of law; you may also use *found* to describe a finding of fact. Do not use *held* or *ruled* to describe any part of an opinion other than a holding, that is, to describe dicta. Use *reasoned, stated, explained, concluded*, or similar words to describe a court's reasoning. Alternatively, you may present the substance of both the holding and the reasoning directly, without referring the court—especially if the corresponding main point does not refer to the courts, either. (See §8.3.2.3.) Refer to the parties in the cases by appropriate generic descriptions (*homeowner, resident, neighbor, concrete plant, paddlewheel boat, hiring law firm, mother, son*, etc.), not by their party titles (*plaintiff, defendant, appellant*, etc.) or by their proper names, unless the titles or names are necessary to avoid confusion or save a lot of space. Use the same reference for the same party consistently.

8.5.4 Multiple-sentence descriptions

In many of your Rule Explanation paragraphs, you will need to use two or more sentences to describe how a case illustrates the main point. State the relevant holding or finding, the key material facts, and any important judicial reasoning—in that order. Use the same sequence whether the description expressly refers to the court or just presents its holding and reasoning directly.

8.5.4.1 Relevant holding or finding

Begin each description by stating the court's holding or finding as to the subject of the main point. That part of the opinion carries the greatest precedential value for your analysis, so begin your description with it; do not begin by reciting the facts alone. Even at this level within a single paragraph, state the most important information first—why or how the case illustrates the main point. (See Introduction §iii.iii.) Use the same or similar terms from the main point to emphasize how the relevant holding or finding relates to that point.

8.5.4.2 Key material facts

Next, describe the key facts, beyond those in the holding or finding, upon which the court relied. Do not describe the facts by quoting at length from the opinion, unless a quotation can present certain facts more clearly, concisely, or effectively than you can, using your own words. (See §8.6.) Try to limit your description of the facts to one or two sentences. If you need more than two sentences to cover a complicated fact pattern, use them.

8.5.4.3 Important judicial reasoning

End the description by identifying any important judicial reasoning—why or how the court arrived at its holding or finding—in a way that relates the example back to the main point. You may, if necessary, use more than one sentence to describe the reasoning, and you may, but need not, include a quotation. You may omit this part of the description altogether if there is no important reasoning in the opinion on the subject of the main point or if the reasoning is not directly relevant to the point.

Example 8.5.4.3.1 (three-sentence case description).

The more residential the neighborhood, the more strictly will the courts evaluate the noise that may be permissible in it. See Smith, 158 N.W.2d at 468; Restatement (Second) of Torts § 821F cmt. e. ("The location, character and habits of the particular community are to be taken into account in determining what is offensive or annoying to a normal individual living in it.") [1] In O'Connor, where the neighborhood was *highly residential*, the court found that nighttime *noise* from a creamery was *impermissible* because it disturbed the residents' peace and comfort in their homes. 248 N.W. at 558-59. [2] Although the neighborhood was not restricted against business use, it was densely populated; the creamery was the only business in the immediate vicinity; its property directly abutted the property of one of the residents; and multiple residents were subjected throughout the night to noise from the truck drivers' shouting and from the starting, stopping, loading, and unloading of the trucks. Id. at 557-58. [3] The court concluded that the owner's right to conduct the business could not "justify the invasion of a residential district" and resulting disturbance to the inhabitants. Id. at 558-59.

(Sample Legal Memorandum 13:3-18) (emphasis and bracketed numbers added)

Comment. Example 8.5.4.3.1 contains the main point and first case law example from a Rule Explanation paragraph about the character of the neighborhood, one of the factors bearing on unreasonable interference. The writer uses three sentences to show how the case illustrates the main point. • Sentence 1 states the finding in the case on the subject of the main point. It uses the same or similar terms from the main point—*highly residential*; *noise*; *impermissible*—to emphasize how the finding relates to that point. • Sentence 2 uses the writer's own words, and a series of clauses linked by semicolons, to condense a large number of material facts into a single, manageable sentence. In other descriptions, shorter, less complicated sentences will suffice to present the facts. • Sentence 3 explains how the court weighed competing considerations to arrive at the relevant finding, which links the example back to the main point. The writer quotes just a key phrase from the court's reasoning, rather than the court's complete, but more discursive, sentence. • The entire description focuses on the subject of the main point; there is no extraneous or unrelated information.

Example 8.5.4.3.2 (extended case description).

The courts do not find significant harm, however, if the conduct would not cause actual physical discomfort to an ordinary person. Id. at 470. [1] In Smith, the Michigan Supreme Court found *no significant harm* where noise from a gun shooting range *would not cause actual physical discomfort to an ordinary person*. Id. at 471. [2] After neighboring residents submitted conflicting testimony about the effect of the noise, the trial judge attended a special shooting demonstration to experience the noise directly, from the homes of various plaintiffs. Id. at 468, 470-71. [3] The judge noted that the harms alleged had to be objectively reasonable. Id. at 469-70.

> [4] Whether the noise is sufficient to constitute a nuisance depends upon its effect upon an ordinary reasonable man, that is, a normal person of ordinary habits and sensibilities. [5] Relief cannot be based solely upon the subjective likes and dislikes of a particular plaintiff. [6] To be workable, relief must be based upon an objective standard of reasonableness.

Id. at 470. [7] Having personally experienced the noise, the judge concluded that it was not such "as would shock a person of ordinary sensibilities or cause actual physical discomfort." Id. at 470-71. [8] The Supreme Court agreed, adopting the trial judge's opinion in full. Id. at 465, 472-73.

(Sample Legal Memorandum 5:21-6:13) (emphasis and bracketed numbers added)

Comment. Example 8.5.4.3.2 contains the main point and first case law example from a Rule Explanation paragraph about actual physical discomfort, one of two factors bearing on substantial harm. *Smith* is the leading case for the main point, and it is complicated to describe—especially, as in this paragraph, for the first time in the memorandum. The writer needs eight sentences to show how the case illustrates the main point. • Sentence 1 states the finding by the Michigan Supreme Court on the subject of the main point. It uses the same or similar terms from the main point—*no significant harm*; *would not cause actual physical discomfort to an ordinary person*—to emphasize how the finding relates to that point. • Sentence 2 introduces key facts at the trial court level. The writer includes only those facts relevant to the main point. • Sentences 3 through 7 introduce, quote, and describe the trial court's important reasoning about the relevant legal standard and its application to the facts. • Ordinarily, a case description would end with sentence 7, which explains how the trial court arrived at its conclusion and links the example back to the main point. Here, Sentence 8 is necessary to return to the Supreme Court opinion that is the case law example. • Despite its eight sentences, the description stays focused on the main point and contains no extraneous information. It leaves room for another case description in the second half of the paragraph.

Example 8.5.4.3.3 (two-sentence case descriptions).

Similarly, the social benefits of noise-producing activity tend to lessen the overall unreasonableness of any disturbance the noise causes. Adams, 602 N.W.2d at 219 & n.10, 223 (noting doctrine of nuisance requires "public-policy assessment of [the] overall value" of defendant's conduct). In Cunningham, "the *benefit* that [high school] students, parents, faculty and the community derived from" Friday evening football games *outweighed the disturbance* certain neighbors experienced from the spectators' *noise*. 2001 WL 716882, at *4. Among other things, the games fostered a stronger sense of community, provided Friday evening activities for students, and permitted lacrosse, soccer, and track events to be scheduled on other, early-weekday evenings when more parents could attend them. Id. In Childs, the *benefits* of constructing a Super K-Mart store in place of a crime-filled lot in Detroit *outweighed the "noise pollution"* the store allegedly created for a nearby family. 2001 WL 1199901, at *3-4. The store reduced neighborhood crime, increased commerce in the area, and was likely to increase local property values. Id. at *4. In Radziewicz, the *benefits* of whistle soundings from a paddlewheel boat *outweighed the disturbance* one riverside property owner experienced from the noise. 2009 WL 2974733, at *3. Not only did the soundings ensure the safe operation of the boat and other watercraft using the river, but they also facilitated a tourist business of economic value to the community at large. Id. at *2-3. . . .

(Sample Legal Memorandum 21:20-22:10) (emphasis added)

Comment. Example 8.5.4.3.3 contains the main point and three case law examples from a Rule Explanation paragraph about the social value of noise-producing conduct, which is half of a compound factor bearing on unreasonable interference. (The other half concerns the necessity of the conduct in question.) The writer is able to use just two sentences to show how each case illustrates the main point. • The first sentence in each description states the finding on the subject of the main point. It uses the same or similar terms from the main point—*benefits*; *outweighed*; *disturbance*; *noise*—to emphasize how the finding relates to that point. • The second sentence in each description combines the key material facts and the important judicial reasoning. It identifies the facts each court relied on to conclude that the benefits outweighed the disturbance, thereby linking each example back to the main point. • These two-sentence descriptions stay focused on the main point and contain no extraneous information. • Note that the components of multiple-sentence case descriptions apply in the same sequence—relevant holding or finding first, followed by key facts and important reasoning—both when a description expressly refers to the court and when, as in these three examples, a description directly presents the result of the courts' analysis.

Example 8.5.4.3.4 (bad example: description beginning with the facts).

In Radziewicz, noise from a paddlewheel boat's whistle soundings disturbed a riverside property owner, but the soundings ensured the safe operation of the boat and other watercraft using the river and facilitated a tourist business of economic value to the community at large. 2009 WL 2974733, at *2-3. On balance, the benefits of the whistle soundings outweighed the disturbance they caused the property owner. Id. at *3.

Comment. The two-sentence description of *Radziewicz* in Example 8.5.4.3.4, a variation of the description that appears in Example 8.5.4.3.3, inverts the standard sequence for describing a case. It begins with the facts and reasoning and only identifies the relevant finding at the end. A reader would not immediately know why or how the case illustrates the main point of the paragraph. But why or how the case illustrates the main point—which the relevant finding discloses—is the most important information to include in each description. It should be the first thing you tell your reader about each case, not the last.

Example 8.5.4.3.5 (bad example: description focused on overall legal issue).

In Radziewicz, noise from a paddlewheel boat's whistle soundings was not a private nuisance, even though it disturbed a riverside property owner. 2009 WL 2974733, at *3. The soundings ensured the safe operation of the boat and other watercraft using the river, and they facilitated a tourist business of economic value to the community at large. Id. at *2-3. The benefits of the soundings outweighed the disturbance they caused the property owner.

Comment. The description in Example 8.5.4.3.5 begins with the holding in *Radziewicz* on the overall issue of private nuisance. The Rule Explanation paragraph for which the description is intended, however, concerns the more specific issue of balancing the public benefits of a noise-producing activity against the disturbance the activity causes. The first sentence of the description, therefore, diverts the reader's attention from the subject of the paragraph. Only the last sentence, stating the finding on the specific issue, identifies the connection between the case law example and the subject of the paragraph. The description should begin with that connection—and omit the reference to private nuisance.

8.5.5 Single-sentence descriptions

In some Rule Explanation paragraphs, you may be able to describe how a case illustrates the main point in a single sentence. State the relevant holding or finding at the start of the sentence—the most important information still comes first—and, if necessary, cover additional facts or important reasoning at the end. If the additional facts or reasoning would make the sentence too long (see §13.3.1), use a multiple-sentence description, instead.

Example 8.5.5.1 (single-sentence case descriptions).

The courts tend to find significant harm only if the conduct in question causes actual physical discomfort to multiple people. In O'Connor v. Jersey Creamery Co. of Detroit, 248 N.W. 557, 558 (Mich. 1933), *the court found significant harm* where smoke, odors, and noise from a creamery plant adversely affected the health of twenty-two neighbors. In Mackenzie v. Frank M. Pauli Co., 174 N.W. 161, 161, 163-64 (Mich. 1919), *the court found significant harm* where machinery noise from a lumberyard and interior trim factory adversely affected the health of twelve neighbors. In Smith, however, *the court found no significant harm*, in part because there was conflicting testimony from the plaintiff residents and other neighbors as to whether noise from the gun shooting range caused them actual physical discomfort. 158 N.W.2d at 469. Similarly, in Radziewicz v. Frankenmuth Paddlewheel Tours, No. 282648, 2009 WL 2974733, at *1, *3 (Mich. Ct. App. Sept. 17, 2009) (per curiam), *the court found no significant harm* to the single complaining property owner, who experienced only "minor annoyance"—not actual physical discomfort—from a paddlewheel boat's whistle soundings.

(Sample Legal Memorandum 6:27-7:10) (emphasis added)

> **Comment.** The Rule Explanation paragraph in Example 8.5.5.1 presents four case law examples to illustrate the main point about the number of people who must experience actual physical discomfort for the harm to be substantial. The two positive supporting examples, *O'Connor* and *Mackenzie*, precede the two negative supporting examples, *Smith* and *Radziewicz*. • The writer describes each case in a single sentence. The first two descriptions state the relevant finding alone. The second two include additional facts or reasoning, without unduly lengthening each sentence. • All four sentences begin with the most important information, whether or not the court found find significant harm based on the number of people affected.

8.5.6 Explanatory parentheticals

Use citations with explanatory parentheticals sparingly in your Rule Explanation paragraphs. Do not use them to substitute for textual descriptions of the best illustrative cases for each main point. Use citations with explanatory parentheticals only when necessary to do the following: (i) provide ancillary information about a case you describe in one or more sentences; (ii) incorporate supplemental cases succinctly, as a way to control paragraph length; or (iii) include an important quotation, where it is not necessary to describe the rest of the case. In many, if not most, Rule Explanation paragraphs, you will not need to use citations with explanatory parentheticals at all. Of course, you should use *citing*, *quoting*, *weight-of-authority*, and other non-explanatory parentheticals as prescribed by the rules of legal citation.

Example 8.5.6.1 (explanatory parenthetical providing ancillary information about case).

Courts find greater evidence of unreasonable interference the higher the volume of a noise and the more abrasive its sound. See Smith, 158 N.W.2d at 468 (citing Borsvold, 81 N.W.2d at 382). In Smith, the court agreed that explosive noises from a gun shooting range could unreasonably interfere with the neighbors' peace and quiet if the noises exceeded 88-1/4 decibels at one-quarter-mile distance. See id. at 472 (*enjoining noise in excess of that level*). . . .

(Sample Legal Memorandum 16:5-11) (emphasis added)

Comment. Example 8.5.6.1 contains the main point and first case law description from a Rule Explanation paragraph about the character of the noise, one of the factors bearing on unreasonable interference. The writer is able to use a single sentence to describe how *Smith* illustrates the main point about loud noise providing evidence of unreasonable interference. • The explanatory parenthetical that follows the description, noting the court's injunction against loud noise, provides information that is related but not directly pertinent to the primary subject matter of the description. (The information will become the primary subject of a subsequent main point, about the time when loud noises occur.) To include that information within the description would draw the focus away from the main point of the paragraph. The explanatory parenthetical acknowledges the ancillary information but properly subordinates it.

Example 8.5.6.2 (explanatory parenthetical incorporating supplemental case).

Written notice. In general, the Eastern District courts construe the "written notice" language strictly: oral notice is not acceptable. In the Cobb litigation, the court disqualified the hiring firm on the partial ground that it failed to provide written notice to the court when it employed the infected attorney. Cobb I, 907 F. Supp. at 1049. In Faith Baptist Church, the court disqualified the hiring firm on the sole ground that it failed to provide written notice when it hired the opposing client's primary attorney—even though the firm had screened him as soon as he started work. 2009 WL 3756891, at *2. The attorney's timely motion to withdraw as plaintiff's counsel did not disclose his new employer, and although he had notified a magistrate judge in the case of his new employment at a motion hearing on the day before, "he did not do so in writing, as required by the rule." Id. at *1-2; see also Nat'l Union Fire Ins. Co. of Pittsburgh, Pa. v. Alticor, Inc., 472 F.3d 436, (6th Cir.

2007) (*holding, in case arising in Western District, that hiring firm's failure to provide court with written notice of infected attorney's employment required firm's disqualification*).

(Sample Informal Memorandum 4:39-5:9) (emphasis added)

Comment. The Rule Explanation paragraph in Example 8.5.6.2 contains two case descriptions that illustrate the main point stated in the first sentence of the paragraph, about Eastern District courts requiring written notice of a law firm's measures to screen a newly hired attorney from a matter as to which the attorney has a conflict of interest. • Following the second description, the paragraph cites a third case, *Alticor*, which arose in a different district court and was decided on appeal by the Sixth Circuit. *Alticor* does not directly illustrate the main point of the paragraph, which is about *Eastern District* courts, but provides a highly analogous example of it. The explanatory parenthetical incorporates that example without disrupting the focus of the paragraph. It helps keep the paragraph concise, too.

Example 8.5.6.3 (explanatory parenthetical including important quotation).

In addition, courts find less evidence of unreasonable interference the more the noise is confined to adults' waking hours and times when other, ordinary noise occurs. . . . For example, in Smith, the court found that noise from a gun shooting range was not unreasonable, in part because it was masked by the sounds of birds and cars in the background. 158 N.W.2d at 470; see also Borsvold, 81 N.W.2d at 382 *("No one is entitled to absolute quiet in the enjoyment of his property; he may only insist upon a degree of quietness consistent with the standard of comfort prevailing in the locality in which he dwells.")*.

(Sample Legal Memorandum 17:15-18:6) (emphasis added)

Example 8.5.6.4 (bad example: explanatory parentheticals substitute for case descriptions).

The other factor courts consider in evaluating significant harm is whether the conduct interferes with the use and enjoyment of property. Adams, 602 N.W.2d at 222. Where noise is concerned, the courts find significant harm if the interference is pervasive, inside and outside the home. Id. at 722; see Restatement (Second) of Torts § 821F cmt. c ("[T]here must be a real and appreciable invasion of the plaintiff's interests before he can have an action."); see, e.g., Mackenzie, 174 N.W. at 163 (finding significant harm where machinery noise from lumberyard and interior trim factory caused pervasive interference with neighbors' use and enjoyment of their property); Wilke, 2007 WL 1828788, at *4 (finding significant harm where rock-crushing noise from concrete plant caused pervasive interference with neighbors' "[ability] to function inside their homes"); cf. Smith, 158 N.W.2d at 468-69 (finding no harm where evidence showed noise from gun shooting range prevented only some homeowners but not others from concentrating, engaging in conversation, watching television, or remaining at home). But see Childs, 2001 WL 1199901, at *4 (finding no significant harm where vehicle and pedestrian noise from Super K-Mart store caused only minimal interference with neighboring family's use of its property); see also id. (rejecting as minimal harm plaintiffs' claims that excessive light made it difficult to sleep, read, work, or concentrate inside their home and that exhaust fumes made it difficult to plant flowers and socialize outside).

Comment. The Rule Explanation paragraph in Example 8.5.6.4, a modified version of the paragraph from Example 8.2.3.1, uses citations and explanatory parentheticals exclusively to describe the case law examples illustrating the main point. The unrelieved telegraphic style of successive parentheticals makes the content hard to absorb, and the parentheticals necessarily omit key material facts and reasoning. Remember that your job in the Rule Explanation is to help the reader learn about the case law and be able to anticipate how it will apply to the client's facts. The best way to do that is to use textual descriptions of the supporting cases, not explanatory parentheticals.

8.5.7 Multiple case descriptions

8.5.7.1 Consistency

The content of each case description in a Rule Explanation paragraph—the holding or finding; the key facts; any important judicial reasoning—should relate to the single main point around which that paragraph is organized. Do not include content that relates to a different point. (See §8.5.1.) Do not introduce a new main point in the middle of a paragraph. (See §8.2.2.) The main point stated at the beginning of the paragraph should be consistent with the case law examples that follow, and vice versa. If necessary, revise your main point to encompass the cases that follow, or select different cases to illustrate your point.

8.5.7.2 Sequence

Describe positive case law examples before negative ones. (See §8.4.1.) You may use case descriptions of different lengths within the same Rule Explanation paragraph, but try to present the most important or complex positive examples—which require the longer descriptions—first; do the same for any negative examples. If you derive a main point from a specific case, and if that case provides a positive example of the point, describe the case first, right after citing it to support the main point.

Example 8.5.7.2.1 (positive case law example, cited for main point, described first).

One factor courts consider in evaluating significant harm is whether the conduct causes actual physical discomfort. Smith, 158 N.W.2d at 468 (citing Borsvold, 81 N.W.2d at 378). The courts do not find significant harm, however, if the conduct would not cause actual physical discomfort to an ordinary person. Id. at 470. In Smith, the Michigan Supreme Court found no significant harm where noise from a gun shooting range would not cause actual physical discomfort to an ordinary person. Id. at 471. . . .

(Sample Legal Memorandum 5-19-25)

Comment. *Smith* is the case from which the main point of the Rule Explanation paragraph in Example 8.5.7.2.1, about the ordinary person standard for substantial harm, derives. The writer cites it after stating the main point and, because it provides a positive example of that point, the writer describes it first. • *Smith* is also a Michigan Supreme Court decision and a complex case to describe. For those additional reasons, the writer describes it first. • Note that *Smith* provides a positive case law example of a substantively negative main point. (See Example 8.4.1.2.)

8.5.8 Subject focus in case descriptions

Subject focus refers to the grammatical subject in a series of successive sentences. (See §13.3.5.) When you are describing an individual case, keep the sentences in the description focused, as much as possible, on the same subject, so your reader can concentrate on the case-specific details that follow the subject. You may focus the sentences on the court that issued the opinion you are describing—what the court found; what the court examined; what the court reasoned; what the court concluded. Alternatively, you may focus on the underlying substance of the opinion, rather than framing the description by focusing on the court. Sometimes, a change of subject focus may be unavoidable, such as when you shift from describing the court's finding in an opening sentence to the relevant facts in the next sentence. Where possible, however, try to return to the subject you used in the opening sentence for any remaining or concluding sentences in the case description. Try to use the same subject focus for all the case descriptions in the same Rule Explanation paragraph; you may use a different subject focus for the case descriptions in other Rule Explanation paragraphs. (See §9.12 on subject focus and other unifying techniques in Rule Explanation and Rule Application paragraphs.)

Example 8.5.8.1 (subject focus on court).

In Guaranty Residential, *the court* found that the hiring firm "effectively complied" with the requirements of Rule 1.10(b) by screening an infected attorney from the start of his employment, even though the firm did not provide written notice to the court until eight days after the firm entered an appearance in the case. U.S. Dist. Lexis 35275, at *4-5. At an evidentiary hearing on the motion to disqualify, *the court* assured itself that "extensive protections" had been and still were in place and that the hiring firm and the infected attorney were committed to honoring them. Id. Based on those protections, *the court* decided that the eight-day delay was "not a fatal flaw." Id. at *5.

(Sample Informal Memorandum 5:14-24) (emphasis added)

Example 8.5.8.2 (opening and closing subject focus on court).

In O'Connor, where the neighborhood was highly residential, *the court* found that nighttime noise from a creamery was impermissible because it disturbed the residents' peace and comfort in their homes. 248 N.W. at 558-59. Although the neighborhood was not restricted against business use, it was densely populated; the creamery was the only business in the immediate vicinity; its property directly abutted the property of one of the residents; and multiple residents were subjected throughout the night to noise from the truck drivers' shouting and from the starting, stopping, loading, and unloading of the trucks. Id. at 557-58. *The court* concluded that the owner's right to conduct the business could not "justify the invasion of a residential district" and resulting disturbance to the inhabitants. Id. at 558-59.

(Sample Legal Memorandum 13:9-18) (emphasis added)

Example 8.5.8.3 (subject focus on substance of opinion).

Similarly, the social *benefits* of noise-producing activity tend to lessen the overall unreasonableness of any disturbance the noise causes. Adams, 602 N.W.2d at 219 & n.10, 223 (noting doctrine of nuisance requires "public-policy assessment of [the] overall value" of defendant's conduct). In Cunningham, "the [A] *benefit* that [high school] students, parents, faculty and the community derived from" [B] *Friday evening football games* outweighed the disturbance certain neighbors experienced from the spectators' noise. 2001 WL 716882, at *4. Among other things, [B] *the games* fostered a stronger sense of community, provided Friday evening activities for students, and permitted lacrosse, soccer, and track events to be scheduled on other, early-weekday evenings when more parents could attend them. Id. In Childs, the [A] *benefits* of constructing a [B] *Super K-Mart store* in place of a crime-filled lot in Detroit outweighed the "noise pollution" the store allegedly created for a nearby family. 2001 WL 1199901, at *3-4. The [B] *store* reduced neighborhood crime, increased commerce in the area, and was likely to increase local property values. Id. at *4. In Radziewicz, the [A] *benefits* of [B] *whistle soundings* from a paddlewheel boat outweighed the disturbance one riverside property owner experienced from the noise. 2009 WL 2974733, at *3. Not only did the [B] *soundings* ensure the safe operation of the boat and other watercraft using the river, but [B] *they* also facilitated a tourist business of economic value to the community at large. Id. at *2-3. Conversely, in Wilke, the [A] *benefits* of a [B] *concrete plant* were outweighed by the extremely loud and continuous rock-crushing noise it produced, even though the [B] *plant* was "undoubtedly valuable to the surrounding community." 2007 WL 1828788, at *4.

(Sample Legal Memorandum 21:20-22:13) (emphasis and bracketed letters added)

Comment. In Example 8.5.8.3, all four case descriptions begin by focusing on the substance of the courts' analysis—the social benefits of different noise-producing activities—rather than on the courts doing the analyzing. • The first sentence of each description uses the same grammatical subject, *benefits* (or, in one sentence that includes a short quotation from the opinion, *benefit*), denoted by *[A]*. • Note that the source of the noise in question, introduced later on in the first sentence and denoted by *[B]*, becomes the grammatical subject of the second sentence in each description, also denoted by *[B]*. (In the fourth, single-sentence description, the source becomes the grammatical subject of the dependent clause in the second half of the sentence.) As a result, there is a consistent subject focus at a secondary level across the descriptions, too. • The consistent subject focus—at both levels—in the four descriptions makes it very easy for the reader to compare the different fact patterns that led to the positive and negative legal outcomes in the cases. • Note, too, that the main point of this paragraph also focuses on the substance of the courts' analysis. Using the same subject focus in the main point and the case law descriptions brings even greater unity, and clarity, to a Rule Explanation paragraph.

8.6 Quotations

Present your legal analyses primarily in your own words. Use quotations to support and illustrate your analyses, not to substitute for them. Use quotations sparingly and prefer succinct quotations to lengthy ones. Where it is necessary to include a lengthy quotation, be sure to explain in your own words how it relates to, supports, or illustrates the point you are discussing—either before you include the quotation, afterwards, or both. Use the indented, single-spaced block format for quotations of fifty words or more. Remember that the block format itself tells the reader you are quoting your source; omit the open and close quotation marks for the text of the quotation.

Example 8.6.1 (lengthy quotation preceded by explanatory sentence).

The courts do not find significant harm, however, if the conduct would not cause actual physical discomfort to an ordinary person. Id. at 470. In Smith, the Michigan Supreme Court found no significant harm where noise from a gun shooting range would not cause actual physical discomfort to an ordinary person. Id. at 471. After neighboring residents submitted conflicting testimony about the effect of the noise, the trial judge attended a special shooting demonstration to experience the noise directly, from the homes of various plaintiffs. Id. at 468, 470-71. *The judge noted that the harms alleged had to be objectively reasonable.* Id. at 469-70.

> Whether the noise is sufficient to constitute a nuisance depends upon its effect upon an ordinary reasonable man, that is, a normal person of ordinary habits and sensibilities. Relief cannot be based solely upon the subjective likes and dislikes of a particular plaintiff. To be workable, relief must be based upon an objective standard of reasonableness.

Id. at 470. Having personally experienced the noise, the judge concluded that it was not such "as would shock a person of ordinary sensibilities or cause actual physical discomfort." Id. at 470-71. The Supreme Court agreed, adopting the trial judge's opinion in full. Id. at 465, 472-73.

(Sample Legal Memorandum 5:21-6:13) (emphasis added)

Comment. Example 8.6.1 contains the main point and first case description from the first Rule Explanation paragraph in Section I.A of the Sample Legal Memorandum. The block quotation appears in the middle of the description. The sentence that precedes the quotation alerts the reader to the key content of the language to follow, which sets forth the court's reasoning. By explaining the reasoning in advance—that the court requires objectively reasonable harm—the introductory sentence expedites the writer's analysis of how the case supports the main point of the paragraph.

Example 8.6.2 (bad example: lengthy quotation not preceded by explanatory sentence)

The judge noted:

> Whether the noise is sufficient to constitute a nuisance depends upon its effect upon an ordinary reasonable man, that is, a normal person of ordinary habits and sensibilities. Relief cannot be based solely upon the subjective likes and dislikes of a particular plaintiff. To be workable, relief must be based upon an objective standard of reasonableness.

Id. at 470.

Comment. In this variation of the case description from Example 8.6.1, the sentence that precedes the block quotation does not alert the reader to the key content of the language to follow. It forces the reader to figure out what is most important about the court's reasoning and how that relates to the subject of the Rule Explanation paragraph. It slows down, and may even obscure, the writer's analysis.

8.7 Templates

Template 8A: Organization of Single Section (Through Rule Explanation).

[X.] Subject heading for section[1]

¶1: Conclusion[2]

¶2: Rule Statement[2,3]; First Rule Explanation Paragraph
- First main point[4,5]
- Case law examples illustrating first main point[6]

¶3: Second Rule Explanation Paragraph, if any
- Second main point[4,5]
- Case law examples illustrating second main point[6]

¶4: Third Rule Explanation Paragraph, if any[7]
- Third main point[4,5]
- Case law examples illustrating third main point[6]

---

[1] Adjust the font style for the level of heading. (See §5.3.5.3.)

[2] Alternatively, you may present the Rule Statement and Conclusion, in that order, within a combined opening paragraph. If you do, begin the first Rule Explanation paragraph directly with your first main point about the law. (See §7.2.2, Template 7B.)

[3] You *may* use a short overview paragraph instead of a combined opening paragraph if it would be helpful to the reader to introduce the topics you will cover in successive paragraphs in the section to follow. You *should* use an overview paragraph if you subdivide the section into subsections. (See §6.7, Template 6B.)

[4] Generally, present your most important main point first, if you have more than one point to make about the case law. Other sequences may be appropriate, however. (See §8.3.3.)

[5] If you derive a main point from a specific judicial decision, cite that decision after stating the point. If you derive a main point from multiple decisions, just cite the decisions as you describe them in the rest of the paragraph. (See §8.3.4.)

[6] Include supporting case law examples first within each Rule Explanation paragraph and any important contrary case law examples second. Include positive supporting case law examples before negative supporting case law examples. (See §8.4.1.)

[7] If you have more than three main points to make about the case law, consider subdividing your section into shorter, more manageable subdivisions. (See §8.2.3.)

Template 8B: Multiple-Sentence Case Description.

Sentence 1: *Holding or finding* as to subject of main point[1] [2]

Sentence 2: *Key material facts*, beyond those in holding or finding, upon which court relied[3]

Sentence 3: *Important judicial reasoning*, to relate case law example back to main point[4] [5]

[1] Use the same or similar terms from the main point to emphasize how the relevant holding or finding relates to that point. (See §8.5.4.1.)

[2] Use the same subject focus to state the relevant holding or finding in successive case descriptions within the same Rule Explanation paragraph. (See §8.5.8.)

[3] Generally, describe key facts in your own words. You may use additional sentences if necessary to describe more complex fact patterns. (See §8.5.4.2.)

[4] Explain why or how the court reached the relevant holding or finding. You may use more than one sentence to describe the important reasoning or to include a helpful quotation. You may omit the reasoning altogether if there is no important reasoning in the opinion on the subject of the main point. (See §8.5.4.3.)

[5] In the context of some Rule Explanation paragraphs, you may be able to describe certain case law examples using one or two sentences. For two-sentence descriptions, use the first sentence to state the relevant holding or finding; use the second sentence to cover the key material facts or any important reasoning, or both. (See §8.5.1.) For single-sentence descriptions, use the first part of the sentence to state the relevant holding or finding; use the second part to cover the facts or reasoning, or both. (See §8.5.5.)

Chapter 9
How to Write the Rule Application and Restated Conclusion for an Individual Section or Subsection

9.1 Purpose

The Rule Application and Restated Conclusion are the final two parts in the standard small-scale organizational sequence of components within a single section or subsection in the Discussion. The Rule Application completes the analysis that the previous parts began, by telling your reader how you think a new court would apply the specific part of the rule you are addressing to your own facts and why. The Restated Conclusion tells your reader again, at the end of a divided or lengthy undivided section or subsection. (See §9.10.)

9.2 Format

The Rule Application is the mirror image of the Rule Explanation. For each main point about the case law you include in a separate Rule Explanation paragraph, use a corresponding Rule Application paragraph to predict how that point would apply to your facts. Begin the first Rule Application paragraph after the last Rule Explanation paragraph ends.

9.2.1 Paragraphs

Organize each Rule Application paragraph around a single main point about the case law—the same one you identified in the corresponding Rule Explanation paragraph. Begin with your conclusion about how that point would apply to your facts. (See §9.3.) Use the rest of the paragraph to support your conclusion, by analyzing the relevant facts (see §9.4) and comparing them to analogous or distinguishable facts in the case law (see §9.5). You may discuss your facts first and compare them to those in the cases second, discuss the facts in the cases first and compare them to your facts second, or interweave the two. However you choose to present them, the case comparisons are essential. They demonstrate that your substantive conclusions are consistent with the applicable legal precedents in your jurisdiction. For attorneys working in a common-law system, that is the essence of legal analysis.

9.2.2 Sequence

Present the Rule Application paragraphs in the same sequence as that of the corresponding Rule Explanation paragraphs. Where possible, present your most important main point or points first in the Rule Explanation (see §8.3.3), so your Rule Application will begin with your conclusions about those points. Do not alternate Rule Explanation and Rule Application paragraphs within an undivided section or subsection, that is, introduce and illustrate one point about the case law, immediately apply it to your facts, introduce and illustrate another point, apply that point to your facts, etc. If it is necessary to cover a lot of main points about the part of the rule you are addressing—generally, four or more—cover them in shorter, more manageable subdivisions within the section or subsection. (See §8.2.3.) Present the Rule Explanation paragraphs in each subdivision before the Rule Application paragraphs.

9.2.3 Length

Generally, the Rule Application will be as short or as long as the corresponding Rule Explanation. Use the same number of Rule Application paragraphs as the number of different Rule Explanation paragraphs—except, in rare instances, where you need a second Rule Application paragraph to present a particularly complex or detailed analysis of how the main point would apply to your facts. Be sure to use the first sentence of the second paragraph to make it very clear that you are continuing the analysis from the prior paragraph. For the most part, however, use only one Rule Application paragraph to present your conclusion and support for each main point. Use a separate Rule Application paragraph—as opposed to omitting it or combining it with the corresponding Rule Explanation paragraph—even where the application of the main point to your facts seems obvious. Your analysis in such a Rule Application paragraph can be succinct.

<u>Example 9.2.3.1</u> (Rule Application for single main point).

A court would likely find that Mr. Lambert experiences only minimal harm, not pervasive interference, from the disruption to his seasonal backyard entertaining. In both Mackenzie and Wilke, where the courts found significant harm, noise from the defendants' businesses prevented the plaintiffs from using and enjoying both the outside and the inside of their homes, much if not all of the time—five days a week in Mackenzie, 174 N.W. at 163, and seven days a week in Wilke, 2007 WL 1828788, at *4. Here, the noise from Mr. Hendricks's business only affects Mr. Lambert's backyard entertaining, only on weekends, and only during warm weather—which, in southeastern Michigan, is limited to half the year or less. In Childs, where the court found no significant harm, there was insufficient evidence that ordinary vehicular noise prevented the complaining family members from using and enjoying their property. 2001 WL 1199901, at *4. Similarly, there is insufficient evidence that the noise from Mr. Hendricks's business prevents Mr. Lambert from using and enjoying his property, too, especially because no other neighbors have complained that the noise prevents them from using their backyards. See Radziewicz, 2009 WL 2974733, at *3 (finding no significant harm where single property owner complained). Altogether, a court is likely to find that the interference with Mr. Lambert's backyard entertaining represents, at most, a diminution in the enjoyment of his property, not anything more significant.

(Sample Legal Memorandum 10:26-11:16)

Comment. The single Rule Application paragraph in Example 9.2.3.1 corresponds to the single Rule Explanation paragraph in Example 8.2.3.1. • It begins with the writer's conclusion about how the main point from the Rule Explanation paragraph would apply to the client's facts, that is, whether the alleged interference with the use and enjoyment of property is pervasive. • Then it references two cases illustrating pervasive interference, contrasts the facts in those cases with the client's facts, and analogizes to the similar facts in a third case, which did not support a conclusion of pervasive interference. • In this Rule Application paragraph, the factual analysis and case comparisons are interwoven throughout the text. For a Rule Application paragraph in which the factual analysis precedes the case comparisons, see Example 9.4.1.

Example 9.2.3.2 (Rule Application for several main points).

Here, a court would probably find that any harm to Mr. Lambert is not significant because the noise from Mr. Hendricks's motorcycle repair business would not cause actual physical discomfort to an ordinary person. . . .

A court would also likely find no significant harm because Mr. Lambert is the only person to complain about the noise. . . .

Finally, a court would likely find no significant harm because the noise would not deprive most adults in the neighborhood of sleep. . . .

(Sample Legal Memorandum 8:4-6, 17-18, 9:1-2)

> **Comment.** Example 9.2.3.2 contains the first sentence of the Rule Application paragraphs that correspond to the three Rule Explanation paragraphs referenced in Example 8.2.3.2. • The writer uses the first sentence in each paragraph to state a conclusion about how the main point introduced in each corresponding Rule Explanation paragraph would apply to the client's facts. • The rest of each Rule Application paragraph (omitted in this example) discusses the client's facts and analogizes them to, or distinguishes them from, the facts in the cases illustrating the main points in the Rule Explanation paragraphs.

Example 9.2.3.3 (two Rule Application paragraphs for single main point).

Nor would a court be likely to find evidence of unreasonable interference in Mr. Hendricks's evening and weekend hours of operation. *First*, the noise ends before most adults go to bed. Mr. Hendricks stops work in the evenings by 10:00 p.m. or 11:00 p.m., an hour or two later than 9:00 p.m., the last time each day when the paddlewheel boat blew its whistle in Radziewicz, which the court found reasonable. 2009 WL 2974733, at *3. He stops work no later than 11:00 p.m., the time when the court in O'Connor deemed it necessary to enjoin noise from the creamery so it would not disturb the neighbors. 248 N.W. at 558. The court in Radziewicz did not have to decide whether noises later than 9:00 p.m. might disturb the neighbors, see 2009 WL 2974733, at *2-3, whereas the court in O'Connor did address the question and found that 11:00 p.m. was the time when interference from noise in the neighborhood could become unreasonable, 248 N.W. at 558. Implicit in O'Connor's reasoning is the assumption that most adults do not go to bed earlier than 11:00 p.m.; the creamery's noise became unreasonable only when adults went to bed. Id. Mr. Hendricks stops working before most adults in his neighborhood go to bed. A court would likely find no evidence that his hours of operation lead to unreasonable interference.

Second, other noises fill the neighborhood at the same times when Mr. Hendricks runs his motorcycles. The court in Smith found that in a given location, ambient noise of various kinds can minimize the interference from one particular source of noise. 158 N.W.2d at 470. In North Ypsilanti, the residents are subject to ordinary, suburban noise from multiple sources during the evenings and on the weekends, such as music from the college students living in the area, voices from other neighbors' outdoor entertaining, and the sound of motorcycle owners in the

> neighborhood—probably more than just the five or six who are Mr. Hendricks's customers—starting and driving their machines. A court would likely find that the motorcycle noise is no more unreasonable than any other ordinary aural interference to which Mr. Lambert is subject before 11:00 p.m. and on weekends.
>
> (Sample Legal Memorandum 19:15-20:14) (emphasis added)
>
> **Comment.** In Example 9.2.3.3, the writer uses two Rule Application paragraphs where the corresponding main point covered two related subjects: *courts find less evidence of unreasonable interference the more the noise is confined to <u>adults' waking hours</u> and <u>times when other, ordinary noise occurs</u>.* (Sample Legal Memorandum 17:15-17) (emphasis added). • It would have been unwieldy to use one long, continuous paragraph for all the factual and legal information necessary to cover both subjects. Instead, the writer uses a second paragraph to cover the second subject and clearly signals the division by using *first* and *second* to introduce the specific conclusion for each subject. • Alternatively, the writer could have divided the main point in two and used separate Rule Explanation and Rule Application paragraphs for each new point.

9.3 The conclusion

Begin each Rule Application paragraph with your conclusion about how the main point of the corresponding Rule Explanation paragraph would apply to your facts. Use a single, succinct sentence.

9.3.1 Relation to the main point

State each conclusion so it clearly relates to the corresponding main point. Repeat the key terms or phrases from the main point—or use recognizable variations. In sections or subsections with multiple Rule Explanation and Rule Application paragraphs, several pages may separate each conclusion from the corresponding main point. Repeating the key language in the conclusion not only identifies which main point you are addressing in the Rule Application paragraph but also reinforces the content of that point for your reader.

9.3.2 Substance

State a specific, substantive conclusion about each main point: *Conversely, a court would probably find no evidence of unreasonable interference in the infrequency and short duration of the motorcycle noise.* (See Sample Legal

Memorandum 18:24-26.) Avoid conclusions that stop short of providing a real answer to the question of how the main point would apply to your facts: *Conversely, a court would probably find that the infrequency and short duration of the motorcycle noise have a strong bearing on whether there is evidence of unreasonable interference.* Such conclusions force your reader to do your work for you.

9.3.3 Degree of certainty

Try to state your conclusion about each main point with reasonable certainty. Use verbs such as *would* or *should*; avoid verbs such as *could* or *might*, which convey uncertainty. For most conclusions, add a qualifier such as *probably* or *likely*. For conclusions about which you are especially confident, you may add a stronger qualifier, such as *almost certainly* or *very likely*. (Of course, the substance of any conclusion can be negative as well as positive. Just add *not* or equivalent language.) Avoid qualifiers that undermine the certainty of your conclusion: *A court would possibly find that ....* Avoid unqualified conclusions, too: *A court will find that ....* The legal analysis in a memorandum represents your prediction about how a court would apply the law to your facts—not your guarantee. (See §3.4.4.)

9.3.4 Supporting reason or detail

You may state your conclusion alone, include a short supporting reason at the end of the conclusion—generally introduced by *because*—or embed a few supporting details throughout the conclusion. Do not include a lengthy supporting reason or extensive supporting details; save them for the remaining sentences in the paragraph. Do not refer to individual cases in the conclusion, either; discuss those in the rest of the paragraph, too.

9.3.5 Consistency

Be sure that your conclusion is consistent with the factual analyses and case law comparisons in the rest of the paragraph, and vice versa. Keep the conclusion focused on the specific main point, not on a broader, narrower, or different point or on the larger legal issue. (See §§7.3.1, 9.6.1.)

Example 9.3.5.1 (conclusion alone).

Main point. The courts are likely to find that a *neighborhood is residential* even if some businesses are interspersed among the dwellings.

Conclusion. Here, a court would likely find that North Ypsilanti, where Mr. Hendricks and Mr. Lambert live, is a *residential neighborhood.*

(Sample Legal Memorandum 12:18-19, 14:18-19) (emphasis added)

Example 9.3.5.2 (conclusion with supporting detail).

Main point. Where noise is concerned, the courts find significant harm if the *interference is pervasive, inside and outside the home.*

Conclusion. A court would likely find that Mr. Lambert experiences only minimal harm, *not pervasive interference*, from the disruption to his *seasonal backyard entertaining.*

(Sample Legal Memorandum 9:24-25, 10:26-28) (emphasis added)

Example 9.3.5.3 (conclusion with supporting reason).

Main point. Courts find greater evidence of unreasonable interference *the higher the volume of a noise and the more abrasive its sound.*

Conclusion. Here, a court would almost certainly find some evidence of unreasonable interference *because the motorcycle noise* from Mr. Hendricks's business *is loud and potentially disruptive*.

(Sample Legal Memorandum 16:5-6, 18:12-14) (emphasis added)

Comment. Each conclusion in Examples 9.3.5.1 through 9.3.5.3 repeats key language from the corresponding main point, to identify the point to which it relates and reinforce the substance of that point for the reader. The repetition is especially helpful in the first and third examples, in which the conclusion is separated from the corresponding main point by two full pages of text, containing two other main points and Rule Explanation paragraphs. • The conclusion in the first two examples is presented with reasonable certainty: *a court would likely find* . . . . The conclusion in the third example is presented with greater confidence but still with some qualification: *a court would almost certainly find* . . . . • The conclusion in the first example omits a supporting reason or detail but just identifies the specific neighborhood to which the main point applies; the rest of the paragraph covers the reasons and the details. The conclusions in the second and third examples, which do include either supporting detail or a supporting reason, remain short enough for a reader to grasp right away.

Example 9.3.5.4 (bad example: conclusion with lengthy supporting reason).

Conclusion. Here, a court would almost certainly find some evidence of unreasonable interference because the motorcycle noise from Mr. Hendricks's business is loud and potentially disruptive, given that the noise is probably at least as great as that of a power lawn mower, if not quite as great as that from a jet engine—both of which the courts have said might produce unreasonable interference.

> **Comment.** The conclusion in Example 9.3.5.4 varies the conclusion in Example 9.3.5.3 by adding substantially more detail to the supporting reason. By lengthening the sentence, the additional detail draws the reader's attention away from the most important information it contains, the basic conclusion itself. The additional detail could be presented more effectively in a separate sentence that follows the conclusion (as it is in the Sample Legal Memorandum: see 18:14-19).

Example 9.3.5.5 (bad example: conclusion focused on narrower main point).

Conclusion. Here, a court would almost certainly find some evidence of unreasonable interference because the motorcycle noise from Mr. Hendricks's business is loud.

> **Comment.** The conclusion in Example 9.3.5.5 varies the conclusion in Example 9.3.5.3 by focusing on only half of the main point from the corresponding Rule Explanation paragraph, about the volume of the noise. It does not refer to the other half, about the abrasiveness of the noise. • If the rest of the Rule Application paragraph addressed both volume and abrasiveness, the conclusion would be inconsistent with it. If the rest of the Rule Application paragraph did not address abrasiveness, either, the entire paragraph would be inconsistent the corresponding Rule Explanation paragraph.

9.4 Factual analysis

Within each Rule Application paragraph, explain how your conclusion about the main point applies to the facts in your matter—including any key documents—and how and why those facts support your conclusion. Include only facts that are relevant to the main point and your conclusion about it. Link the facts back to your conclusion explicitly; do not just describe the facts and stop.

Example 9.4.1 (factual analysis supporting conclusion about main point).

Conversely, a court would probably find no evidence of unreasonable interference in the infrequency and short duration of the motorcycle noise, and those characteristics would tend to outweigh the volume and abrasiveness of the noise. We do not know exactly how often Mr. Hendricks tests the engines he repairs or how long he runs them. Judging from the number of customers he has, however—five or six from the immediate neighborhood and some others from surrounding areas—Mr. Hendricks may not be fully occupied at work even when he is open for business. When he does have work, he must spend more time disassembling the engines, identifying what needs to be fixed, obtaining or repairing the parts, and reassembling the engines than he does running the engines to diagnose them at the start of a job or to test them when he has finished. Moreover, not every motorcycle Mr. Hendricks accepts to work on requires engine repair; for those jobs, it would not be necessary to run the engines at all. Thus, a court would likely find the noise from Mr. Hendricks's business is more analogous to the bursts of noise from the football spectators in Cunningham, 2001 WL 716882, at *3, loud but infrequent and brief, than it is to the loud and continuous noise from the lumberyard machinery in Mackenzie, 174 N.W. at 166, or from the stone-crushing machinery at the cement plant in Wilke, 2007 WL 1828788, at *4. *As such, the noise would not unreasonably interfere with Mr. Lambert's household activities.*

(Sample Legal Memorandum 18:24-19:14) (emphasis added)

Comment. Example 9.4.1 contains the Rule Application paragraph that corresponds to the Rule Explanation paragraph in Example 8.3.2.7.1. • It begins with the writer's conclusion about how the main point from the Rule Explanation paragraph, with its two related insights, would apply to the client's facts, that is, whether the noise is sufficiently infrequent and brief to outweigh its loud and potentially disruptive nature. • The paragraph continues with an extensive analysis of the facts that pertain to the first insight, about the probable number of the client's repair jobs and the probable amount of time he spends generating noise. • Then, and more concisely, it compares that noise to the noise in one case, which was also loud but infrequent and brief, and contrasts it with the noises in two other cases, which were both loud and continuous. (The prior Rule Application paragraph analyzed the facts that pertained to the second insight, about the volume and nature of the noise, so no further analysis of those facts is required in this paragraph.) • The paragraph ends by linking the factual analysis back to the opening conclusion, to leave no doubt about how the facts support that conclusion.

9.4.1 Consistency

Be sure that the facts you discuss in each Rule Application paragraph are consistent with the facts you included in the Statement of Facts—and in the other Rule Application paragraphs throughout the memorandum. Do not introduce any facts that you did not include in the Statement of Facts. (See §4.2.3.)

9.4.2 Citations

For your reader's convenience, cite the specific provisions of any documents you discuss or in which your facts appear, such as a deposition transcript. Otherwise, you do not need to cite the facts that appear in the Statement of Facts.

9.5 Case comparisons

Within each Rule Application paragraph, also include one or more comparisons between your facts and those in the case law, to support your conclusion about how the main point would apply to your facts. Where your facts are similar to those in the case law, the legal outcome based on your facts should be similar to the legal outcome based on the facts in the cases; where your facts are dissimilar, the legal outcome should be dissimilar.

9.5.1 Length

Use one or more complete sentences to present each case comparison. One sentence can be sufficient, but if a single sentence becomes too long, use two sentences. Occasionally, you may need to use three or more sentences for comparisons that are especially important or complex. You will often use the same case for comparisons in more than one Rule Application paragraph throughout the memorandum; the length of those comparisons will vary according to how much you need to say about the case and your facts to support your conclusion in each paragraph. For every case comparison, include only the information about the case and your facts that is necessary to support your conclusion.

9.5.2 Specificity

Compare your specific facts to the specific facts in the cases and, where appropriate, explain how the courts' reasoning in the cases would support your conclusion. Make your comparisons self-explanatory by including the analogous or distinguishable facts or reasoning from the cases. Do not just refer to a case name and assume that your reader will remember the details. Spell them out, so the reader will not have to go back to the Rule Explanation paragraph to find them. Make the point of your comparisons explicit, too. Do not just present your facts and the facts in the cases, without explaining—within the comparison itself or by the end of the paragraph—how the comparison supports your conclusion. Do not just say that your facts are like or unlike the facts in some case, without explaining why or how or what that means for your analysis.

9.5.3 Language

Present each case comparison primarily in your own words. You may quote a key term or phrase from the decision to facilitate the comparison, but avoid lengthy quotations, which force the reader to interpret the court's language. That is your job. (If your description of the case in the Rule Explanation paragraph included a lengthy quotation, you may refer back to it more selectively—with a succinct quotation or paraphrase—in the Rule Application comparison.) Continue to use the past tense to describe the content of individual cases, as you did in the corresponding Rule Explanation paragraphs. (See §8.5.3.)

9.5.4 Accuracy

Be sure your case comparisons are accurate. Do not strain an analogy or distinction. Do not overstate or misrepresent the facts, the law, or the analysis in any of the cases you include in your comparisons—or anywhere else in the memorandum. Do not use a quotation from a case out of context. Be scrupulous about distinguishing what the courts *held*, *ruled*, or *found* in the cases from what they *reasoned*, *stated*, or *explained*. (See §8.5.3.)

<u>Example 9.5.4.1</u> (single-sentence comparison to analogous case).

Just as the court in <u>Rose</u> found no significant harm in the complaining neighbor's respiratory discomfort, where she was extra-sensitive to smoke and fumes, 2009 WL 3276431, at *4, a court would probably find no significant harm in Mr. Lambert's migraines, where he happens to be extra-sensitive to noise.

(Sample Legal Memorandum 8:8-12)

> **Comment.** The comparison in Example 9.5.4.1 is self-explanatory: it identifies certain analogous facts from the *Rose* decision and

compares them to the relevant facts in the client's matter. • The point of the comparison is explicit, too: the same legal result should follow in the client's matter based on the similarity of the facts. • Note the similarity between the two halves of the sentence: the writer uses the same subject (*court*), similar verbs (*found* or *would . . . find*), and similar material facts (extra-sensitivity to stimuli). Parallel structure of this kind makes the case comparison clear and comprehensible. See §13.4.1 for other, effective applications of parallel structure within a legal memorandum.

Example 9.5.4.2 (bad example: comparison without relevant facts about case).

As in Rose, 2009 WL 3276431, at *4, a court would probably not find significant harm in Mr. Lambert's migraines, where he happens to be extra-sensitive to noise.

Comment. The comparison in Example 9.5.4.2, a variation of the comparison in Example 9.5.4.1, is no longer self-explanatory. By omitting the analogous facts from the *Rose* decision, it would force a reader to go back to the Rule Explanation paragraph to find out what they were.

Example 9.5.4.3 (two-sentence comparison to distinguishable cases).

In both Mackenzie and Wilke, where the courts found significant harm, *noise* from the defendants' businesses *prevented* the plaintiffs from using and enjoying both the outside and the inside of their homes, much if not all of the time— five days a week in Mackenzie, 174 N.W. at 163, and seven days a week in Wilke, 2007 WL 1828788, at *4. Here, the *noise* from Mr. Hendricks's business only *affects* Mr. Lambert's backyard entertaining, only on weekends, and only during warm weather—which, in southeastern Michigan, is limited to half the year or less.

(Sample Legal Memorandum 10:28-11:5) (emphasis added)

Comment. The two-sentence comparison in Example 9.5.4.3 is still self-explanatory. It identifies certain distinguishable facts from the *Mackenzie* and *Wilke* decisions and contrasts them with the relevant facts in the client's matter. • The point of the comparison is explicit, too, but it comes at the end of paragraph, after the writer contrasts the distinguishable facts from a third decision with the client's facts: *Altogether, a court is likely to find that the interference with Mr. Lambert's backyard entertaining represents, at most, a diminution in the enjoyment of his property, not anything more significant.*

(Sample Legal Memorandum 11:14-16) • Note the similarity between the two sentences: the writer uses the same subject (*noise*), verbs expressing causation (*prevented* or *affects*), and similar material facts (the effect of the noise on the residents' ability to use and enjoy their property). As in Example 9.5.4.1, the parallel structure makes the comparison clear and comprehensible. (See §13.4.1.)

Example 9.5.4.4 (three-sentence comparison involving analogous and distinguishable cases).

The *court* in O'Connor *found* significant harm where *twenty-two neighbors complained*, 248 N.W. at 558, and the *court* in Mackenzie *found* significant harm where *twelve neighbors complained*, 174 N.W. at 161. The *courts* in Rose and Radziewicz, however, *found* no significant harm where a *single property owner complained*. Rose, 2009 WL 3276431, at *4; Radziewicz, 2009 WL 2974733, at *2. Here, *in the absence of multiple plaintiffs*, a *court would* probably *find* that the motorcycle noise, however bothersome to Mr. Lambert, does not constitute significant harm for purposes of a private nuisance lawsuit.

(Sample Legal Memorandum 8:22-30) (emphasis added)

Comment. The comparison in Example 9.5.4.4 presents the specific, analogous or distinguishable facts about the cases and the client's matter in three sentences. • The third sentence states the point of the comparison, that client's facts are more like the facts in the cases in which just a single property owner complained, and so the legal result should follow the legal result in those cases. • Again, note the similarity between the three successive sentences: the writer uses the same subject (*court*, singular or plural), similar verbs (*found* or *would . . . find*), and similar material facts (the number of plaintiffs). The parallel sentence structure makes it easy to compare the similarities and differences between the facts and legal outcome in the four cases and the facts and probable outcome in the client's matter. (See §13.4.1.)

9.5.5 Explanatory parentheticals

As in your Rule Explanation paragraphs, use citations with explanatory parentheticals sparingly in your Rule Application paragraphs. Your job in the Rule Application paragraphs is to tie together the applicable law and the relevant facts to support your conclusions; the compressed, telegraphic style used in explanatory parentheticals works against such clear exposition just when you need it most. For that reason, do not use citations with explanatory parentheticals to substitute for fully articulated case comparisons. Use them only when necessary to supplement your comparisons with additional information or support. As in your Rule Explanation paragraphs, you should not need to use citations with explanatory parentheticals very often in your Rule Application paragraphs. You should continue to use non-explanatory parentheticals as prescribed by the rules of legal citation.

Example 9.5.5.1 (explanatory parenthetical supplements textual case comparison).

A court would likely find that Mr. Lambert experiences only minimal harm, not pervasive interference, from the disruption to his seasonal backyard entertaining. In both Mackenzie and Wilke, where the courts found significant harm, noise from the defendants' businesses prevented the plaintiffs from using and enjoying both the outside and the inside of their homes, much if not all of the time—five days a week in Mackenzie, 174 N.W. at 163, and seven days a week in Wilke, 2007 WL 1828788, at *4. Here, the noise from Mr. Hendricks's business only affects Mr. Lambert's backyard entertaining, only on weekends, and only during warm weather—which, in southeastern Michigan, is limited to half the year or less. In Childs, where the court found no significant harm, there was insufficient evidence that ordinary vehicular noise prevented the complaining family members from using and enjoying their property. 2001 WL 1199901, at *4. Similarly, there is insufficient evidence that the noise from Mr. Hendricks's business prevents Mr. Lambert from using and enjoying his property, too, especially because no other neighbors have complained that the noise prevents them from using their backyards. *See Radziewicz, 2009 WL 2974733, at *3 (finding no significant harm where single property owner complained)*. Altogether, a court is likely to find that the interference with Mr. Lambert's backyard entertaining represents, at most, a diminution in the enjoyment of his property, not anything more significant.

(Sample Legal Memorandum 10:26-11:16 (emphasis added)

Comment. The Rule Application paragraph in Example 9.5.5.1 (also discussed in Example 9.2.3.1) presents the writer's conclusion that noise from a motorcycle repair business does not sufficiently interfere with the plaintiff's use and enjoyment of his property to constitute significant harm. The case comparisons that follow address the extent of the interference with ordinary activities on the property. • The first comparison distinguishes the pervasive interference in the *Mackenzie* and *Wilke* cases from the limited interference the plaintiff, Mr. Lambert, experiences. The second comparison analogizes the limited interference in the *Childs* case to the equally limited interference Mr. Lambert experiences. • The second comparison ends with an observation—about the number of people whose activities are affected—that is related but subordinate to the primary subject of the comparison (and of the Rule Application paragraph as a whole), the ordinary activities that are affected. The citation and explanatory parenthetical that follow, succinctly describing the *Radziewicz* finding about significant harm and the number of people affected, supplement the comparison without drawing the reader's focus away from the primary subject of the rest of the paragraph.

Example 9.5.5.2 (bad example: explanatory parentheticals substitute for textual case comparisons).

A court would likely find that Mr. Lambert experiences only minimal harm, not pervasive interference, from the disruption to his seasonal backyard entertaining. Mr. Lambert complains of noise affecting only his backyard entertaining, only on weekends, and only during warm weather—which, in southeastern Michigan, is limited to half the year or less. The courts require more pervasive interference than Mr. Lambert experiences to support a claim for significant harm. Compare Mackenzie, 174 N.W. at 163 (finding significant harm based on residents' inability to use inside and outside of home five days a week), and Wilke, 2007 WL 1828788, at *4 (finding significant harm based on residents' inability to use inside and outside of home seven days a week), with Childs, 2001 WL 1199901, at *4 (finding no significant harm based on minimal interference with residents' ability to use home). Cf. Radziewicz, *2009 WL 2974733, at *3* (finding no significant harm based on single complaining resident).

Comment. The Rule Application paragraph in Example 9.5.5.2, a modified version of the paragraph in Example 9.5.5.1, relies exclusively on citations and explanatory parentheticals to identify the case law that supports the writer's conclusion. The parentheticals force the reader to complete the connections between the client's facts and the distinguishable or analogous facts in the cases. It is the writer's job, not the reader's, to make those connections, using fully articulated, textual comparisons.

9.5.6 Subject focus in case comparisons

Using consistent subject focus in the case comparisons in your Rule Application paragraphs is just as important as it is in the case descriptions in your Rule Explanation paragraphs. (See §8.5.8; see also §9.12.) When you are comparing your client's facts to analogous or distinguishable facts in the case law, keep both parts of the comparison focused on the same grammatical subject—courts and courts, findings and findings, facts and facts; reasoning and reasoning (apples and apples, in other words)—so your reader can concentrate on the specific details that follow the subjects. Do not focus one part of a comparison on one subject and the other part on a different subject. In a single-sentence comparison, use the same subject for the parts of the sentence doing the comparing: an independent clause and a dependent clause, two independent clauses, or an independent clause and a phrase. (See §§13.2.1, 13.2.3.) In a multiple-sentence comparison, use the same subject for each sentence. For both types of comparison, you may use words from the same subject category, rather than the exact same word, if the correspondence between your matter and the case or cases is not exact. (See Example 9.5.6.4.) You may use a different subject focus in different case comparisons that appear in the same Rule Application paragraph, but be sure to use a consistent focus within each comparison.

<u>Example 9.5.6.1</u> (consistent subject focus in single-sentence comparison: courts).

Just as the *court* in <u>Rose</u> found no significant harm in the complaining neighbor's respiratory discomfort, where she was extra-sensitive to smoke and fumes, 2009 WL 3276431, at *4, a *court* would probably find no significant harm in Mr. Lambert's migraines, where he happens to be extra-sensitive to noise.

(Sample Legal Memorandum 8:8-12) (emphasis added)

> **Comment.** The comparison in Example 9.5.6.1 focuses on the same grammatical subject, *court,* in both parts of the sentence. (The first part, beginning with *Just as,* is a dependent clause; the second part, beginning with *a court,* is an independent clause.) The consistent subject focus makes it easy for the writer to illustrate the similarity of the rest of each part of the sentence, that is, the similar findings based on similar facts. • Consistent subject focus would make it just as easy, in a different case comparison, to illustrate dissimilar findings based on dissimilar facts.

<u>Example 9.5.6.2</u> (consistent subject focus in single-sentence comparison: facts).

Here, a court would likely find that North Ypsilanti, where Mr. Hendricks and Mr. Lambert live, is a residential neighborhood. It consists of homes inhabited by families, working people, and college students. The nearest *stores* are located on two main streets, a half-mile away, unlike the *commercial district* within two or three blocks of the plaintiffs' homes in Moore, which helped give the neighborhood a "semibusiness" character, 222 N.W. at 121-22.

(Sample Legal Memorandum 14:18-24) (emphasis added)

Comment. The comparison in the third sentence of Example 9.5.6.2 focuses on the same subject category, *stores* and *commercial district*, rather than on identical words. (The first part of the comparison, from *The nearest stores* through *streets*, is an independent clause; the second part, from *unlike* through *Moore*, is a phrase.) The facts in a client's matter will rarely be identical to those in the cases, but you maintain a consistent subject focus when you compare, or distinguish, facts and facts by focusing the parts of your comparison on the same category of facts.

Example 9.5.6.3 (bad example: inconsistent subject focus in single-sentence comparison).

Just as *the court* in Rose found no significant harm in the complaining neighbor's respiratory discomfort, where she was extra-sensitive to smoke and fumes, 2009 WL 3276431, at *4, *the motorcycle noise* would cause no significant harm to Mr. Lambert, who gets migraines because he is extra-sensitive to noise.

Comment. Example 9.5.6.3, a variation of Example 9.5.6.1, presents a poorly constructed case comparison. The first part of the sentence focuses on *the court* in an analogous case, which found no significant harm, but the second part focuses directly on *motorcycle noise*, without framing the legal conclusion in terms of what a new court would find about significant harm arising from that noise. The writer is not comparing apples and apples. • Note how the inconsistent subject focus also misaligns the other important information in the sentence. Instead of the parallel presentation contained in both parts of Example 9.5.6.1—*court* | *found no harm* | *symptom* | *reason* | *stimulus*—the presentation in the second part of Example 9.5.6.3 is no longer parallel to that in the first part—*stimulus* | *would cause no harm* | *symptom* | *reason* | *stimulus*. A reader would have to make more effort to line up the details of the comparison, and to reinsert the missing detail about the court, than if the writer had done it in the first place, by using consistent subject focus. • Further, the comparison in Example 9.5.6.3 contains a grammatical error. The second part of the sentence is modified by the first part: It says that something performs an action *just as the* *court in Rose* performs an action. (See §13.2.6.) The grammatical subject of the second part of the sentence, which the first part modifies, is *noise*. Noise cannot perform the same kinds of action that a court can perform, to find or not find. It can only perform the kinds of action than another noise can perform, to cause an effect—and the only thing that can perform the same actions as a court is another court. • So be sure that your case comparisons, both single-sentence and multiple-sentence, use a consistent subject focus. If you do not, your reader may be disoriented.

Example 9.5.6.4 (consistent subject focus in multiple-sentence comparison: courts).

The *court* in O'Connor found significant harm where twenty-two neighbors complained, 248 N.W. at 558, and the *court* in Mackenzie found significant harm where twelve neighbors complained, 174 N.W. at 161. The *courts* in Rose and Radziewicz, however, found no significant harm where a single property owner complained. Rose, 2009 WL 3276431, at *4; Radziewicz, 2009 WL 2974733, at *2. Here, in the absence of multiple plaintiffs, a *court* would probably find that the motorcycle noise, however bothersome to Mr. Lambert, does not constitute significant harm for purposes of a private nuisance lawsuit.

(Sample Legal Memorandum 8:22-30) (emphasis added)

Comment. The consistent subject focus in Example 9.5.6.4 on *courts* makes it very easy to compare a series of similar and dissimilar findings in four cases and the probable finding in the client's matter. (The two parts of the first sentence, joined by *and*, are independent clauses. The independent clause in the second sentence begins with *The courts* and ends with *harm*. The independent clause in the third sentence begins with *a court* and ends with *harm*. Each independent clause uses the same grammatical subject, *court* or *courts*.)

9.6 Consistency with the Rule Explanation

Each Rule Application paragraph should be consistent—in its focus, content, and analysis—with the Rule Explanation paragraph to which it corresponds.

9.6.1 Main point

Apply the same main point that you identified in the Rule Explanation paragraph when you present and support your conclusion in the corresponding

Rule Application paragraph. Do not change the scope or substance of the main point when you apply it. Do not introduce a main point you did not cover in the Rule Explanation. If another main point is important to your analysis, add a new Rule Explanation paragraph to introduce and illustrate it and a new Rule Application paragraph to apply it to your facts.

9.6.2 Material facts

Do not introduce the basic facts about any case for the first time in a Rule Application paragraph. Introduce the facts when you describe the case in the Rule Explanation paragraph, and refer back to them, as necessary, in the corresponding Rule Application paragraph.

9.6.3 Key analytical terms and concepts

If you introduce an important definition, term or phrase, legal principle, judicial rationale, or policy statement in a main point or during the course of describing the case law examples in a Rule Explanation paragraph, be sure to show how it would apply to your facts in the corresponding Rule Application paragraph.

9.7 Consistency with other conclusions

Your conclusion in each Rule Application paragraph should be consistent with any related conclusion you present elsewhere in the memorandum. A reader will expect to find your conclusions in multiple locations: (i) in the Brief Answer; (ii) in the main Overview to the Discussion; (iii) in the first paragraph of each section and subsection; (iv) in the first sentence of each Rule Application paragraph; (v) in the Restated Conclusion at the end of a lengthy or subdivided section (see §9.10); and (vi) in the final Conclusion to a lengthy memorandum (see Chapter 10). Be sure the conclusions you include in each location are consistent with one another, in terms of their substance and the degree of certainty or qualification with which you express them.

9.8 Counterarguments

A research memorandum must inform the reader of the strengths and weaknesses of your client's legal position. If there is a *credible* counterargument to any part of your analysis, you need to address it. Do not, however, manufacture a counterargument for any part of the applicable rule, just for the sake of including one.

9.8.1 Indirect rebuttal

Sometimes, you can rebut a potential counterargument indirectly, simply by distinguishing the factual or legal basis for it within the larger Rule Application paragraph.

Example 9.8.1.1 (indirect rebuttal of counterargument).

Nor would a court be likely to find evidence of unreasonable interference in Mr. Hendricks's evening and weekend hours of operation. First, the noise ends before most adults go to bed. Mr. Hendricks stops work in the evenings by 10:00 p.m. or 11:00 p.m., an hour or two later than 9:00 p.m., the last time each day when the paddlewheel boat blew its whistle in Radziewicz, which the court found reasonable, 2009 WL 2974733, at *3. He stops work no later than 11:00 p.m., the time when the court in O'Connor deemed it necessary to enjoin noise from the creamery so it would not disturb the neighbors, 248 N.W. at 558. The court in Radziewicz did not have to decide whether noises later than 9:00 p.m. might disturb the neighbors, see 2009 WL 2974733, at *2-3, whereas the court in O'Connor did address the question and found that 11:00 p.m. was the time when interference from noise in the neighborhood could become unreasonable, 248 N.W. at 558.

(Sample Legal Memorandum 19:15-27)

Comment. In Example 9.8.1.1, the writer does not directly address the potential counterargument, based on *Radziewicz*, that noise after 9:00 p.m. is unreasonable. The writer rebuts it indirectly, and effectively, by distinguishing *Radziewicz* from *O'Connor*, to show that courts draw the line for unreasonable noise at 11:00 p.m.

9.8.2 Direct rebuttal

At other times, however, you may need to confront the counterargument directly. If you do not believe the counterargument is persuasive, try to introduce it by stating why it is not persuasive; at a minimum, introduce it by stating that it would not persuade a court. Otherwise, you will leave the reader guessing about its merit relative to your main analysis. That is, do not introduce a counterargument with language along the lines of, *On the other hand, opposing counsel could argue that* . . . . If, in your honest estimation, the counterargument is stronger than the argument favoring your client, you must phrase your opening conclusion and organize your Rule Application paragraph to present it as the probable outcome. Do try your best to find and include support for your client's position, even if you must acknowledge that the position will not prevail. The senior colleague who gave you the research assignment and the client will expect you to do that.

Example 9.8.2.1 (direct rebuttal of counterargument).

A possible counterargument, that truckers have the alternative of using credit cards, does not account for all the needs that truckers have for cash. First, not every trucker will be able to obtain credit, and these truckers in particular should not have to bear the risk of carrying cash for long distances. Second, Triathlon offers discounts for cash at its truck stops. Filling a truck's tank costs over $400, and truckers have tight operating budgets; many truckers are under a practical necessity to seek these discounts. Third, truckers will need to pay tolls as they continue on the highway, and many toll booths only accept cash.

> **Comment.** This rebuttal of a counterargument, from a memorandum addressing the unconscionability of a contract under California law, begins by identifying the counterargument and suggesting why it is not persuasive. (The memorandum was written before the widespread adoption of electronic payments at tollbooths.) • In the rest of the paragraph, which has been omitted here, the writer includes comparisons to the relevant case law, to show how the available precedents helped to refute the counterargument. (See §9.8.4.)

9.8.3 Placement within paragraph

Try to dispense with a counterargument within the same Rule Application paragraph in which you present your main analysis, if that does not make the paragraph too long. Present the main analysis first, and then dispense with the counterargument. If you need a separate paragraph, you may use it, but be sure the first sentence clarifies that the new paragraph continues the analysis of the main point from the prior paragraph. (See §9.2.3, Example 9.2.3.3.)

9.8.4 Substantive analysis

If you need to rebut a counterargument directly, use the same methods that you use to present any Rule Application. Analyze the facts and incorporate comparisons to the legal precedents.

9.9 Additional information

If an important part of your analysis would turn on factual information you do not have, note the absence of the potentially relevant facts, but present your analysis based on the facts you do have. Be sure to identify any missing material facts in the Statement of Facts. (See §4.5.5.)

Example 9.9.1 (Statement of Facts identifies missing material facts).

Mr. Hendricks lives in North Ypsilanti. The surrounding neighborhood consists of small and medium-sized houses occupied by families, working-class people, and local college students. The closest stores are a half-mile away, on Cross Street and Michigan Avenue. As a result of the bad economy, many people in the neighborhood have lost their jobs; some have lost their homes, too. To make ends meet, a number of residents have started home businesses, *the natures of which we do not currently know*. . . .

To diagnose and repair motorcycles with engine problems, Mr. Hendricks needs to start, run, and stop them. The engines are loud, so Mr. Hendricks tries to limit the number of startups each day. *We do not know exactly how loud the engines are, however, or for how long Mr. Hendricks runs them.* Other kinds of repairs do not require Mr. Hendricks to run the engines.

(Sample Legal Memorandum 2:1-8, 22-27) (emphasis added)

Example 9.9.2 (Rule Application paragraph notes missing facts but bases analysis on available facts).

Even the recent proliferation of home businesses has not altered North Ypsilanti's residential character. The presence of scattered stores, shops, and other businesses, including some home businesses, did not alter the generally residential character of the urban locale in Mackenzie. 174 N.W. at 162-63. *We do not know the exact nature of the other home businesses in North Ypsilanti*, but their presence would not likely change a court's view that the neighborhood is generally residential, too.

(Sample Legal Memorandum 14:24-30) (emphasis added)

Example 9.9.3 (Rule Application paragraph notes missing facts but bases analysis on available facts).

We do not know the decibel level of the noise, but the volume is probably at least as great as that of a power lawn mower, if not quite as great as that from a jet engine—both of which the courts have said might produce unreasonable interference. Wilke, 2007 WL 1828788, at *4 (jet engine); Cunningham, 2001

WL 717882, at *4 n.5 (power mower).

(Sample Legal Memorandum 18:14-19) (emphasis added)

> **Comment.** Example 9.9.1 contains two extracts from the Statement of Facts in the Sample Legal Memorandum, which identify facts potentially important to the legal analysis—material facts—that the writer does not have. • Examples 9.9.2 and 9.9.3 contain extracts from two Rule Application paragraphs in the Discussion, in which the writer acknowledges the missing facts but analyzes how the law would apply to the facts the writer does have.

9.10 Restated Conclusion

The Restated Conclusion is optional. If the analysis within an undivided section or subsection is lengthy or complex, add a short paragraph after the final Rule Application paragraph to restate your conclusion about the subject of the section or subsection. Similarly, if the analysis within a section or subsection is divided into more manageable subdivisions (see §9.2.2), add a short paragraph after the final subdivision to restate your conclusion about the subject of the larger section or subsection. In either case, a single sentence generally suffices for the Restated Conclusion; no separate heading is needed. Note that if the last in a series of subdivisions requires its own Restated Conclusion, use a single, combined paragraph at the end of the subdivision for both that conclusion and the Restated Conclusion for the larger section or subsection; do not use two successive, single-sentence paragraphs to restate each conclusion separately.

Example 9.10.1 (Restated Conclusion at end of lengthy undivided subsection).

Accordingly, a court would probably find no significant harm because the noise from Mr. Hendricks's motorcycle repair business does not cause Mr. Lambert and his family actual physical discomfort, objectively considered.

(Sample Legal Memorandum 9:15-18)

> **Comment.** Example 9.10.1 contains the final paragraph of Section I.A of the Sample Legal Memorandum, the subsection that addresses actual physical discomfort, the first factor for the significant harm element in the Michigan rule on private nuisance. • The subsection contains three Rule Explanation paragraphs and three Rule Application paragraphs—long enough for a Restated Conclusion, in a final paragraph at the end, to be helpful to the reader.

Example 9.10.2 (Restated Conclusion at end of divided section).

For all of these reasons, a court would probably conclude that the noise from Mr. Hendricks's business does not constitute an unreasonable interference.

(Sample Legal Memorandum 23:23-25)

Comment. Example 9.10.2 contains the final paragraph of Section II of the Sample Legal Memorandum, which addresses the unreasonable interference element of the Michigan rule on private nuisance. • The last of the three subsections, addressing the necessity and value of the conduct in question, contains two Rule Explanation paragraphs and two Rule Application paragraphs—short enough so that a reader does not need a Restated Conclusion in a final paragraph. • Accordingly, Example 9.10.2, the paragraph that follows the third subsection, just presents the Restated Conclusion for Section II as a whole.

Example 9.10.3 (successive Restated Conclusions at end of divided section).

On balance, a court would probably find that the character of the noise from Mr. Hendricks's business provides little evidence of unreasonable interference. Considering all three factors, a court would probably conclude that the noise from Mr. Hendricks's business does not constitute an unreasonable interference.

Comment. Example 9.10.3 is what Example 9.10.2, the final paragraph of Section II of the Sample Legal Memorandum, might look like if the third factor bearing on unreasonable interference was the character of the noise, not the necessity and value of the conduct. • The first sentence in the paragraph presents the Restated Conclusion for the subsection—now the last one—on the character of the noise. The subsection contains three Rule Explanation and three Rule Application paragraphs and is long enough for the first Restated Conclusion to be helpful to the reader. • The second sentence in the paragraph presents the Restated Conclusion for the entire section on unreasonable interference. The section contains three subsections and a total of eight pairs of Rule Explanation and Rule Application paragraphs—more than long enough for the second Restated Conclusion to be helpful to the reader. • The paragraph efficiently combines both Restated Conclusions, rather than using two successive, single-sentence paragraphs.

9.11 Template

Template 9: Organization of Single Section (Through Rule Application).

[X.] Subject heading for section[1]

¶1: Conclusion[2]

¶2: Rule Statement[2 3]; First Rule Explanation Paragraph
- First main point[4 5]
- Case law examples illustrating first main point[6]

¶3: Second Rule Explanation Paragraph, if any
- Second main point[4 5]
- Case law examples illustrating second main point[6]

¶4: Third Rule Explanation Paragraph, if any[7]
- Third main point[4 5]
- Case law examples illustrating third main point[6]

¶5: First Rule Application Paragraph
- Conclusion: how first main point applies to client's facts[8 9]
- Analysis of client's facts and comparisons to case law[10 11]

¶6: Second Rule Application Paragraph, if necessary
- Conclusion: how second main point applies to client's facts[8 9]
- Analysis of client's facts and comparisons to case law[10 11]

¶7: Third Rule Application Paragraph, if necessary
- Conclusion: how third main point applies to client's facts[8 9]
- Analysis of client's facts and comparisons to case law[10 11]

¶8: Restated Conclusion[12]

[1] Adjust the font style for the level of heading. (See §5.3.5.3.)

[2] Alternatively, you may present the Rule Statement and Conclusion, in that order, within a combined opening paragraph. If you do, begin the first Rule Explanation paragraph directly with your first main point about the law. (See §7.2.2, Template 7B.)

[3] You *may* use a short overview paragraph instead of a combined opening

paragraph if it would be helpful to the reader to introduce the topics you will cover in successive paragraphs in the section to follow. You *should* use an overview paragraph if you subdivide the section into subsections. (See §6.7, Template 6B.)

[4] Generally, present your most important main point first, if you have more than one point to make about the case law. Other sequences may be appropriate, however. (See §8.3.3.)

[5] If you derive a main point from a specific judicial decision, cite that decision after stating the point. If you derive a main point from multiple decisions, just cite the decisions as you describe them in the rest of the paragraph. (See §8.3.4.)

[6] Include supporting case law examples first within each Rule Explanation paragraph and any important contrary case law examples second. Include positive supporting case law examples before negative supporting case law examples. (See §8.4.1.)

[7] If you have more than three main points to make about the case law, consider subdividing your section into shorter, more manageable subdivisions. (See §8.2.3.)

[8] Use a single sentence that clearly relates to the subject of the corresponding main point. (See §§9.3, 9.3.1.)

[9] You may state the conclusion alone, add a concise supporting reason, or embed a few supporting details. (See §9.3.4.)

[10] You may present the factual analysis first and the case comparisons second, present the case comparisons first and the factual analysis second, or interweave the two throughout the paragraph. (See §9.2.1.)

[11] Cover any credible counterargument after presenting the factual analysis and case comparisons supporting your conclusion. (See §§9.8, 9.8.3.) You may rebut the counterargument indirectly or directly. (See §§9.8.1, 9.8.2.)

[12] Use a short, separate paragraph to restate the conclusion after a lengthy or complex undivided section or subsection or after a section or subsection divided into subdivisions. (See §9.10.)

9.12 Exhibit

Exhibit 9: Subject Focus and Other Unifying Techniques in Rule Explanation and Rule Application Paragraphs.[1]

One factor **courts** consider in evaluating significant harm is whether the conduct causes <u>actual physical discomfort</u>. <u>Smith,</u> 158 N.W.2d at 468 (citing <u>Borsvold</u>, 81 N.W.2d at 378). **The courts** do not find significant harm, however, if the conduct would not cause <u>actual physical discomfort</u> to an ***ordinary person***. <u>Id.</u> at 470. In <u>Smith,</u> **the Michigan Supreme Court** found no significant harm where noise from a gun shooting range would not cause <u>actual physical discomfort</u> to an ***ordinary person***. <u>Id.</u> at 471. After neighboring residents submitted conflicting testimony about the effect of the noise, **the trial judge** attended a special shooting demonstration to experience the noise directly, from the homes of various plaintiffs. <u>Id.</u> at 468, 470-71. **The judge** noted that the harms alleged had to be objectively reasonable. <u>Id.</u> at 469-70.

> Whether the noise is sufficient to constitute a nuisance depends upon its effect upon an ***ordinary reasonable man***, that is, a ***normal person of ordinary habits and sensibilities***. Relief cannot be based solely upon the *subjective likes and dislikes of a particular plaintiff*. To be workable, relief must be based upon an objective standard of reasonableness.

<u>Id.</u> at 470. Having personally experienced the noise, **the judge** concluded that it was not such "as would shock a ***person of ordinary sensibilities*** or cause <u>actual physical discomfort</u>." <u>Id.</u> at 470-71. **The Supreme Court** agreed, adopting tbe trial judge's opinion in full. <u>Id.</u> at 465, 472-73. Similarly, in <u>Rose v. Braciszewski</u>, No. 285316, 2009 WL 3276431, at *4 (Mich. Ct. App. Oct. 13, 2009) (per curiam), **the court** found no significant harm where smoke from burning yard waste on a neighboring property and exhaust fumes from the neighbor's automobiles would not cause <u>actual physical discomfort</u> to an ***ordinary person***. The neighbor burned leaves only a few times a year and ran his old cars in a barn on the property for a couple of hours each on two or three

[1] Different styles of emphasis in the text represent the following:
- <u>Underline</u> (excluding case names and signals): the part of the rule under discussion
- **Bold**: a court or a judge
- ***Bold italics***: the key subject of the main point
- *Italics*: the opposite of the key subject of the main point

They are included for pedagogical purposes only; do not use them in your memoranda.

days. Id. The complaining homeowner may have been "*particularly susceptible* to the smoke and fumes," but **the court** concluded that her discomfort was not sufficient to satisfy the objective standard for harm, i.e., that a ***person of ordinary sensibilities*** would have suffered adverse health effects, too. Id.; see also Restatement (Second) of Torts § 821F cmt. d ("*idiosyncrasies of the particular plaintiff*" not enough to establish significant harm). . . .

Here, **a court** would probably find that any harm to Mr. Lambert is not significant because the noise from Mr. Hendricks's motorcycle repair business would not cause actual physical discomfort to an ***ordinary person***. An ***ordinary person*** does not have an *underlying propensity* to experience migraine headaches. Just as **the court** in Rose found no significant harm in the complaining neighbor's respiratory discomfort, where she was *extra-sensitive* to smoke and fumes, 2009 WL 3276431, at *4, **a court** would probably find no significant harm in Mr. Lambert's migraines, where he happens to be *extra-sensitive* to noise. In both cases, the conduct complained of falls short of the objective standard for significant harm, which requires "actual physical discomfort to ***persons of ordinary sensibilities***." Id. **A court** would probably conclude that Mr. Lambert's migraines, although unfortunate, are *unique to him*.

(Sample Legal Memorandum 5:19-6:26, 8:4-16) (emphasis added)

Comment. The corresponding Rule Explanation and Rule Application paragraphs in Exhibit 9, from Section I.A of the Sample Legal Memorandum, are unified individually and unified with each other in several ways, suggested by the guidelines in Chapters 8 and 9.

Consistent grammatical subject focus. First, the two paragraphs maintain a consistent subject focus on the same (or a synonymous) grammatical subject, the courts (or the individual by whom a court acts, a judge):

- in the second sentence of the Rule Explanation paragraph, which states the main point;
- in every sentence of the multiple-sentence case description of *Smith* (except the three sentences quoted from the opinion) and in the first and last sentence of the multiple-sentence case description of *Rose*;
- in the first sentence of the Rule Application paragraph, which states the writer's conclusion as to how the main point would apply to the client's facts;

- in both clauses that make up the single-sentence case comparison; and
- in the last sentence of the paragraph, which restates the basis for the writer's conclusion.

(Note, too, that the first sentence in the Rule Explanation paragraph, the rule statement, introduces the subject, *courts*, which many of the following sentences will focus on, although *factor*, not *courts*, is the grammatical subject of that sentence.) The consistent subject focus in both paragraphs allows the reader to concentrate on the details that follow, about the law, the cases, and the facts. (See §§8.5.8, 9.5.6.)

Repeated references to subject of rule. Second, the content of the two paragraphs consistently relates back to the part of the rule the writer is addressing in Section I.A—which the rule statement establishes—that is, the requirement, for the significant harm, of actual physical discomfort:

- in the second sentence of the Rule Explanation paragraph, which states the main point (see §8.3.2.1);
- in the first sentence of each case description in that paragraph, which states the relevant finding (see §8.5.4.1);
- in the last or next-to-last sentence of each description, which relates the case law example back to the main point about actual physical discomfort (see §8.5.4.3);
- in the first sentence of the Rule Application paragraph, which states the writer's conclusion as to how the main point about this part of the rule would apply to the client's facts (see §9.3.1);
- in both clauses of the case comparison, which identify the actual physical discomfort the plaintiff and Mr Lambert experience; and
- in the last two sentences, which restate the requirement of actual physical discomfort in the part of the rule under discussion and which restate that Mr. Lambert's discomfort is legally insufficient.

These repeated references keep the overall subject of Section I.A, the part of the rule the writer is addressing, in focus for the reader.

Repeated references to subject of main point. Third, and similarly, the content of the two paragraphs consistently relates back to the insight about the case law on this part of the rule—which the main point establishes—that actual physical discomfort is measured by an ordinary-person standard:

- in the first sentence of each case description in the Rule

Explanation paragraph, which states the relevant finding (see §8.5.4.1);

- in the first sentence quoted from the *Smith* decision's reasoning, which articulates the ordinary person requirement;
- in the last or next-to-last sentence of each description, which relates the case law example back to the main point (see §8.5.4.3);
- in the first sentence of the Rule Application paragraph, which states the writer's conclusion as to how the main point would apply to the client's facts (see §9.3.1); and
- in the next-to-last sentence, which restates the ordinary person test that the main point identified.

These repeated references keep the subject of the main point in this pair of Rule Explanation and Rule Application paragraphs in focus for the reader.

Repeated references to opposite of main point. Finally, and by way of contrast, the two paragraphs also introduce and then refer back to the opposite of the main point—that actual physical discomfort is not measured subjectively, based on a specific person's extra-sensitivity to stimuli:

- in the second sentence quoted from the *Smith* decision's reasoning, which distinguishes the objective, ordinary person requirement from the subjective likes and dislikes of a particular plaintiff;
- in the last sentence of the *Rose* description, which identifies the plaintiff's particular susceptibility to smoke and fumes;
- in the explanatory parenthetical that follows the *Rose* description, which quotes a comment that the particular idiosyncrasies of a particular plaintiff are legally insufficient
- in the second sentence of the Rule Application paragraph, which emphasizes that ordinary people do not have an underlying propensity to experience migraine headaches;
- in both halves of the case comparison, which emphasize that the plaintiff's extra-sensitivity to smoke and fumes in *Rose* and Mr. Lambert's extra-sensitivity to migraines are legally insufficient.; and
- in the last sentence of the paragraph, which, in restating the basis for the writer's conclusion, identifies Mr. Lambert's unique propensity to experience migraines.

These repeated references to subjective conditions that do not satisfy the main point help keep that point in focus for the reader.

Rule Explanation and Rule Application paragraphs unified by these several techniques are easier for the reader to follow and, accordingly, communicate the writer's analysis more clearly and efficiently. Consciously or unconsciously, a reader will appreciate such assistance in a legal memorandum of any length.

Chapter 10
How to Write the Final Conclusion

10.1 Purpose

The final Conclusion is the optional, sixth component of a legal memorandum. When it is appropriate to use one, the final Conclusion reminds the reader of the key points in your analysis at the end of your memorandum.

10.2 When to use it

Use a final Conclusion at the end of your memorandum if the Discussion as a whole is lengthy or complex. Omit a final Conclusion if the Discussion is shorter and more straightforward. If you are unsure where your Discussion falls within that spectrum, use a final Conclusion if you think it would be helpful to your reader.

10.3 Format

The final Conclusion follows the Discussion at the end of the memorandum. It is a separate component of the memorandum and requires its own heading. Use a heading printed in bold, capital letters and centered on the page, as you did for the other components of the memorandum, the Question Presented, the Brief Answer, the Statement of Facts, and the Discussion. (See §5.3.5.) (Of course, if your employer or the assigning attorney prefers a different format for the headings, follow it.) The final Conclusion after a lengthy or complex Discussion should be no longer than the Brief Answer—about half of a page, at most. The final Conclusion after a Discussion of moderate length and complexity should be even shorter.

10.4 Content

Restate your overall conclusion, and include no more than a few key points from your analysis. You may cover some of the same information you covered in the Brief Answer, but do not repeat it verbatim—in part, because the final Conclusion follows, rather than precedes, the Discussion. You do not need to reintroduce the applicable rule, for example, but you should continue to use the same specific names and descriptions you used in the Discussion, rather than the generic references you used in the Brief Answer. Do not repeat every key point from your analysis in the Discussion, unless you can do that succinctly. Do not use multiple paragraphs, unless your memorandum addresses multiple legal issues. In particular, do not introduce new facts, conclusions, or legal analyses. If appropriate, you may repeat important information about the operation of the rule, but focus primarily on your conclusions.

Example 10.4.1 (final Conclusion from complex memorandum).

CONCLUSION

A Michigan court would probably determine that the noise produced by Mr. Hendricks's motorcycle repair business is not a private nuisance. Neither key element of the test for private nuisance is present. The noise does not create significant harm because Mr. Lambert's migraines and his children's interrupted sleep do not represent actual physical discomfort to ordinary persons, and the interference with his backyard entertaining represents only minimal harm. Nor does the noise create an unreasonable interference. The noise is loud and the neighborhood is residential, but the sound is a type of ordinary street noise that is sporadic, brief, and limited to adults' waking hours. Moreover, the social utility of Mr. Hendricks's business far outweighs the interference with Mr. Lambert's rights.

(Sample Legal Memorandum 23:26-24:7)

Example 10.4.2 (final Conclusion from complex memorandum, with note about operation of rule).

CONCLUSION

A court would likely determine that Triathlon's $4.00 ATM fee is unconscionable under California law. Although no court has specified to what degree the procedural and substantive elements of the rule on unconscionability must be present, the truckers' case sufficiently satisfies both. During the contract-negotiation process, the truckers do not have an opportunity to negotiate or amend any terms. Nor do they possess any meaningful choice in the process. As for the contract itself, Triathlon's higher-than-market fee yields enormous profits, at no risk or inconvenience to Triathlon. With both elements of the rule present to a high degree, a court would likely conclude that the ATM fee is unconscionable.

(Final Conclusion to memorandum analyzing unconscionability of ATM fee under California law)

Comment. Examples 10.4.1 and 10.4.2 contain the final Conclusion from two complex memoranda, each one more than twenty pages long. • Each Conclusion restates the overall conclusion from the memorandum and includes the most important points from the writer's analysis. • Each one covers information similar to that in the corresponding Brief Answer, but each uses specific, not generic, references. • Each Conclusion is no longer than the corresponding Brief Answer and no longer than half a page. • Neither Conclusion restates the applicable rule, but the Conclusion in Example 10.4.2, in the second sentence, repeats important information about the operation of the rule: The courts have not identified a minimum threshold for satisfying either element. Having repeated that information, Example 10.4.2 refers back to it in the final sentence, which restates the overall conclusion in terms of the operation of the rule.

Chapter 11
How to Organize and Write an Informal or E-mail Memorandum

11.1 Purpose

Attorneys write informal or e-mail memoranda to answer more specific or more narrowly focused questions than are typically the subject of formal, comprehensive legal research memoranda—as well as to address other matters arising in a law office that do not involve legal research. Attorneys usually need to produce informal or e-mail memoranda on shorter deadlines, too, often within twenty-four hours or less. As with any legal memorandum, an informal or e-mail memorandum must be objective and enable the reader to act on its contents and conclusions (see Introduction §iii.i), but it also must be especially clear and to the point.

11.2 Format

For these reasons, use a more streamlined organizational structure for your informal and e-mail memoranda.

11.2.1 Degree of formality

There is no page limit or word count below which a memorandum automatically requires the more streamlined organizational structure. Instead, the limited scope or different nature of the assignment and the shorter deadline will make an informal or e-mail structure better suited to your work product. Sometimes, the assigning attorney may specifically ask for a short memorandum or an e-mail, leaving no doubt as to the structure you should use.

11.2.2 Delivery

You may deliver an informal memorandum in hard copy or as an attachment to an e-mail, unless the assigning attorney has requested, or office logistics dictate, one or the other. If you deliver an informal memorandum as an attachment to an e-mail, use the text of the e-mail to describe it succinctly, in just a few sentences. The e-mail recipient may not always be able to read your memorandum right away but will always appreciate the preview. For the recipient's benefit, too, make the subject line in the e-mail self-explanatory, for example, *Eastern District's Construction of MRPC 1.10(b)*—not *Memorandum You Requested* or the like. Similarly, make the file name for the memorandum self-explanatory: Attachments often get separated from the e-mails that transmit them. When you deliver a stand-alone e-mail memorandum—electronically, of course—make the subject line self-explanatory.

Example 11.2.2.1 (e-mail transmitting informal memorandum).

I am attaching the memorandum you requested, analyzing the Eastern District courts' construction of the screening and notice requirements of MRPC 1.10(b). In almost all cases, the courts construe both requirements very stringently.

Example 11.2.2.2 (e-mail transmitting informal memorandum).

I have read the transcript of Richard Riley's deposition and summarized its contents in the attached memorandum. Richard's testimony covers his relationship with Wanda and Billy Lee and his fifteen-month absence, about which we knew very little. Not surprisingly, some of his testimony contradicts Wanda's statements to us.

> **Comment.** Example 11.2.2.1 contains the text of an e-mail transmitting the Sample Informal Memorandum as an attachment. Example 11.2.2.2 contains the text of an e-mail transmitting an informal memorandum summarizing the deposition testimony of the respondent to an involuntary termination of parental rights proceeding. The text of both e-mails, in only two or three sentences, identifies the attached memorandum and previews its contents for the benefit of the e-mail recipient.

11.2.3 Length

There is no maximum page limit or word count to which an informal or e-mail memorandum must adhere. The assigning attorney will expect a work product commensurate in length and detail with the more limited scope or nature of the assignment. Try not to write an informal memorandum longer than about ten double-spaced pages; often, you can keep it shorter. You may also single-space an informal memorandum to make it physically as well as textually concise. (The Sample Informal Memorandum is single-spaced, to keep it to five pages.) When you write an e-mail memorandum—which lacks page divisions and will be read on the screen of an electronic device—you should include even less text than in an informal memorandum. (The Sample E-mail Memorandum has fewer than half the number of words in the Sample Informal Memorandum.) If you start writing an e-mail memorandum but it becomes longer and longer, rewrite it as a separate informal memorandum and attach it to an e-mail. (See §11.2.2.)

11.2.4 Informal memorandum

When you write an informal memorandum, condense the three introductory components of a formal memorandum, the Question Presented, the Brief Answer, and the Statement of Facts, into just an Introduction and a Summary. (See §§11.4, 11.5.) Include a Discussion component, but use fewer levels of sections and subsections than you would typically use in a longer, formal memorandum. (See §11.7.) Identify each major component in your memorandum with a separate, stand-alone heading in the text. (See §12.6.) If your employer or the assigning attorney prefers different names for the components of an informal memorandum or a different format altogether, you should—as always—comply with those different preferences.

11.2.5 E-mail memorandum

When you write an e-mail memorandum, you have even greater flexibility as to its organizational structure. You may include an Introduction and a Summary; you may combine them into a single component; or you may dispense with them altogether—as long as you incorporate other organizational techniques to establish a clear and accessible structure from the start of the e-mail. (See §11.9.1.) You should always include a Discussion component or its equivalent. Unless the text of your Discussion is just a few paragraphs long, divide it into short, clearly labeled parts that will be easy to read on a computer, tablet, or mobile phone. (See §11.9.3.)

11.2.6 Degree of repetition

In an informal or e-mail memorandum, there is less need than in a longer, formal memorandum to repeat information in different places throughout the document and in different levels of detail. A range of readers may still consult an informal or e-mail memorandum (see §5.5), but its more limited scope, simpler organizational structure, and shorter overall length make it easier for those readers both to find the information they need to know and to keep specific conclusions, rules, and other key information in mind as they read through the document. More of the readers are likely to read the entire document, too, so the individual parts need not be as self-sufficient as in a formal memorandum. Your readers will still appreciate a high-level preview, in the Summary or an equivalent paragraph, of a few key points or topics from the analysis or discussion to follow. Little or no repetition should be necessary in the rest of the document.

11.3 Heading

Begin your informal or e-mail memorandum with the name of the person to whom you are writing it, your name as the author, and the date and subject matter of the memorandum. For an informal memorandum, use the same heading format that you use at the start of a formal memorandum, with the word *MEMORANDUM* at the top of the page, bolded (but not italicized), followed by two columns for the four categories of information—*TO*, *FROM*, *DATE*, and *RE*, with those words also bolded (but not italicized). (See Chapter 1.) For an e-mail memorandum, fill in the *To* and *Subject* fields; the *From* and *Date* fields will be filled in automatically. Do not type a separate heading at the beginning of the text of the e-mail.

11.4 Introduction

The first major component of an informal memorandum is the Introduction. (An e-mail memorandum may include a separate Introduction, too.) State the relevant background for the assignment, followed by the specific question you have been asked to answer or the specific matter you have been asked to address. In other words, state the facts and factual context (see §4.4) first. Do not include a detailed statement of facts, however. If you need to cover a lengthy set of facts, use a formal memorandum with a separate Statement of Facts. Alternatively, you may include a separate statement or summary of the facts as an attachment or supplement to an informal or e-mail memorandum, although that tends to defeat the purpose, and effectiveness, of writing a shorter memorandum in the first place. Consistent with the more informal nature of these memoranda, you may state the assigned question or matter more informally, too, rather than using a yes-or-no question format. (See §11.8.) Use specific names and descriptions, not generic references, for both the facts and the assigned question or matter. Try to limit the Introduction to no more than a few short paragraphs.

Example 11.4.1 (Introduction to informal memorandum).

INTRODUCTION

One of our new associates, John Gillespie, split his 2009 summer between our firm and opposing counsel in the Minton Mobile litigation, Torin & Conover. While at Torin, Mr. Gillespie did some legal work for Defendant Clark Monroe on a matter involved in the case. Mr. Gillespie is personally disqualified from working on the case for us, and today, on his first day of work, we notified the Eastern District that we have screened him from any involvement in the case. Nevertheless, the Torin firm may move to disqualify us from continuing to represent Minton Mobile in the lawsuit.

You have asked me to determine how stringently the Eastern District courts apply the screening and notification requirements of Michigan Rule of Professional Conduct 1.10(b) to law firms subject to a motion to disqualify counsel.

(Sample Informal Memorandum 1:10-24)

Example 11.4.2 (Introduction to informal memorandum).

INTRODUCTION

On Thursday, October 27, I deposed Richard Riley at the office of his counsel, Sam Phillips, of Legal Action of Wisconsin, in Green Bay. Richard is the Respondent in the involuntary proceeding to terminate parental rights to his son, Billy Lee Riley, which we are handling on behalf of Wanda Jackson, who has had exclusive custody of Billy Lee since mid-December 2015. Including a short lunch break, the deposition lasted about four hours. Yesterday, we received the deposition transcript from the reporter.

As you requested, I have summarized Richard's deposition testimony.

(Introduction from informal memorandum summarizing deposition testimony)

Comment. The Introductions contained in Examples 11.4.1 and 11.4.2 succinctly summarize the key facts giving rise to the assignment in the first paragraph, and they identify the assignment itself in the second paragraph. • Both Introductions use specific, not generic, facts and descriptions.

11.5 Summary

The second major component of an informal memorandum is the Summary. (An e-mail memorandum may include a separate Summary, too.) Provide a short answer or response to the assignment, in a single paragraph. For an assignment that calls for legal research and analysis, state your conclusion and no more than two or three supporting reasons, previewing key points in the analysis to follow; save the applicable law to introduce in the Overview to the Discussion. For an assignment that does not call for legal research or analysis, briefly describe the core content or import of the matter you addressed. As in the Introduction, use specific names and descriptions, not generic references, in the Summary.

Example 11.5.1 (Summary from informal memorandum).

SUMMARY

In general, the Eastern District courts strictly construe both requirements. The courts require "timely" screening, which obliges the hiring firm to implement effective screening measures at least as soon as the firm becomes aware of the potential conflict. Similarly, the courts insist on written notice; oral notice will not do. The courts require notice prompt enough to allow them to oversee the proper screening of the infected attorney, but in an exceptional case, they may overlook a delayed notice if the screening was timely and effective and the delay was not very long.

(Sample Informal Memorandum 1:26-35)

Example 11.5.2 (Summary from informal memorandum).

SUMMARY

In his deposition testimony, Richard blames Wanda for the break-up of their relationship. He did not take Billy Lee with him when he left because he did not have the means to support him. Richard moved to Florida, where he lived with a friend and picked up the friend's cocaine habit. He sent occasional cards to Wanda and Billy Lee while he was away; some of them included money. Richard went through rehab in Florida and returned to Wisconsin in March of this year. He is working part-time and taking college courses, and he wants Billy Lee to come live with him.

(Summary from informal memorandum summarizing deposition testimony)

> **Comment.** Example 11.5.1 contains the Summary from the Sample Informal Memorandum. The first sentence states the conclusion to the research question the writer was asked to answer. The supporting reasons in the next three sentences preview key points in the analysis to follow in the Discussion. • Example 11.5.2 contains the Summary from an informal memorandum summarizing the deposition testimony of the respondent to an involuntary termination of parental rights proceeding. The Summary describes the core content of the testimony in six concise sentences. • Both Summaries use specific names and descriptions.

11.6 Discussion

The final major component of an informal memorandum is the Discussion. (An e-mail memorandum always includes a Discussion component or equivalent text.) Use the Discussion to present your substantive analysis or information. Use the same organizational strategies and techniques that you would use in a formal memorandum, but with some modifications appropriate for a shorter document and the range of different subjects.

11.6.1 Overview

For assignments that call for legal research and analysis, begin the Discussion with an Overview before the first section, to introduce the applicable rule. (See §6.4.) Do not repeat your overall conclusion or supporting reasons in the Overview: The immediately preceding Summary component will have stated them both. For assignments that do not call for legal research or analysis, you may begin the Discussion with a paragraph or two before the first section, to cover any helpful preliminary topics.

> **<u>Example 11.6.1.1</u> (Overview to Discussion presenting legal analysis).**
>
> **DISCUSSION**
>
> The Michigan Rules of Professional Conduct (MRPC) apply in the Eastern District of Michigan. E.D. Mich. LR 83.22(b). Rule 1.10(b) governs the imputed disqualification of a hiring law firm when a new attorney at the firm would be personally disqualified from representing a client with interests adverse to those of the attorney's old client. MPRC 1.10(a).
>
> > (b) When a lawyer becomes associated with a firm, the firm may not knowingly represent a person in the same

> or a substantially related matter in which that lawyer, or a firm with which the lawyer was associated, is disqualified under Rule 1.9(b), unless:
>
> (1) the disqualified lawyer is screened from any participation in the matter and is apportioned no part of the fee therefrom; and
>
> (2) written notice is promptly given to the appropriate tribunal to enable it to ascertain compliance with the provisions of this rule.

Id. 1.10(b). The rule allows the hiring firm to avoid disqualification if it screens the infected attorney from all participation in and compensation from the matter from which the attorney is disqualified, id. 1.10(b)(1), and if the firm "promptly" gives written notice of its compliance with the rule to the court adjudicating the litigation, id. 1.10(b)(2).

(Sample Informal Memorandum 1:37-2:17)

Comment. Example 11.6.1.1 contains the Overview to the Discussion in the Sample Informal Memorandum. The Overview introduces the rule on law firm disqualification, which the individual Discussion sections that follow analyze in detail. The Overview omits the overall conclusion and supporting reasons because the Summary, just before the Overview, already supplied them.

Example 11.6.1.2 (Overview to Discussion not presenting legal analysis).

DISCUSSION

As we anticipated, Richard was not cooperative during his deposition. He is angry at the prospect of losing his son, and he took out his anger in various ways during my questioning. Eventually I was able to get him to provide the information we needed. At one point, Richard's counsel persuaded him to be more forthcoming, as my notes below will indicate. I have also identified a number of subjects where Richard's testimony appears to conflict with the facts that Wanda has given us.

I have presented the subjects to which Richard testified in approximate chronological order, rather than in the more elliptical order in which we covered the subjects during the deposition. For your convenience, I have included cross-references to the transcript pages on which Richard's statements appear.

(Overview from informal memorandum summarizing deposition testimony)

> **Comment.** Example 11.6.1.2 contains the Overview to the Discussion in an informal memorandum summarizing the deposition testimony of the respondent to an involuntary termination of parental rights proceeding. The Overview provides certain preliminary, explanatory information about the conduct of the deposition, its content, and the sequence in which the writer presents the content within the rest of the Discussion.

11.6.2 Large-scale organization

To present a traditional legal analysis, organize the Discussion using most of the same large-scale organizational strategies that apply to the Discussion in a formal memorandum. (See §5.3.) To cover other matters—whether proposing a litigation strategy or a transactional structure, summarizing a deposition or the edits to a contract, or anything other than explaining and applying the law—incorporate alternate organizational strategies to present your subject clearly and effectively. Depending on the subject of your memorandum, select from the following organizational sequences, combine one or more of them, or use a different sequence that is better suited to the content of your Discussion.

11.6.2.1 Rule structure

For a traditional legal analysis, divide the Discussion into sections and subsections that correspond to the structure of the applicable rule, just as you would in the Discussion component of a formal memorandum. (See §5.3.3.)

> <u>**Example 11.6.2.1.1**</u> **(large-scale organization by rule structure).**
>
> **DISCUSSION**
>
> [Overview]
> **A. The Screening Requirement: Rule 1.10(b)(1)**
> **B. The Notice Requirement: Rule 1.10(b)(2)**
>
> (Sample Informal Memorandum 1:37, 39, 2:19, 4:32)
>
> **Comment.** The Discussion in the Sample Informal Memorandum is divided into two main sections, which correspond to the two-part structure of the applicable law firm disqualification rule.

11.6.2.2 Thematic structure

Divide the Discussion into sections and subsections that correspond to important themes or topics within the subject matter of your memorandum.

<u>Example 11.6.2.2.1</u> (large-scale organization by rule structure and thematic structure).

DISCUSSION

[Overview]

A. The Screening Requirement: Rule 1.10(b)(1)

Timely screening

Relation to disqualifying event

Risk of confidence sharing

Comprehensive screening

B. The Notice Requirement: Rule 1.10(b)(2)

Written notice

Prompt notice

(Sample Informal Memorandum 1:37, 39, 2:19, 24, 43, 3:26, 4:6, 32, 39, 5:11)

Comment. The Discussion in the Sample Informal Memorandum combines two organizational sequences. • The first level of organization follows a rule structure: The two main sections correspond to the structure of the applicable rule on law-firm disqualification. • The second level of organization follows a thematic structure: The paragraphs within each section correspond to important topics the courts address when they construe each part of the rule.

<u>Example 11.6.2.2.2</u> (large-scale organization by thematic structure).

[Introductory paragraph]

<u>Model agreement</u>

<u>Michigan law on noncompetition agreements</u>

<u>Key provisions</u>

<u>Other provisions</u>

(Sample E-mail Memorandum 1:8, 17, 29, 44, 3:23)

Comment. The text of the Sample E-mail Memorandum is divided into the four main sections, which correspond to important topics about the draft noncompetition agreement that the memorandum is transmitting.

11.6.2.3 Procedural structure

Divide the Discussion into sections and subsections that correspond to the applicable procedural steps in a matter your office is or may be handling.

Example 11.6.2.3.1 (large-scale organization by procedural structure).

DISCUSSION

[Overview]
A. Petition and summons
B. Hearing on petition
C. Discovery
D. Fact-finding hearing
E. Disposition hearing

(Informal memorandum outlining applicable procedure)

Comment. The Discussion in this informal memorandum is divided into five sections, which correspond to the sequence in which an involuntary proceeding to terminate parental rights moves from start to finish under Wisconsin law. • Note that you may be able to combine organization by procedural structure with organization by rule structure if the procedural steps follow the sequence of provisions in the applicable statute or rule.

11.6.2.4 Other sequential structures

Divide the Discussion into sections and subsections that correspond to the order in which certain actions or events occurred (*chronological structure*), the order in which certain information was acquired or delivered, for example, in an interview or during testimony (*narrative structure*), the order in which certain sections appear in a document (*numerical structure*), or similar sequences.

Example 11.6.2.4.1 (large-scale organization by thematic and numerical structure).

[Introductory paragraph]
Model agreement
Michigan law on noncompetition agreements
Key provisions
Recitals: Competitive business interests
§ 1: Noncompetition (duration)
§ 1: Noncompetition (geographic scope)
§ 1: Noncompetition (type of employment)
§ 2: Nondisclosure
Other provisions
§ 3: Specific performance
§ 4: Severability
§ 7: Governing law
§ 8: Consent to jurisdiction and venue

(Sample E-mail Memorandum 1:8, 17, 29, 44, 46, 2:17, 28, 43, 3:12, 23, 28, 31, 33, 35)

Comment. The text of the Sample E-mail Memorandum combines two organizational sequences. • The first level of organization follows a thematic structure: The four main sections correspond to important topics about the draft noncompetition agreement that the memorandum is transmitting. • The second level of organization incorporates a numerical structure: The paragraphs within the third and fourth sections correspond to the order in which certain key and other noteworthy provisions appear in the draft.

Example 11.6.2.4.2 (large-scale organization by chronological structure).

[Overview]
A. **Richard's life with Billy Lee before meeting Wanda, 2007-2010**
B. **Richard's life with Wanda and their children, 2010-December 2014**
C. **Richard's life in Florida after leaving Wisconsin, December 2014-March 2016**
D. **Richard's life in Wisconsin after his return, March 2016-present**

(Informal memorandum summarizing deposition testimony)

Comment. The Discussion in this informal memorandum is divided into four sections, which track the chronology of events covered during the deposition of the respondent in an involuntary termination of parental rights proceeding. • For the reader's benefit, the writer presents the summary using a chronological sequence, although the deposition itself covered the events more elliptically. (See Example 11.6.1.2.) The writer could have presented the summary using a strict narrative sequence, following the order in which the respondent actually gave his testimony, but that would have made it harder for the reader to get the big picture of what happened when—which, as in most legal proceedings, has important legal implications.

11.6.3 Small-scale organization

To present a traditional legal analysis, organize the sections and subsections in the Discussion using most of the same small-scale organizational strategies that apply to the sections and subsections in a formal memorandum. (See §5.4.) To cover other matters, incorporate alternate organizational strategies to present the information in each section and subsection clearly and effectively.

11.6.3.1 Legal analysis

In a memorandum that presents a legal analysis, begin each section or subsection with your conclusion for the particular part of the rule you are analyzing. Omit the rule statement if the individual sections and subsections are so short that only a few pages separate them from a prior statement of the entire rule. Otherwise, include a rule statement—either following the conclusion or preceding it (see §7.2); include a rule statement in every section if you include one in a single section. Include one or more pairs of Rule Explanation and Rule Application paragraphs, with appropriate main points about the case law, descriptions of individual decisions, and comparisons between the cases and your client's facts. (See Chapters 8 and 9.) Omit the Rule Application paragraphs if you are analyzing a pure question of law, without applying the law to a set of facts. (The Sample Informal Memorandum analyzes a pure question of law and does not contain Rule Application paragraphs.) The sections and subsections in your Discussion should be short enough that you do not need to include a Restated Conclusion at the end of each one.

Example 11.6.3.1.1 (small-scale organization presenting legal analysis).

B. The Notice Requirement: Rule 1.10(b)(2)

The Eastern District courts insist upon receiving written notice of a potential conflict promptly enough for them to oversee the hiring firm's screening measures, but in limited circumstances they may overlook a short delay.

Written notice. In general, the Eastern District courts construe the "written notice" language strictly: oral notification is not acceptable. . . .

Prompt notice. Nevertheless, the Eastern District courts may construe the prompt written notice requirement more leniently in an exceptional case, where the hiring firm fully complied with the screening requirement and its delay in providing written notice was only slight. . . .

(Sample Informal Memorandum 4:32-40, 5:11-14) (citations omitted)

Comment. Example 11.6.3.1.1 contains extracts from the second section of the Discussion in the Sample Informal Memorandum. The section incorporates a small-scale organizational structure appropriate to the presentation of a legal analysis. • The opening paragraph states the writer's conclusion about the second half of the rule on law firm disqualification. • The two Rule Explanation paragraphs that follow begin with a main point about the case law on that half of the rule. They contain descriptions of judicial decisions illustrating each point (not included in the example above). • The section omits a separate rule statement because a statement of the entire rule appears in the Overview to the Discussion, just two pages before. (Had the Sample Informal Memorandum been double-spaced, however—resulting in a Discussion component of about six pages—it would have been acceptable to include a rule statement at the start of each section in the Discussion, for the reader's convenience.) • The section contains no Rule Application paragraphs because the memorandum analyzes a pure question of law, rather than the application of a rule to a set of facts.

11.6.3.2 Non-legal analysis

In a memorandum that covers matters other than legal research and analysis, you have greater flexibility for organizing the individual sections and subsections. Often, the large-scale organizational sequence you select for the Discussion (see §11.6.2) will suggest an appropriate sequence of presentation within the sections and subsections. Where the subject matter permits, begin with the most important information and then add the details.

<u>Example 11.6.3.2.1</u> (small-scale organization presenting non-legal analysis).

D. Richard's life in Wisconsin after his return, March 2016-present

Upon his return to Wisconsin this past March, Richard rented an apartment in Green Bay, found a job as a part-time clerk at a law office there, and began taking courses at a local community college. He began to send cards and money to Wanda and Billy Lee again, but he did not attempt to visit his son. When he telephoned Wanda's house in October and asked to speak to Billy Lee, Wanda refused and told him she was going to see a lawyer about adopting Billy Lee.

Richard's domestic arrangements. Richard testified that he left Florida and returned to Wisconsin in March. . . .

Richard's contacts with Wanda and Billy Lee. Richard testified that as soon as he began to earn money again, he resumed sending cards and money to Wanda and Billy Lee. . . .

(Informal memorandum summarizing deposition testimony)

Comment. Example 11.6.3.2.1 contains extracts from the fourth section in an informal memorandum summarizing the deposition testimony of the respondent to an involuntary termination of parental rights proceeding. • The large-scale organization of the Discussion follows successive chronological periods covered by the deposition. (See Example 11.6.2.4.2.) That organizational structure suggests an appropriate structure for each Discussion section. • Each section begins with a paragraph that identifies key facts from the relevant chronological period. In that way, the opening paragraph states the most important information a reader should learn from the entire section—just as the opening conclusion does in a Discussion section presenting a legal analysis. • The rest of the fourth section divides the relevant deposition testimony into two general subjects, but it presents the testimony within each subject in chronological order, in one or more paragraphs (not included in the example above).

11.6.4 Final Conclusion

Regardless of the large-scale organizational structure you incorporate, do not include a separate component at the end to restate your overall conclusion. It should not be necessary in light of the shorter overall length of your memorandum.

11.7 Sections, headings, lists

For all but the shortest of presentations, divide your Discussion into sections and, where appropriate, subsections. Identify each one with a separate heading. Try not to use more than two levels of sections for informal or e-mail memoranda. You may use embedded headings at the start of related paragraphs within a section or subsection as a way to identify their content without adding further subdivisions. (See §12.6.) You may also use lists, bullet points, and indented text to set off or illustrate different subjects within a section or subsection—and you may use these techniques, as well as embedded headings, even in an undivided Discussion component if they would help make the content easier for your reader to assimilate. Visual clarity is especially important in informal and e-mail memoranda, but do not use more organizational apparatus than necessary to achieve it.

Example 11.7.1 (Discussion section with embedded headings).

B. The Notice Requirement: Rule 1.10(b)(2)

With limited exceptions, the Eastern District courts insist upon receiving written notification of a potential conflict promptly enough for them oversee the hiring firm's screening measures.

Written notice. In general, the Eastern District courts construe the "written notice" language strictly: oral notification is not acceptable. . . .

Prompt notice. Nevertheless, the Eastern District courts may construe the prompt written notice requirement more leniently in exceptional cases, where the hiring firm has implemented the other protections embodied in Rule 1.10(b). . . .

(Sample Informal Memorandum 4:32-40, 5:11-14)

Comment. The Discussion in the Sample Informal Memorandum is divided into two main sections. Each section is preceded by a separate, stand-alone heading. • Within each section, the writer uses paragraphs with embedded headings to present the relevant topics, keeping the content of the section clear but also concise. • Note, however, that if the topics within a section require more than a paragraph or two each to cover, it would be better to use a new level of subsections, instead.

11.8 Paragraphs, writing, citations

For both informal and e-mail memoranda, use well-organized paragraphs—with the most important information in the first sentence, where possible—direct and concise sentence structure, plain but specific words, and, when necessary, accurate citations in the correct format. These features of good legal writing are always appropriate, no matter how short or informal the work product is. Consistent with the informal nature of these memoranda, however, you may write in the first or second person, if appropriate: *in our lawsuit* or *you have asked me to find out*. You should continue to introduce adults by their full name, but in subsequent references you may use their last name only, without a prefix (*Parker*), or even just their first name (*Richard*). Keep your language and tone professional—especially in e-mail memoranda. Do not use the kind of informal language, exclamations or other punctuation marks, acronyms or other abbreviations, or emoticons or emoji that you might use in your personal e-mail correspondence or texts.

11.9 Special issues for e-mail memoranda

Attorneys in all practice areas increasingly communicate by short, informal, e-mail messages and memoranda—most commonly for matters other than traditional legal analysis. These communications do not have a standard organizational structure, although it may be appropriate to incorporate some of the organizational tools you would use in a formal or informal legal memorandum. E-mail memoranda, however, do present several issues unique to their means of delivery.

11.9.1 Letter format

Given the more immediate and personal nature of e-mail correspondence, you may begin the text of your memorandum with a salutation, such as *Dear Mr. Benedetti* or *Dean*, depending on the degree of formality you ordinarily maintain with the recipient. Use the opening paragraphs to state the assignment or identify the purpose of the e-mail, describe the key facts or background, summarize the answer or contents, or preview the topics to follow. Use the rest of the text for your substantive analysis or discussion; organize it to present your subject clearly and effectively within the confines of an e-mail communication. (See §11.9.3.) Note that if you do use the more personal letter format, you can generally omit the Introduction, Summary, and Discussion components and just use a combination of sections, subsections, and lists for your content. (The Sample E-mail Memorandum, which uses the letter format, does that.) Be sure to identify any documents you attach to the e-mail. It is usually a good idea to welcome questions about the substance of your memorandum, to offer to discuss it with the recipient, or both. You may do so at the beginning or at the end of the text, but not in both places. As in a letter, include your name at the end, even though it also appears in the *From* field. Use your full name if you are not on a first-name basis with the recipient.

Example 11.9.1 (opening and closing paragraphs in e-mail memorandum using letter format).

Dean:

As you requested, I have drafted a noncompetition agreement between our client, Woodside Review, and Charlene Parker, the seller's CEO in Woodside's acquisition of the assets of Steeplechase Test Preparation. Parker's execution of the agreement is a condition to Woodside's obligation to close, and Woodside has instructed us to draft the agreement to incorporate the maximum restrictions on Parker's post-closing activities that a Michigan court will enforce. This e-mail summarizes the key provisions I have included in my draft. . . .

Please let me know if you have any questions. I would be happy to meet with you at your convenience to discuss them.

Junior

(Sample E-mail Memorandum 1:6-15, 3:38-41)

Comment. The Sample E-mail Memorandum uses a letter format. • The opening and closing indicate that the writer and the recipient are on a first-name basis. • The opening paragraph identifies the assignment, the transactional context in which it arose, and the memorandum's focus on the key provisions in the draft contract. • Note that the subject matter does not call for a summary, but the memorandum includes two preliminary sections following the opening paragraph (not included in the example above) on the source of the contract the writer used for the assignment and the state law that applies to the draft contract's provisions. In the first of those sections, the writer identifies the two attached documents: the clean and marked-up versions of the draft contract. • In the final paragraph, the writer welcomes questions about the work product and offers to discuss it with the recipient.

11.9.2 Recipients

As with any e-mail message, be very careful about the recipients you include. If you send an e-mail memorandum containing, or attaching, confidential client information or attorney work product to recipients other than the client and the colleagues with whom you are working on the matter, you could be deemed to have waived the evidentiary privileges that otherwise would attach to the information or work product. Add a line to the heading in the *Subject* field or at the start of the e-mail text to identify any applicable privileges. If you send an e-mail memorandum—or any e-mail—in response to an e-mail message you received, do not hit *Reply to All* unless you know who each recipient of the original message was and you intend to send your memorandum—or response—to each one of them.

11.9.3 Visual appearance

Make your e-mail memorandum easy to read on the screen of an electronic device. Use a plain, sans-serif font style, in a *Normal* or slightly larger size. (See §§12.3.1, 12.3.2.) Divide the text into concise sections and paragraphs. Single-space the text, but double-space between sections and paragraphs. Use stand-alone headings for sections; use headings embedded at the start of related paragraphs within the sections. (See §12.6.) Make the headings stand out. Use bold and underlined fonts for the section headings, bold fonts for embedded paragraph headings, and, if necessary, underlined fonts for headings in lists or other subdivisions. Do not use italics: They recede into the text. (See §12.3.4.) Use numbered or bulleted lists to present a series of points about the same subject. Indent the text with each new level within the organizational structure, to create an outline appearance—avoid a dense wall of text aligned at the left margin on the screen. (See §12.9.) Proofread your memorandum before you send it, to catch and fix any typos and format glitches.

Example 11.9.3.1 (e-mail memorandum incorporating techniques to enhance visual clarity).

Michigan law on noncompetition agreements

Michigan permits the use of noncompetition agreements to protect a company's reasonable competitive business interests, provided that the restrictions are reasonable as to duration, geographical area, and type of employment or line of business. Mich. Comp. Laws Ann. § 445.774a(1) (West, Westlaw through P.A. 2015 No. 6) (limited to employment context); Bristol Window & Door v. Hoogenstyn, 650 N.W.2d 670, 680 (Mich. Ct. App. 2002) (clarifying that Michigan courts apply statute to both employment and non-employment contexts). Courts more readily enforce noncompetition agreements entered into during the sale of a business than those signed in ordinary employment relationships. M. Scott McDonald & Jacqueline C. Johnson, Drafting and Enforcing Covenants Not to Compete § 3.II(A), at 49 (2014), Bloomberg Law.

Key provisions

- **Recitals: Competitive business interests.** The Recitals identify several of Woodside's competitive business interests in the underlying transaction:

    - to purchase the goodwill and proprietary, confidential intellectual property associated with the successful Steeplechase test preparation methods and materials;
    - to incorporate those methods and materials into Woodside's own operations and then to expand its operations nationally; and
    - to protect its investment by requiring Parker, who created the intellectual property and made the Steeplechase business successful, not to compete with Woodside while the agreement is in force.

  Courts recognize that these kinds of interests are reasonable to protect by means of a noncompetition agreement. See, e.g., Perceptron, Inc. v. Sensor Adaptive Machs., Inc., 221 F.3d 913, 920 (6th Cir. 2000) (applying Michigan law).

(Sample E-mail Memorandum 1:29-2:15)

Comment. The Sample E-mail Memorandum incorporates a number of techniques to make the text easy to read. • Separate headings, bolded and underlined, identify the main sections. Bolded, embedded headings identify the paragraphs within each section. • Different styles of bullet points—closed and open—mark the individual paragraphs and the items in a list. • The main sections are aligned at the left margin. The paragraphs and the list are indented by the successive levels of bullet points. • The text is single-spaced, but the section headings, sections, paragraphs, and lists are separated by double-spacing, for visual relief. • The two undivided sections in the memorandum are just one paragraph long. The two divided sections contain a series of bulleted individual paragraphs. It may not be possible to be as concise in every e-mail memorandum, but the more concise you can make each part—and the more techniques you can use to make the parts easy to read—the more efficiently will you be able to communicate the contents of your memorandum to the recipient.

Chapter 12
How to Format a Memorandum

12.1 Purpose

The format of a memorandum helps to manage the presentation, appearance, and accessibility of the information you need to communicate. Your memoranda, formal or informal, should always look professional. They should be neat, easy to read and use, and error-free. Do not over-design the format of your memoranda, with wide margins, different or unusual font sizes and styles, or the like. A memorandum is not a book or a journal, and alternate formats that may be acceptable in those publications may only serve to distract—if not annoy—your reader and impede the delivery of your memorandum's content. If the assigning attorney, your law office, or local custom does require different format choices, you should comply with them. Otherwise, follow the guidelines below to create a professional-looking format for your memoranda (but note that that format will differ in various ways from the format you observe in this book, which requires a smaller page size and other modifications).

12.2 Page Size and Margins

Set up your formal and informal memoranda to print on standard, letter-size paper. Use consistent margins of one-and-a-quarter or one-and-a-half inches on each side of the page and on top and bottom. Do not vary the margins within your document, except when you indent lists or block quotations (see §12.9) or successive levels of text in e-mail memoranda (see §11.9.3).

12.3 Fonts

Use a single font style and size for the text, headings, and page numbers throughout your memorandum.

12.3.1 Font style

Use a conservative font style with serifs for formal and informal legal memoranda, which will, or may, be read in hard copy. Serifs add a gravitas to the characters that is appropriate for a hard-copy, professional document. Times New Roman is a good choice of serif font. Use a plain font style without serifs for the text of e-mail memoranda or messages. Sans-serif fonts are easier to read on a computer, tablet, or mobile phone screen. Arial is a good choice.

12.3.2 Font size

Use a font size that is large enough to be read easily. For formal and informal memoranda, use a 12-point font size. For e-mail text, use the *Normal* or a slightly larger setting, unless the primary recipient of your e-mail prefers a different size.

12.3.3 Footnotes and endnotes

Use a smaller, 10-point font size for the text of footnotes or endnotes within a formal or informal memorandum. Use the same font style as that in the regular text of the memorandum.

12.3.4 Headings

Use bold fonts for the headings of the major components in formal and informal memoranda. Use bold fonts for the headings of the main sections and either bold or underlined fonts for the headings of any subsections or further subdivisions. Bold fonts stand out from the text more than underlined fonts. For that reason, you should use them to denote the higher levels in the organizational structure within your document. Use underlined fonts, if at all, to denote the lower levels; underline only the text of each heading, not the letter or number to the left of the text. (The Sample Legal Memorandum uses bold fonts for the main section headings and underlined fonts for the subsection headings. The Sample Informal Memorandum uses bold fonts for both the main section headings and the embedded headings within each section.) Except in e-mail memoranda, where the greater visual clarity can be beneficial, do not combine bold and underlined fonts for any headings in formal and informal memoranda: Such headings are too emphatic. (The Sample E-mail Memorandum uses bold and underlined fonts for the section headings and bold fonts for the embedded headings.) Do not use italic fonts for headings in any memorandum: Italics recede into the text.

12.3.5 Superscripts

Do not use superscript fonts in your legal writing, such as *P.*^{2d}, *9*th *Cir.*, or *5*th *ed.*, except to number footnotes or endnotes. If an automatic formatting function on your computer converts ordinal numbers to superscripts, go to the settings on your computer and turn it off—or correct it manually each time.

12.4 Justification

Use left justification only, including within block quotations. If a colleague, a law office, or a local custom requires full justification, use that. Do not change the justification choice within the same document.

12.5 Spacing

12.5.1 Lines

Double-space lines in a formal legal memorandum, and single-space lines in an e-mail memorandum. You may double-space or single-space lines in an informal memorandum. (See §11.2.3.) Do not leave extra space between lines; set your line spacing options to *0* points before and after each line. Single-space lines for multiple-line headings, items in an indented list, and footnotes. (Do not number the lines in the memoranda you write. Line numbers are included in the sample memoranda in this book for pedagogical purposes only.)

12.5.2 Paragraphs

Double-space between paragraphs in every memorandum; for memoranda that are single-spaced, the double spacing between paragraphs provides helpful visual relief. Do not leave extra space before or after any paragraph.

12.5.3 Headings

Double-space before and after each stand-alone heading in your document.

12.5.4 Lists

If some or all of the items in an indented list require multiple lines, you may double-space between them—including any single-line items—for visual relief.

12.5.5 Sentences

Leave two spaces between sentences, not one. In left-justified text, the two spaces set off each new sentence clearly and make them easier to read.

12.5.6 Ellipsis

Leave a space between the three periods of an ellipsis mark. If an automatic formatting function on your computer closes them up, go to the settings on your computer and turn it off—or correct it manually each time.

12.6 Headings

The headings in a memorandum signal the division of the document into different parts and sub-parts. A *stand-alone heading* appears in a line by itself, separated by double-spacing from the text before and after it. Use stand-alone headings for the major components of your memorandum and for the different levels of sections. An *embedded heading* appears at the start of a paragraph, on the same line as the first sentence of the text. You may use embedded headings to identify the content of a series of related paragraphs within an undivided section or subsection, instead of creating a new organizational level. Unlike a *full-sentence heading*, a *subject heading* contains only a word or a phrase. A full-sentence heading is always a stand-alone heading; a subject heading may be a stand-alone heading or an embedded heading. Note that full-sentence headings are more typically used in briefs than in memoranda.

12.6.1 Titles

Make the headings in your memoranda concise but specific and self-explanatory. For example, use *Actual Physical Discomfort* as a heading, not *First Factor*.

12.6.2 Outline format

Apart from the headings for the major components in your memorandum—which you should center on the page—use an outline format for the different levels of headings in the document. Align the main section headings at the left margin, and indent one-half inch for each new level of subsections or further subdivisions. It is customary in formal memoranda to use Roman numerals (*I*, *II*, etc.) for the main section headings, capital letters (*A*, *B*, etc.) for the subheadings, and Arabic numbers (*1*, *2*, etc.) for the first level of further subdivisions (all without italics). For memoranda with more than three levels of headings, you may use an all-Arabic numbering format—as this book does—to keep the more complex organizational structure clear on any page of the document (for example, *12.6.2*). For informal memoranda with no more than two levels of sections and subsections, you may use the less-formal-looking capital letters instead of Roman numerals for the main headings and Arabic numbers for the subheadings; you may align the main section headings with the half-inch paragraph tab and indent the subheadings another half-inch. (The Sample Informal Memorandum uses indented capital letters for the main headings.) For e-mail memoranda, use the outline format for the headings, but you may omit the number and letter designations. (The Sample E-mail Memorandum uses main headings aligned at the left margins and bulleted, indented, embedded headings within the sections.) Include a period after the number or letter of every heading in your memoranda, before the heading text.

12.6.3 Location on the page

Do not leave a heading alone at the bottom of any page (an *orphan heading*) or split a heading across two pages. Be sure to include at least two lines of text after a heading near the bottom of a page. If necessary, use a hard return to place the heading at the top of the next page.

12.6.4 Punctuation

End full-sentence headings and embedded headings with a period. Omit a period after stand-alone subject headings.

12.6.5 Capitalization

Use all capital letters for the headings of the major components of your formal and informal memoranda. Use initial capitals for the first word and the major words in stand-alone, full-sentence or subject headings (such as the heading of this chapter). Capitalize only the first word in an embedded heading (as in the Sample Informal Memorandum.)

12.7 Page numbering

The page numbering in formal and informal memoranda should be readily accessible but unobtrusive. A good choice is to number every page except the first at the bottom center. For certain documents, with a header on each page, it may be cleaner and more efficient to include the page number on the last line of the header. If it is important to convey the total number of pages in a document, you may use the *Page X of Y* format. Generally, however, just include the numeral alone. E-mail memoranda, without page breaks, do not require page numbers. (Page numbers are included in the Sample E-mail Memorandum in this book for pedagogical purposes only.)

12.8 Page limits

Generally, memoranda do not have page limits. Their length will be dictated by scope of the topic and the brevity or complexity of the facts, the analysis, or the discussion. Should an assigning attorney specify a page limit for a memorandum, try not to exceed it.

12.9 Indentation for paragraphs, lists, and block quotations

For formal and informal memoranda, indent the first line of each paragraph one-half inch—including the first paragraph after any heading; indent the text of lists and block quotations one inch from both margins. Some word processing software automatically adjusts the paragraph indentation to match the indentation for each new level of heading. The result is a distracting line of uneven paragraph indentations throughout the document. Go to your computer's settings and turn that auto-formatting function off—or correct it manually each time. For e-mail memoranda, do not indent the first line of individual paragraphs, but indent successive levels of text—not just the headings—for greater visual clarity on the screen of an electronic device. (See §11.9.3.)

12.10 Emphasis

Use <u>underlined fonts</u>, not *italicized fonts*, to emphasize words or text within your memorandum—even if the text in a source you quote is printed in italics. Underlining stands out more readily than italics, in both hard-copy text and e-mail text. So if you want to emphasize something, use a font that will catch the reader's attention. Certain legal analyses, written for law reviews or other publications with their own format rules, may need to use italics for emphasis (or other purposes). If you are writing a memorandum for a colleague or a client, use underlining for emphasis.

12.11 Citations

Generally, use the citation rules that the attorneys with whom you practice use. Local custom or court rules in different jurisdictions often require unique or individually tailored citation practices. If no such custom or rules apply to you, follow the citation rules contained in current edition of *The Bluebook.*

12.12 Quality control

Take the following precautions before you submit any memorandum, to ensure that it is error-free.

12.12.1 Spelling and grammar

Proofread your memorandum before you submit it. Do not rely exclusively on the *Spell and Grammar Check* function on your computer. It will not catch every word that is misused or recognize every complex, but correct, grammatical structure. Use *Spell and Grammar Check* first, to catch obvious typos and errors. Then proofread your document manually, to catch anything else.

12.12.2 Names, titles, and key language

Be sure you have all the names right in your memorandum, for your client, your colleagues, a judge, other important people and organizations, the titles of statutes and key documents, and so on. Use the *Find* function on your computer to check that each name, title, and key word or phrase, including every abbreviation or defined term, is correct and consistent throughout your memorandum.

12.12.3 Format

Before you submit a formal or informal memorandum, use *Print Preview* or a similar function on your computer to check the appearance of every page and the document as a whole. Look for misaligned margins, paragraphs, and headings; different font styles and sizes; unequal spacing between headings, lines, and paragraphs; orphan or split headings; or any other format errors, glitches, and inconsistencies. It is much easier to spot and fix format problems when you are moving from one full-page view to the next in *Print Preview* than when you are scrolling through the document in regular view on your computer screen or when you are paging through the document in hard copy. Use *Print Preview* even after you make minor edits to a memorandum you previously checked on *Print Preview*, just to be sure the edits do not affect the format. Before you send an e-mail memorandum, scroll through the text on the screen and try to spot and fix any format problems.

Chapter 13
How to Write Clearly

13.1 Purpose

Every attorney must be able to write clearly, regardless of the attorney's area of practice. The most insightful, comprehensive, best-supported written analysis or discussion will not be effective for its organizational purpose if the reader cannot follow the writing, must read a sentence or paragraph several times to understand it, or remains confused or uncertain about the writer's intended meaning. You can improve the overall clarity of your writing by following the five strategies in §13.3 of this chapter for writing clear sentences and paragraphs and the three strategies in §13.4 for presenting related information clearly. You can improve the clarity of your writing, too, by following the thirty guidelines in §13.5 for correct grammar, precise word choice, and clear style. To be able to follow these strategies and guidelines, you should first review §13.2, about the structure and operation of the English language.

13.2 The English language

You will be able to write more clearly if you understand some fundamental points about the parts and mechanics of the English language. You will need to be familiar with a number of basic grammatical terms and rules; where possible, however, this section presents the technical concepts in more general terms.

13.2.1 Independent and dependent clauses

An ***independent clause*** is a group of words that contains a subject and a verb and sometimes the object of the verb: *The courts* [subject] *found* [verb] *significant harm* [object of the verb]. It can stand alone as a complete sentence. A ***dependent clause*** is a group of words that contains a subject, a verb, and sometimes the object of the verb, as well as a subordinating word at the front: *Although* [subordinating word] *the courts* [subject] *found* [verb] *significant harm* [object]. A dependent clause cannot stand on its own. The subordinating word makes the clause depend on another group of words to complete the thought it expresses—hence, it is a *dependent* clause. A dependent clause needs to be attached to an independent clause; together, they can stand as a complete sentence: *Although the court found substantial harm* [dependent clause], *it did not find unreasonable interference* [independent clause]. Independent and dependent clauses may contain many more words than in these simple examples, but the distinction between the two is the same.

13.2.2 Compound and complex sentences

A ***compound sentence*** contains two independent clauses, attached together by a coordinating word: *The court found substantial harm,* [first independent clause] *and* [coordinating word] *it also found unreasonable interference* [second independent clause]. A ***complex sentence*** contains an independent clause and a dependent clause, attached together by the subordinating word at the front of the dependent clause: *Although* [subordinating word] *the court found substantial harm* [dependent clause], *it did not find unreasonable interference* [independent clause]. The dependent clause can follow the independent clause as well as precede it: *The court did not find unreasonable interference* [independent clause], *although* [subordinating word] *it found substantial harm* [dependent clause]. Compound and complex sentences are complete sentences, which can stand on their own; they just contain more groups of words. Both compound and complex sentences may contain more than one clause of each type, as well as other groups of words, but the dependent clause or clauses always need to be attached to at least one independent clause to complete the thoughts they express—to be part of a complete sentence.

13.2.3 Phrases

Phrases are other groups of words that are not independent or dependent clauses. They do not contain a subject and a verb: *before 11:00 p.m.; including vehicular noise; the time of day; to run a motorcycle; loud but infrequent and brief.* Phrases cannot stand alone as complete sentences. They just provide supplemental information about the thoughts expressed in the independent or dependent clauses in the sentences of which they are part.

13.2.4 Nouns, verbs, and pronouns

Nouns are the words in a sentence that represent subjects, objects, or ideas: *court; harm; enjoyment.* ***Verbs*** are the words that convey action: *found.* Verbs require a subject, which performs the action: *The court* [subject] *found* [verb]. Verbs often require an object, too, which receives, is the product or the result of, or is affected by the action: *The court* [subject] *found* [verb] *substantial harm* [object]. Some verbs convey an action that is complete in itself; they do not require an object: *The trial ended.* ***Pronouns*** are words that refer to and substitute for nouns within a sentence, a clause, or a phrase: *Although the court* [noun] *found substantial harm, it* [pronoun, referring to court and taking its place as the subject in the independent clause] *did not find unreasonable interference.* ***Personal pronouns*** refer to and substitute for people: *she, her, hers; The judge* [noun] *issued her* [personal pronoun, referring to the judge] *order.* ***Relative pronouns*** refer to and substitute for people or entities, subjects, ideas, or other inanimate things: *who, which, that.* The pronoun, *who,* should only be used to refer to people; *which* should never be used to refer to people; *that* may be used to refer to people or things.

13.2.5 Active and passive voice

The ***active voice*** refers to a combination of words in which the grammatical subject of a clause is also the subject of the verb: It is performing the action the verb expresses: *The court* [grammatical subject and subject of the verb, performing the action] *found* [verb, conveying the action] *substantial harm* [object of the verb]. The ***passive voice*** refers to a combination of words in which the grammatical subject is not also the subject of the verb: a different word, or an unstated word, is performing the action the verb expresses: *The ruling* [grammatical subject, but not performing the action] *was announced* [verb, conveying the action] *by the judge* [subject of the verb, performing the action]. Sometimes, a combination of words in the passive voice omits the subject of the verb altogether: *The ruling was greeted with applause* [omitting subject of the verb, *the court audience*, performing the action expressed by the verb].

13.2.6 Adjectives, adverbs, and modifiers

An ***adjective*** is a word that modifies a noun by providing information about it: *substantial* [adjective] *harm* [noun]. An ***adverb*** is a word that modifies an adjective, a verb, or another adverb by providing more information about it: *highly* [adverb, modifying adjective] *prejudicial* [adjective]*; very* [adverb, modifying adverb] *highly* [adverb, modifying adjective] *prejudicial* [adjective]*; greatly* [adverb, modifying verb] *prejudices* [verb]. A ***modifier*** is a single adjective or adverb, a combination of adjectives or adverbs, or a larger group of words—including a dependent clause—that provides information about another word or group of words in a sentence: *Although it included a number of actual stores, shops, and other businesses* [dependent clause, modifying the subject that follows], *the urban locale* [the subject modified by the clause] *in* *Mackenzie* *was still generally residential.*

13.2.7 Natural emphasis

Words or groups of words that come at the beginning or the end of a sentence receive greater emphasis than the words or groups of words in the middle.

Similarly, sentences that come at the beginning or the end of a paragraph receive greater emphasis than the sentences in the middle.

13.3 Five essential strategies for writing clear sentences and paragraphs

13.3.1 Sentence load

Limit most of your sentences to just two ideas, a primary idea and a secondary idea or two primary ideas. Express a primary idea in an independent clause; express a secondary idea in a dependent clause or phrase. Use a complex sentence to convey a primary idea and a secondary idea; use a compound sentence to convey two primary ideas. You may include more than two ideas in a sentence, but do so sparingly.

13.3.2 Order of ideas

In general, place the most important idea at the start of a sentence. Establish a pattern of proposition and support—primary idea and secondary idea; independent clause and dependent clause or phrase. You may use a short phrase before the independent clause (as in the first sentence of this paragraph). Occasionally, if you wish to communicate a causal or sequential relationship between your ideas, you may place the most important idea, expressing the result or outcome, at the end of the sentence (as in this sentence). Do not use a back-loaded sentence structure too often, especially in successive sentences, because it will impede the efficient communication of your ideas.

13.3.3 Verbs

Use a precise verb to express the specific action contained in each idea you are trying to communicate. Avoid general verbs that displace the action to a noun ***(nominalization***: see §13.5.19) or an adjective (***adjectivization***: see §13.5.1), The most common general verbs are based on *have*, *be*, *make*, and *do*. Use the active voice most of the time, too—subject performing the action; verb expressing the action; and object of the verb, expressing the result or effect of the action. (See §13.2.5.)

13.3.4 Paragraph unity

Unify every paragraph, except introductory or concluding paragraphs, around a single point, expressed in the first sentence—or in the second sentence, if the first one contains a Rule Statement. (See §8.2.2.) Be sure that the rest of the paragraph addresses, explains, develops, illustrates, and applies only that single point. If necessary, change the opening point to make it consistent with the content of the rest of the paragraph. Do not change, expand, or modify the opening point or introduce a different point in the middle of the paragraph. If necessary, use additional paragraphs to cover the other points.

13.3.5 Subject focus

Maintain a consistent subject focus within each major paragraph. ***Subject focus*** refers to the grammatical subject in a series of successive sentences. Just as you should unify each major paragraph around a single idea, you should begin many, if not most, of the sentences within each paragraph with the same grammatical subject, such as a court, a person, a thing, an idea, or a pronoun referring to that subject. If you keep the opening subjects relatively constant, you will enable your reader to concentrate on the variables that follow the subject—the conclusions, the details, the nuances, and the support for your analyses or discussions. If you cannot maintain a consistent subject focus throughout a paragraph, try to begin and end the paragraph with the same grammatical subject and return to that subject as often as you can. (See §8.5.8 on subject focus in case descriptions, §9.5.6 on subject focus in case comparisons, and §13.4.1 on parallel structure; see also §9.12 on subject focus and other unifying techniques in Rule Explanation and Rule Application paragraphs.)

13.4 Three essential strategies for presenting related information clearly

13.4.1 Parallel structure

Use parallel grammatical or semantic structure to present the same kinds of information, such as successive Rule Statements within the same level of legal analysis, successive main points within a series of Rule Explanation paragraphs, or successive case descriptions within a single Rule Explanation paragraph. Parallel structure allows the writer to remind the reader of what remains constant in the particular analysis—the ideas conveyed through the repeated structure and words—and to direct the reader's attention to the important variables within that analysis or discussion. It is a very helpful tool for communicating the relationship of different items within a larger analytical structure.

Example 13.4.1.1 (parallel structure: Rule Statements).

The first key element of the test for private nuisance is whether the plaintiff suffers significant harm. . . .

The second key element of the test for private nuisance is whether the defendant's conduct unreasonably interferes with the plaintiff's use and enjoyment of the property. . . .

(Sample Legal Memorandum 5:2-3, 11:21-23) (emphasis added)

> **Comment.** The Discussion in the Sample Legal Memorandum contains two main sections, one for each major element of the rule on private nuisance. The overview to each section begins with the applicable Rule Statement. • The writer uses parallel structure in the Rule Statements to keep the primary subject constant—the elements of the test for private nuisance—and to draw the reader's attention to the variables—the substance of each element.

Example 13.4.1.2 (parallel structure: main points).

Courts find greater evidence of unreasonable interference the higher the volume of a noise and the more abrasive its sound. . . .

On the other hand, *courts find less evidence of unreasonable interference* as the frequency and duration of the noise decrease, and they tend to give frequency and duration greater weight than the sheer volume and abrasiveness of the noise. . . .

In addition, *courts find less evidence of unreasonable interference* the more the noise is confined to adults' waking hours and times when other, ordinary noise occurs. . . .

(Sample Legal Memorandum 16:5-6, 22-25, 17:15-17) (emphasis added)

> **Comment.** Section II.B of the Sample Legal Memorandum, on unreasonable interference based on the character of the noise, contains three Rule Explanation paragraphs. Each paragraph begins with a main point about the case law on the character of the noise. • The writer uses parallel structure in the main points to keep the primary subject constant—the evidence of unreasonable interference that the courts find, based on the character of the noise—and to draw the reader's attention to the variables—the substance of each type of evidence.

Example 13.4.1.3 (parallel structure: case descriptions).

For example, *in Mackenzie, the court found significant harm where* machinery *noise* from a lumber yard and interior trim factory *caused pervasive interference* with the neighbors' use and enjoyment of their property. . . . Similarly, *in Wilke, the court found significant harm where* rock-crushing *noise* from a concrete plant *caused pervasive interference* with the neighbors' "[ability] to function inside their homes." . . . Conversely, *in Childs, the court found no significant harm where* vehicle and pedestrian *noise* from a Super K-Mart store *caused only minimal interference* with a neighboring family's use of its property. . . .

(Sample Legal Memorandum 9:28-10:1, 10:4-6, 13-16) (emphasis added)

Comment. Section I.B of the Sample Legal Memorandum, on substantial harm based on inability to use and enjoy property, contains a single Rule Explanation paragraph. That paragraph contains three case descriptions, and the first sentence in each description states the relevant holding. • The writer uses parallel structure in those first sentences to keep the primary subject constant—the holdings about substantial harm based on inability to use and enjoy property—and to draw the reader's attention to the variables—the specific facts in each case that did or did not interfere with the plaintiffs' ability to use and enjoy their property.

13.4.2 Items in a list

If you present a list—of conclusions, the parts of a rule, important insights about how the courts apply a rule, examples supporting your insights, reasons supporting your conclusions, key provisions in a contract, etc.—cover the items in the list in the same order in which you list or introduce them. Your reader will expect you to do that and will be disoriented if you do not. Cover the items in the same order whether you use a formal list, with numbers, letters, or bullets for the items, or an informal list of items within a sentence. If there is a good reason to cover the items in a different order, state the reason clearly—and then cover the items in that different order. Cover the items within the same list in the same order within every part of the memorandum: the Brief Answer, the Overview to the Discussion, the sections and subsections within the Discussion, the paragraphs within a section or subsection, and even individual paragraphs within a section or subsection.

Example 13.4.2.1 (list introduced in overview to Discussion section).

A second factor the courts evaluate when deciding if noise creates an unreasonable interference is the character of the noise itself. Smith, 158 N.W.2d at 468 (citing Borsvold, 81 N.W.2d at 382). The courts balance several considerations: *the nature and volume of the noise, its frequency and duration*, and *the time of day when it occurs*. Id. Here, a court would likely find that the motorcycle noise from Mr. Hendricks's business, although *loud*, is produced only *intermittently*, *does not last long*, and *occurs when adult neighbors are awake and can hear other suburban noise*.

Courts find greater evidence of unreasonable interference *the higher the volume of a noise and the more abrasive its sound*. . . .

On the other hand, courts find less evidence of unreasonable interference *as the frequency and duration of the noise decrease*, and they tend to give frequency and duration greater weight than the sheer volume and abrasiveness of the noise. . . .

In addition, courts find less evidence of unreasonable interference *the more the noise is confined to adults' waking hours and times when other, ordinary noise occurs*. . . .

(Sample Legal Memorandum 15:27-16:6, 16:22-25, 17:15-17) (emphasis added)

> **Comment.** The second sentence in the overview paragraph to Section II.B of the Sample Legal Memorandum introduces a list of considerations the courts balance when determining whether the character of a noise contributes to unreasonable interference. The writer covers the items in the list in the same order three times. • First, the conclusion for Section II.B, in the third sentence of the overview paragraph, covers the supporting reasons in the same order as in the original list, in the second sentence. • Second, the three Rule Explanation paragraphs cover the several considerations in the same order as in the original list, too. • Third, the three corresponding Rule Application paragraphs (not included in this example) cover the conclusions and support for the considerations in the same order as in the original list. • By adhering to the order of items established in the original list, the writer fulfills the reader's expectations.

13.4.3 Transitions

Use a transitional word or phrase at or near the start of a new paragraph or sentence, to emphasize how the main idea in the new paragraph or sentence relates to the main idea in a previous one. For example, you can use a transitional word or phrase at, or near the start of, a new case law example within a Rule Explanation paragraph to emphasize how the example relates to the others in the paragraph. Similarly, you can use a transitional word or phrase at, near the start of, or within, a case comparison in a Rule Application paragraph, to emphasize how the parts of the comparison relate to each other. Of course, you can also use transitional words or phrases in memoranda that do not present a legal analysis, to emphasize how different parts and different ideas within your discussion relate to each other.

Example 13.4.3.1 (transitions between Rule Explanation paragraphs).

Courts find greater evidence of unreasonable interference the higher the volume of a noise and the more abrasive its sound. . . .

On the other hand, courts find less evidence of unreasonable interference as the frequency and duration of the noise decrease, and they tend to give frequency and duration greater weight than the sheer volume and abrasiveness of the noise. . . .

In addition, courts find less evidence of unreasonable interference the more the noise is confined to adults' waking hours and times when other, ordinary noise occurs. . . .

(Sample Legal Memorandum 16:5-6, 22-25, 17:15-17) (emphasis added)

> **Comment.** Section II.B of the Sample Legal Memorandum, on unreasonable interference based on the character of the noise, contains three Rule Explanation paragraphs, each with a different main point about the case law. The first main point identifies case law where the courts find greater evidence of unreasonable interference. The second and third main points identify case law where the courts find less evidence. • At the start of the second paragraph, the writer uses a transitional phrase that expresses contrast, *On the other hand*, to signal that the second main point conveys an insight unlike the insight the first main point conveyed. • At the start of the third paragraph, the writer uses a transitional phrase that expresses similarity, *In addition*, to signal that the third main point conveys an insight that is like the insight the second main point conveyed. • By using these transitions, the writer emphasizes the contrasting content of the second and third main points.

Example 13.4.3.2 (transitions within Rule Explanation paragraph).

The other factor courts consider in evaluating significant harm is whether the conduct interferes with the use and enjoyment of property. Adams, 602 N.W.2d at 222. Where noise is concerned, the courts find significant harm if the interference is pervasive, inside and outside the home. Id. at 722; see Restatement (Second) of Torts § 821F cmt. c ("[T]here must be a real and appreciable invasion of the plaintiff's interests before he can have an action.") *For example*, in Mackenzie, the court found significant harm where machinery noise from a lumberyard and interior trim factory caused pervasive interference with the neighbors' use and enjoyment of their property. 174 N.W. at 163. . . *Similarly*, in Wilke, the court found significant harm where rock-crushing noise from a concrete plant caused pervasive interference with the neighbors' "[ability] to function inside their homes." 2007 WL 1828788, at *4. . . . *Conversely*, in Childs, the court found no significant harm where vehicle and pedestrian noise from a Super K-Mart store caused only minimal interference with a neighboring family's use of its property. . . .

(Sample Legal Memorandum 10:22-11:16) (emphasis added)

> **Comment.** Section I.B of the Sample Legal Memorandum, on substantial harm based on inability to use and enjoy property, contains a single Rule Explanation paragraph. That paragraph begins with the Rule Statement, the main point about the case law, and a quotation from the Restatement—all before the three case descriptions illustrating the main point. • At the start of the first case description, the writer uses the transitional phrase, *For example*, to signal the start of the first case description after the relatively lengthy preliminary content. • At the start of the second case description, the writer uses a transitional word expressing similarity, *Similarly*, to signal that the holding resembles the holding in the first case. • At the start of the third case description, the writer uses a transitional word expressing contrast, *Conversely*, to signal that the holding differs from those in the first two cases. • By using these transitions, the writer emphasizes the contrasting content of the three case descriptions.

Example 13.4.3.3 (transition within case comparison in Rule Application paragraph).

In Childs, where the court found no significant harm, there was insufficient evidence that ordinary vehicular noise prevented the complaining family members from using and enjoying their property. 2001 WL 1199901, at *4. *Similarly*, there is insufficient evidence that the noise from Mr. Hendricks's business prevents Mr. Lambert from using and enjoying his property, too, especially because no other neighbors have complained that the noise prevents them from using their backyards.

(Sample Legal Memorandum 11:5-12) (emphasis added)

> **Comment.** Example 13.4.3.3 contains a two-sentence case comparison from the Rule Application paragraph that corresponds to the Rule Explanation paragraph in Example 13.4.3.2. • The first sentence identifies a case where the court found no significant harm, based on a lack of evidence that noise unreasonably interfered with the use and enjoyment of property. • At the start of the second sentence, the writer uses a transitional word expressing similarity, *Similarly*, to signal the same lack of evidence in the client's matter. • By using the transition, the writer emphasizes the analogy within the case comparison.

13.5 Thirty guidelines for correct grammar, precise word choice, and clear style

Attorneys can improve the clarity of their writing in scores of specific ways, too. Some of the following guidelines address common grammatical errors, although a comprehensive list of common grammatical errors is beyond the scope of this chapter. The other guidelines address semantic and stylistic problems; they are intended to make your writing easier to read and understand.

13.5.1 Adjectivization

An ***adjectivization*** is an action expressed as an adjective, not as the part of speech designed to convey action, a verb: *The noise was disturbing* [adjectivization] *to the nearby residents*, instead of *The noise disturbed* [verb] *the nearby residents.* Adjectivization also lengthens your writing because you must include one or more other words to complete the sentence—*was* and *to* in the prior example. (See §13.3.3.) Avoid adjectivization; use a precise verb, instead. (See also §13.5.19 **Nominalization**, §13.5.28 **Verbalization**.)

13.5.2 Agreement: subject-pronoun

Use singular pronouns to refer to singular nouns and plural pronouns to refer to plural nouns. Do not use a plural pronoun to refer to a singular noun. Change the singular noun to a plural, or revise the sentence in other ways. You could revise the following sentence in at least three different ways to address the subject-pronoun mismatch: *Courts find substantial harm where noise interferes with a <u>resident's</u>* [singular noun] *ability to sleep or function inside <u>their</u>* [plural pronoun] *own home*. First, you could substitute a phrase to make the pronoun unnecessary: *interferes with a resident's ability to sleep or function <u>at home</u>*. Second, you could make the subject plural, to agree with the pronoun: *interferes with the <u>residents'</u>* [plural noun] *ability to sleep or function inside <u>their</u>* [plural pronoun] *own homes* [conforming change to plural]. Third, you could repeat the noun and omit the pronoun: *interferes with a <u>resident's</u>* [singular noun] *ability to sleep or function inside the <u>resident's</u>* [singular noun] *own home*. Use singular pronouns for collective nouns, too, unless you are referring to the members of the entity as individuals. Collective nouns for which plural pronouns are commonly misused include *court, jury*, and businesses, law firms, and other organizations: *At the time, Mr. Gillespie worked for <u>Torin & Conover</u>* [singular collective noun], *in <u>their</u>* [plural pronoun] *litigation department*. (The singular pronoun, *its*, would be correct.)

13.5.3 Agreement: subject-verb

Use singular verbs with singular subjects and plural verbs with plural subjects. Gaps between subject and verb can result in agreement errors, where a noun closer to the verb leads the writer to choose a verb that agrees in number with that noun, instead of the prior noun that is the subject of the verb—as in the following sentence: *Mr. Lambert has complained that the noises* [plural subject] *created by Mr. Hendricks's motorcycle repair business* [singular noun at the end of gap between subject and verb] *ruins* [singular verb] *his ability to entertain in his backyard.* (The plural verb, *ruin*, would be correct.)

13.5.4 *As*

Do not use *as* when you mean *because. As* is potentially ambiguous because it could express a temporal relationship—its primary meaning—or a causal one. In the following sentence, a reader might be confused about which type of relationship to expect after the opening clause: *As the defendant was driving out of town around midnight, he could not have been at home during the burglary.* A reader might reasonably expect a temporal relationship: *As the defendant was driving out of town around midnight, he realized he left his briefcase at home.* The second half of the actual sentence, however, states a causal, not a temporal, relationship. If you want to express a causal relationship unambiguously, use *because.* You may need to rearrange the parts of your sentence, too: *The defendant could not have been at home during the burglary because he was driving out of town around midnight.* (See also §13.5.25 **Since**, §13.5.30 **While**.)

13.5.5 *As such*

Avoid this phrase. It is usually unnecessary and almost always misused, as a transition between two subjects that modifies one subject with information that applies to the other subject. *Thus, a court would likely find the noise from Mr. Hendricks's business is more analogous to the bursts of noise from the football spectators in Cunningham, 2001 WL 716882, at *3, loud but infrequent and brief, than it is to the loud and continuous noise from the lumberyard machinery in Mackenzie, 174 N.W. at 166, or from the stone-crushing machinery at the cement plant in Wilke, 2007 WL 1828788, at *4. As such, the court found that the noise would not unreasonably interfere with Mr. Lambert's household activities.* In the second sentence, *as such* modifies *the court,* but it really refers to information in the first sentence about noise, not about the court. The second sentence is using *as such* as a shorthand reference for that information, but, grammatically, it is incorrect. You could correct the sentence as follows: *As such, the noise would not unreasonably interfere with Mr. Lambert's household activities.* Now, *as such* correctly modifies *the noise*, based on information about the noise in the first sentence. Alternatively, you could substitute a different, and correct, transitional phrase at the start of the second sentence: *Accordingly, the court found . . .* , or you could just omit *as such* from the original sentence altogether. (See §13.5.18 **Misplaced modifiers**.)

13.5.6 Clients and other parties

In formal memoranda, refer to clients and other adult parties formally, unless you are instructed to do otherwise. State their full name when you introduce them. In subsequent references, use *Mr., Mrs., Ms., Dr.,* or similar titles with each person's last name. Your clients may see your work product and could be offended if you refer to them casually—especially if your clients are older than you are. In informal and e-mail memoranda, you may be able to omit the titles before people's last name or even use their first name, if your work product will not be distributed outside your law office. In all memoranda, you may refer to children by their first name only, after you introduce them using their full name.

13.5.7 Comma in a series

Always include a comma after the next-to-last item in a series of three or more items: *The surrounding neighborhood consists of small and medium-sized houses occupied by families, working-class people,* [comma after next-to-last item] *and local college students.* As a series becomes longer and more complex, it becomes easier for a reader to be uncertain where the next-to-last item ends and the last item begins, without a final comma to separate the two. In laws and legal documents, that kind of ambiguity can lead to disputes and litigation. If you get in the habit of including the final comma in all your series, you will never have to worry about potential ambiguity. For series with complex individual items, use semicolons to separate the items, use an indented, bulleted list, or use both. The following sentence contains a simple series (underlined) within a complex series, both punctuated correctly: *Where an alleged nuisance involves noise, the courts consider the residential make-up of the neighborhood; <u>the nature and volume, the frequency and duration,</u>* [comma after next-to-last item the simple series] *<u>and the time of day of the noise</u>;* [semicolon after next-to-last item in the complex series] *and the necessity and value of the conduct responsible for the noise.*

13.5.8 Comparisons with *like* or *as*

Use ***like*** to compare subjects: *Like the daughter's treatment in <u>MPI</u>, . . . Billy Lee's treatment . . . .* Use ***as*** to compare actions: *As in <u>MPI</u>, where the doctors [did A], in Billy Lee's case, the doctors [did B].* Do not use *like* to compare actions: *Just <u>like</u> the employment restrictions in <u>Whirlpool</u> prohibited* [action 1] *the defendant from doing business with new customers, <u>id.</u>, the employment restrictions here would prohibit* [action 2] *Ms. Parker from doing business with new customers.* Use *as*: *Just <u>as</u> the employment restrictions in Whirlpool prohibited . . . , the employment restrictions here would prohibit . . . .*

13.5.9 Contractions

Do not use contractions in formal and informal memoranda, unless you are quoting someone who used them. You may use them in very informal e-mail memoranda, but even then, do so sparingly.

13.5.10 *Court* and *courts*

If you are describing a series of decisions in a jurisdiction, do not introduce a generalization about the decisions with *the court.* Often, your analyses will be covering decisions from courts of different levels within the jurisdiction—the highest court, intermediate appellate courts, and even trial courts. It is inaccurate to refer to them collectively as *the court.* Refer to them as *the courts* or, for example, *Sixth Circuit courts* (to include the federal district courts as well as the appellate courts in the Sixth Circuit) or *Michigan courts.* Even if all of the decisions you are describing were decided by the same level of court, introduce that case law by referring to *the courts* or *the Sixth Circuit,* rather than *the court.* Save *the court* for your description of an individual decision.

13.5.11 Dates

Do not mix cardinal and ordinal numbers when you write or refer to a date containing the month, the day, and the year. Use cardinal numbers exclusively: *On October 27, 2016, I deposed Richard Riley at the office of his counsel*—not *On October 27th, 2016.* Use cardinal numbers, too, when you refer to the month and the day, especially in a series: *On October 27, I deposed Richard Riley at the office of his counsel, and on November 1, I defended Wanda Jackson in her deposition at our office.* In very informal e-mail memoranda, with their more personal tone of address, you may use an ordinal number to refer to a day by itself, as if you were speaking to the recipient: *Richard's deposition is coming up on the 27th.* Otherwise, use cardinal numbers.

13.5.12 First- and second-person

Writing in the first person uses the singular *I* or the plural *we* as the subject; writing in the second person uses the singular or plural *you* as the subject. Avoid both in formal memoranda. You may be able to use them in informal and e-mail memoranda, however. (See §11.8.)

13.5.13 *Impact*

Do not use *impact* as a verb: *The economic downturn <u>impacted</u> many people's incomes.* Use *affected* or, better still, another verb with more precise meaning about how the object of the verb is affected by the action the verb expresses: *The economic downturn* <u>*decreased*</u> *many people's incomes.* (See §13.5.28 **Verbalization**.)

13.5.14 *In fact*; *indeed*

Avoid both.

13.5.15 Inexact equation

Be sure you compare or contrast the same categories of things in your legal writing: decisions and decisions, courts and courts, people and people, actions and actions, apples and apples—not apples and oranges. In a case comparison, write, *Like* <u>*the court*</u> [apple 1] *in* <u>*Childs,*</u> *which found that noise emanating from the ordinary operation of a Super K-Mart store was not unreasonable absent any zoning restrictions, 2001 WL 1199901, at *4,* <u>*a court*</u> [apple 2] *here would probably find that noise produced by the ordinary operation of Mr. Hendricks's business is not unreasonable, either—and that there are no zoning restrictions on the use of North Ypsilanti residential properties for home businesses.* Do not write, *Like* <u>*Childs*</u> [orange; a decision, not a court], *which found that . . . ,* <u>*a court*</u> [apple] *here would probably find that . . . .* Inexact equations can result, as in this example, when the first subject is separated from the second subject by a lot of intervening text. They can also result without the intervening text: *Like* <u>*Childs*</u> [orange; a decision, not a court], *2001 WL 1199901, at *4,* <u>*a court*</u> [apple] *here would probably find that. . . .*

13.5.16 *Inter alia*

Avoid. If you must convey this idea, do it in English: *among other things*.

13.5.17 Jargon

Avoid jargon, including most Latin phrases and unnecessary abbreviations and acronyms for institutions and people, such as *SCOTUS* or *RBG*. Legal analysis has enough specialized terminology. Do not make your work product any harder to read than necessary by incorporating even more specialized, technical, or idiomatic language. Use plain English wherever possible. (See §11.8.)

13.5.18 Misplaced modifiers

Be sure that a word, phrase, or clause that modifies an adjacent noun or subject is intended to modify it and not a different noun or subject later in the sentence. *Cruising up and down the river with its whistle blasting, the court found that the steamboat created an unreasonable interference.* The phrase that begins the sentence, *Cruising up and down the river with its whistle blasting,* is intended to modify *steamboat,* but, grammatically, it modifies the nearest noun, *court.* Place the modifier adjacent or closer to the word it is intended to modify, or rewrite the sentence in other ways to avoid the inadvertent mischaracterization: (i) *Cruising up and down the river with its whistle blasting, the steamboat created an unreasonable interference* or (ii) *The court found that the steamboat created an unreasonable interference as it cruised up and down the river with its whistle blasting.*

13.5.19 Nominalization

A ***nominalization*** is an action expressed as a noun, not as the part of speech designed to convey action, a verb: *The noise caused a disturbance* [nominalization] *to the nearby residents,* instead of *The noise disturbed* [verb] *the nearby residents.* Nominalization also lengthens your writing because you must include one or more other words to complete the sentence—*caused a* and *to* in the prior example. (See §13.3.3.) Occasionally, you may use a nominalization to help you emphasize another idea or to state a legal phrase verbatim: *The noise was an unreasonable interference* [nominalization; part of a legal phrase] *with the residents' use and enjoyment* [nominalizations; part of another legal phrase] *of their property.* Otherwise, avoid nominalization. Use a precise verb, instead. (See also §13.5.1 **Adjectivization**, §13.5.28 **Verbalization**.)

13.5.20 Numbers

In general, spell whole numbers up to ninety-nine; use numerals for whole numbers starting at 100 and above. Spell combinations of whole numbers and fractions below 100 if you can do so concisely (*two-and-a-half*); use numerals if you cannot (*88-1/4*). Use numerals for combinations of whole numbers and fractions starting at 100 and above. Use numerals in a list or a series of sentences that contains numbers both below 100 and 100 or above. Spell stand-alone fractions, without a preceding whole number, if you can do so concisely (*one-quarter*). Spell ordinal numbers, if you can do so concisely (*fourth visit,* not *4th visit*). For other rules and exceptions involving numbers, consult the current edition of *The Bluebook.*

13.5.21 Parenthetical insertions

Try to avoid parenthetical insertions, especially long ones, to convey additional information within textual sentences: *The engines are loud (we do not know exactly how loud or for how long Mr. Hendricks runs them), so Mr. Hendricks tries to limit the number of startups each day.* Revise the sentence, instead, or add another one: *The engines are loud, so Mr. Hendricks tries to limit the number of startups each day. We do not know exactly how loud the engines are, however, or for how long Mr. Hendricks runs them.* At most, use parenthetical insertions within a sentence for short clarifications.

13.5.22 Past and present tense

Use the ***past tense*** to describe the facts and the courts' actions and reasoning in your case descriptions and case comparisons. Use the ***present tense*** to identify the content of a rule, by itself, in a Rule Statement, or in the context of a case description: *The court <u>held</u>* [past tense] *that an "equivalent employment position" <u>means</u>* [present tense] *a position with equivalent compensation, benefits, working shift, hours of employment, job status, responsibility, and authority.* Use the present tense to state your main points about the case law, too: *The courts <u>tend</u> to find significant harm only if the conduct in question <u>causes</u> actual physical discomfort to multiple people.*

13.5.23 *Per*

Avoid, except in common expressions, such as *miles per hour.* In particular, avoid *per your request* and similar constructions. Write *as you requested.*

13.5.24 Quoting ordinary phrases

Once you quote an ordinary phrase that is part of a legal rule, you do not need to keep quoting it. Examples include *substantial harm, unreasonable interference, procedural unconscionability, substantive unconscionability, equivalent employment position,* and many other, similar terms and phases.

13.5.25 *Since*

Do not use *since* when you mean *because*. *Since* is potentially ambiguous because it could express a temporal relationship—its primary meaning—or a causal one. In the following sentence, a reader might be confused about which type of relationship to expect after the opening clause: *Since he accepted our firm's offer of employment, Mr. Gillespie had to decline an offer to work for the State Attorney General.* A reader might reasonably expect a temporal relationship: *Since he accepted our firm's offer of employment, Mr. Gillespie has been effectively screened from the litigation against Clark Monroe.* The second half of the actual sentence, however, states a causal, not a temporal, relationship. If you want to express a causal relationship unambiguously, use *because.* You may need to rearrange the parts of your sentence, too: *Mr. Gillespie had to decline an offer to work for the State Attorney General <u>because</u> he accepted our offer of employment.* (See also §13.5.4 ***As***, §13.5.30 ***While***.)

13.5.26 Slash constructions

Avoid slash constructions, such as *24/7* or *family/medical leave.* Choose one term or the other; use a third, more encompassing term or phrase; use an alternative term or phrase that conveys the same meaning (*twenty-four hours a day*); or state the terms without the slash (*family and medical leave*).

13.5.27 *This* and *that*

Do not use *this* or *that* alone to refer back to a prior subject, statement, or idea. It may not be obvious to your reader which prior subject, statement, or idea you mean, as in the following example. *The firm's failure to implement a timely screen created the risk that confidential information about the attorney's old client could have been disclosed to his new firm—a risk "that the provisions of M.R.P.C. 1.10(b) were intended to eliminate." Id. at 1050 n.9. This led the court to find . . . .* A reader might be confused about the subject or subjects in the first sentence to which *This*, at the start of the second sentence, refers. Add a succinct word or phrase after *this* or *that* to clarify your intended meaning: *This combination of delay and risk led the court to find . . . .*

13.5.28 Verbalization

Verbalization is the opposite of nominalization, in which an action is expressed as a noun, not as the part of speech designed to convey action, a verb. In verbalization, nouns are forced to convey actions for which they are not well suited—for example, *impact*—often in an attempt to write or speak informally. (See §13.5.13.) Verbalizations, like other types of informal expressions and slang, do enter the language, and eventually some of them may be considered acceptable for formal writing and speech. Resist the temptation to use verbalizations in your own legal writing, even in informal and e-mail memoranda. You never know whether a senior colleague, a client, or another reader might dislike or be distracted by them. (See also §13.5.1 **Adjectivization**, §13.5.19 **Nominalization**.)

13.5.29 *Via*

Avoid. Use *through, by,* or another, more precise word.

13.5.30 *While*

Do not use *while* when you mean *although* or *whereas. While* is potentially ambiguous because it could express a temporal relationship—its primary meaning—or a contrasting one. In the following sentence, a reader might be confused about which type of relationship to expect after the opening clause:

While Ms. Parker met with the board of directors, she refused to meet with the shareholders. A reader might reasonably expect a temporal relationship: *While Ms. Parker met with the board of directors, she outlined her plan for the acquisition*. The second half of the actual sentence, however, states a contrasting, not a temporal, relationship. If you want to express a contrasting relationship, unambiguously, use *although* or *whereas*: *Although Ms. Parker met with the board of directors, she refused to meet with the shareholders.* (See also §13.5.4 ***As***, §13.5.25 ***Since***.)

Sample Memoranda

Sample Legal Memorandum
Sample Informal Memorandum
Sample E-mail Memorandum

MEMORANDUM

TO: Partner
FROM: Associate
DATE: November 29, 2010
RE: Jon Hendricks: Private Nuisance Lawsuit

QUESTION PRESENTED

Does a home motorcycle repair business create a private nuisance under Michigan law where it operates on evenings and weekends and the intermittent noise it produces aggravates one neighbor's migraines, wakes the neighbor's young children, and interferes with the neighbor's backyard entertaining?

BRIEF ANSWER

No. A Michigan court would probably conclude that the home motorcycle repair business does not create a private nuisance. Under Michigan law, private nuisance requires proof of significant harm resulting from unreasonable interference with the use or enjoyment of property. The neighbor would not be able to establish either requirement. A court would likely find no significant harm because the noise would not cause physical discomfort to persons of ordinary sensibilities and it causes only minimal disruption to the neighbor's use of his backyard. A court would also likely find that any interference is not unreasonable. Although the neighborhood is residential, the noise is sporadic and ends by 11:00 p.m., the noise is a necessary part of the repair business, and the business contributes to the social and economic well-being of the neighborhood.

STATEMENT OF FACTS

Jon Hendricks has asked our firm to defend him in a lawsuit filed in Washtenaw County Circuit Court. Mr. Hendricks's next-door neighbor, Dave Lambert, is suing him for private nuisance in connection with a motorcycle repair business that Mr. Hendricks operates at his home.

Mr. Hendricks lives in North Ypsilanti. The surrounding neighborhood consists of small and medium-sized houses occupied by families, working-class people, and local college students. The closest stores are a half-mile away, on Cross Street and Michigan Avenue. As a result of the bad economy, many people in the neighborhood have lost their jobs; some have lost their homes, too. To make ends meet, a number of residents have started home businesses, the natures of which we do not currently know.

Mr. Hendricks works as a music teacher in the Ypsilanti public schools. His wife is a waitress and earns a salary and tips. At the start of the 2009-10 academic year, the school system reduced hours for teachers in the music program. Mr. Hendricks had to take a pay cut and lost his benefits. He began to have trouble paying his bills.

To supplement his income, Mr. Hendricks began to repair motorcycles in late 2009. He operates his business, Popity Pop Motorcycle Repair, out of his garage and driveway. There are no zoning restrictions or local ordinances limiting the use of his property for this business. He works weekday evenings after school and on weekends. He stops working each day by 10:00 or 11:00 p.m. The business has acquired a good reputation, and Mr. Hendricks now has five or six customers from the neighborhood and some other customers from surrounding areas.

To diagnose and repair motorcycles with engine problems, Mr. Hendricks needs to start, run, and stop them. The engines are loud, so Mr. Hendricks tries to limit the number of startups each day. We do not know exactly how loud the engines are, however, or for how long Mr. Hendricks runs them. Other kinds of repairs do not require Mr. Hendricks to run the engines.

Mr. Lambert, the next-door neighbor, complained about the noise from the repair business right away. He has migraines, and the noise aggravates them. He has two young children, who go to bed early; the noise wakes them up, and they have trouble going back to sleep. In addition, he likes to entertain in his backyard on weekends when the weather is warm, but the motorcycle noise spoils his parties. He asked Mr. Hendricks to curtail the noise several times, and Mr. Hendricks has tried to minimize it while still conducting his business. No one else in the neighborhood has complained about the noise.

In his lawsuit, Mr. Lambert is seeking an injunction and damages.

DISCUSSION

A Michigan court would probably conclude that Mr. Hendricks's home motorcycle repair business does not create a private nuisance.

"A private nuisance is a nontrespassory invasion of another's interest in the private use and enjoyment of land." Restatement (Second) of Torts § 821D (1979). Following the Restatement's analysis, most Michigan courts find one person liable to another for private nuisance if

> (a) the other has property rights and privileges in respect to the use or enjoyment interfered with,
> (b) the invasion results in significant harm,
> (c) the actor's conduct is the legal cause of the invasion, and
> (d) the invasion is either (i) intentional and unreasonable, or (ii) unintentional and otherwise actionable under the rules governing liability for negligent, reckless, or ultrahazardous conduct.

Adkins v. Thomas Solvent Co., 487 N.W.2d 715, 720 (Mich. 1992) (citing Restatement (Second) of Torts §§ 821D-F); Capitol Props. Grp. v. 1247 Ctr. St., LLC, 770 N.W.2d 105, 112 (Mich. Ct. App. 2009). Although all four elements are required, see Capitol Props. Grp., 770 N.W.2d at 112, the courts tend to concentrate on just two, significant harm and unreasonable interference, because the other elements, property rights and causation, are usually not in dispute. See, e.g., id.; Adams v. Cleveland-Cliffs Iron Co., 602 N.W.2d 215, 222 (Mich. Ct. App. 1999).

Where an alleged nuisance involves noise, the courts evaluate significant harm by considering two factors: whether the noise causes the plaintiff "actual physical discomfort" and whether it prevents the plaintiff from using and enjoying the property. Smith v. W. Wayne Cty. Conservation Ass'n, 158 N.W.2d 463, 468, 470 (Mich. 1968) (per curiam) (citing Borsvold v. United Dairies, 81 N.W.2d 378, 382 (Mich. 1957) (en banc)); Adams, 602 N.W.2d at 222. The courts evaluate unreasonable interference by considering a number of factors, including the character of the neighborhood in which the noise occurs, the character of the noise itself, and the necessity and value of the conduct that produces the noise. Smith, 158 N.W.2d at 468.

A Michigan court would probably conclude that Mr. Hendricks's motorcycle repair business does not satisfy either key element for a private nuisance claim. A court would probably find no significant harm because Mr. Lambert's aggravated migraines and his children's interrupted sleep would not cause actual physical discomfort to ordinary persons. In addition, a court would probably find that interference with Mr. Lambert's backyard entertaining represents just a minimal harm.

Similarly, a Michigan court would probably find no unreasonable interference because the motorcycle noise is sporadic, brief, and confined during the week to evening hours when most adults are awake. A court would find that Mr. Hendricks's neighborhood is residential and subject to stricter limits on noise; however, a court would also find that the production of noise is unavoidable for a motorcycle repair business and that the value this successful business confers on its customers and the community at large outweighs the harms of which Mr. Lambert complains.

There is no dispute as to the other two elements of the private nuisance rule, property rights and causation. This memorandum will not address them.

I. Significant Harm

The first key element of the test for private nuisance is whether the plaintiff suffers significant harm. Adkins, 487 N.W.2d at 720. For this element, the courts use an objective standard to evaluate whether a plaintiff experiences actual physical discomfort or is unable to use and enjoy the property. Smith, 158 N.W.2d at 468, 470; see also Restatement (Second) of Torts § 821F cmt. d ("If normal persons in th[e] locality would not be substantially annoyed or disturbed by the situation," the harm is not significant, "even though the idiosyncrasies of the particular plaintiff may make it unendurable to him.") Here, a court would likely conclude that the noise from Mr. Hendricks's motorcycle repair business does not cause significant harm. "Normal persons" in the neighborhood would not experience migraines or loss of sleep as a result of the noise or be "substantially disturbed" by the noise while entertaining in the backyard.

A. Actual Physical Discomfort

A court would likely find that Mr. Lambert's aggravated migraines and his children's problems sleeping are too unique to them to satisfy an objective standard of harm.

One factor courts consider in evaluating significant harm is whether the conduct causes actual physical discomfort. Smith, 158 N.W.2d at 468 (citing Borsvold, 81 N.W.2d at 378). The courts do not find significant harm, however, if the conduct would not cause actual physical discomfort to an ordinary person. Id. at 470. In Smith, the Michigan Supreme Court found no significant harm where noise from a gun shooting range would not cause actual physical discomfort to an ordinary person. Id. at 471. After neighboring residents submitted conflicting testimony about the effect of the noise, the trial judge attended a special shooting demonstration to experience the noise directly, from the homes of various plaintiffs. Id. at 468, 470-71. The judge noted that the harms alleged had to be objectively reasonable. Id. at 469-70.

> Whether the noise is sufficient to constitute a nuisance depends upon its effect upon an ordinary reasonable man, that is, a normal person of ordinary habits and sensibilities. Relief cannot be based solely upon the subjective likes and dislikes of a particular plaintiff. To be workable, relief must be based upon an objective standard of reasonableness.

Id. at 470. Having personally experienced the noise, the judge concluded that it was not such "as would shock a person of ordinary sensibilities or cause actual physical discomfort." Id. at 470-71. The Supreme Court agreed, adopting the trial judge's opinion in full. Id. at 465, 472-73. Similarly, in Rose v. Braciszewski, No. 285316, 2009 WL 3276431, at *4 (Mich. Ct. App. Oct. 13, 2009) (per curiam), the court found no significant harm where smoke from burning yard waste on a neighboring property and exhaust fumes from the neighbor's automobiles would not cause actual physical discomfort to an ordinary person. The neighbor burned leaves only a few times a year and ran his old cars in a barn on the property for a couple of hours each on two or three days. Id. The complaining homeowner may have been "particularly susceptible to the smoke and fumes," but the court concluded that her discomfort was not sufficient to satisfy the objective standard for harm, i.e., that a person of ordinary sensibilities would have suffered adverse health effects, too. Id.; see also Restatement (Second) of Torts § 821F cmt. d ("idiosyncrasies of the particular plaintiff" not enough to establish significant harm).

The courts tend to find significant harm only if the conduct in question causes actual physical discomfort to multiple people. In O'Connor v. Jersey Creamery Co. of Detroit, 248 N.W. 557, 558 (Mich. 1933), the court found significant harm where smoke, odors, and noise from a creamery plant adversely affected the health of twenty-two neighbors. In Mackenzie v. Frank M. Pauli Co., 174 N.W. 161, 161, 163-64 (Mich. 1919), the court found significant harm where machinery noise from a lumberyard and interior trim factory adversely affected the health of twelve neighbors. In Smith, however, the court found no significant harm, in part because there was conflicting testimony from the plaintiff residents and other neighbors as to whether noise from the gun shooting range caused them actual physical discomfort. 158 N.W.2d at 469. Similarly, in Radziewicz v. Frankenmuth Paddlewheel Tours, No. 282648, 2009 WL 2974733, at *1, *3 (Mich. Ct. App. Sept. 17, 2009) (per curiam), the court found no significant harm to the single complaining property owner, who experienced only "minor annoyance"—not actual physical discomfort—from a paddlewheel boat's whistle soundings.

The courts are especially likely to find significant harm if noise causes actual physical discomfort to multiple adults by depriving them of sleep. See Smith, 158 N.W.2d at 468-69 (summarizing case law). For example, in O'Connor, the court found significant harm where noise from the creamery's operations kept neighboring residents awake during the night hours, when they had "a right to repose in sleep without being disturbed." 248 N.W. at 557 (enjoining operations after 11:00 p.m.). Similarly, in Wilke v. Adkins, No. 268685, 2007 WL 1828788, at *3-4 (Mich. Ct. App. June 26, 2007) (per curiam), the court found significant harm where rock-crushing noise from a concrete plant kept neighboring residents awake at night, sometimes to 1:00 a.m. When assessing significant harm, however, the courts do not consider the effect of noise upon children, even when the conduct occurred in or near a residential neighborhood, where at least some families with children probably lived. See, e.g., O'Connor, 248 N.W. at 557-59 (finding significant harm without mentioning children); Mackenzie, 174 N.W. at 162-64 (same); Wilke, 2007 WL 1828788, at *3-4 (same); Childs v. K-Mart Corp., No. 220870, 2001 WL 1199901, at *3-4 (Mich. Ct. App. Oct. 9, 2001) (per curiam) (finding no significant harm to adult neighbors from superstore's vehicle and pedestrian noise, without mentioning children). The courts only analyze the effect of noise upon adults; when applying the objective standard for significant harm, they appear to equate "a person of ordinary habits and sensibilities" with "an ordinary reasonable man." See Smith, 158 N.W.2d at 470 (emphasis added).

Here, a court would probably find that any harm to Mr. Lambert is not significant because the noise from Mr. Hendricks's motorcycle repair business would not cause actual physical discomfort to an ordinary person. An ordinary person does not have an underlying propensity to experience migraine headaches. Just as the court in Rose found no significant harm in the complaining neighbor's respiratory discomfort, where she was extra-sensitive to smoke and fumes, 2009 WL 3276431, at *4, a court would probably find no significant harm in Mr. Lambert's migraines, where he happens to be extra-sensitive to noise. In both cases, the conduct complained of falls short of the objective standard for significant harm, which requires "actual physical discomfort to persons of ordinary sensibilities." Id. A court would probably conclude that Mr. Lambert's migraines, although unfortunate, are unique to him.

A court would also likely find no significant harm because Mr. Lambert is the only person to complain about the noise. Other neighbors within hearing distance of the motorcycle repair business are exposed to the same noise, at the same times, but they have not sued Mr. Hendricks. Courts are skeptical that significant harm exists where just a single plaintiff complains. The court in O'Connor found significant harm where twenty-two neighbors complained, 248 N.W. at 558, and the court in Mackenzie found significant harm where twelve neighbors complained, 174 N.W. at 161. The courts in Rose and Radziewicz, however, found no significant harm where a single property owner complained. Rose, 2009 WL 3276431, at *4; Radziewicz, 2009 WL 2974733, at *2. Here, in the absence of multiple plaintiffs, a court would probably find that the motorcycle noise, however bothersome to Mr. Lambert, does not constitute significant harm for purposes of a private nuisance lawsuit.

Finally, a court would likely find no significant harm because the noise would not deprive most adults in the neighborhood of sleep. Mr. Hendricks stops working at 10:00 or 11:00 p.m., before most adults go to bed. Even the court in O'Connor, which emphasized the neighbors' right to sleep undisturbed in their homes at night, only enjoined the operation of the nearby creamery after 11:00 p.m. 248 N.W. at 557. Although we do not know the exact bedtime of Mr. Lambert's children, it is before 11:00 p.m. Thus, a court, following O'Connor, would probably conclude that the motorcycle noise would not deprive Mr. Lambert's adult neighbors of sleep before 11:00 p.m. Mr. Lambert's children may go to bed earlier than the adults, but their interrupted sleep would not satisfy the objective standard courts apply for significant harm, which only considers how the alleged conduct affects an ordinary reasonable "man." See Smith, 158 N.W.2d at 470.

Accordingly, a court would probably find no significant harm because the noise from Mr. Hendricks's motorcycle repair business does not cause Mr. Lambert and his family actual physical discomfort, objectively considered.

B. Inability to Use and Enjoy Property

A court would likely find that the disruptions to Mr. Lambert's backyard entertaining on warm weekends represent only minimal harm.

The other factor courts consider in evaluating significant harm is whether the conduct interferes with the use and enjoyment of property. Adams, 602 N.W.2d at 222. Where noise is concerned, the courts find significant harm if the interference is pervasive, inside and outside the home. See Restatement (Second) of Torts § 821F cmt. c ("[T]here must be a real and appreciable invasion of the plaintiff's interests before he can have an action.") For example, in Mackenzie, the court found significant harm where machinery noise from a lumberyard and interior trim factory caused pervasive interference with the neighbors' use and enjoyment of their property. 174 N.W. at 163. The noise lasted all day, it went through the neighbors' homes, whether the windows were closed or not, and people could not escape from it. Id. One neighbor even had to leave his home. Id. Similarly, in Wilke, the court found significant harm where rock-crushing noise from a concrete plant caused pervasive interference with the neighbors' "[ability] to function inside their homes." 2007 WL 1828788, at *4. The noise began early in the morning, ended late at night, and continued unabated on the weekends. Id. at *3-4. Several neighbors were unable to sit in their backyards, use portions of their houses, or hear the television or radio inside their homes. Id.; cf. Smith, 158 N.W.2d at 468-69 (finding no harm where evidence showed noise from gun shooting range prevented only some homeowners but not others from concentrating, engaging in conversation, watching television, or remaining at home). Conversely, in Childs, the court found no significant harm where vehicle and pedestrian noise from a Super K-Mart store caused only minimal interference with a neighboring family's use of its property. 2001 WL 1199901, at *4. The family members complained that the honking horns, squealing brakes, loud radios, and noise from freight delivery vehicles caused them significant harm. Id. at *3. The court disagreed: "By describing their alleged injuries merely as 'problems' and 'diminution' of the use [and] enjoyment . . . of their property, plaintiffs failed to set their claims apart from minimal damages insufficient to support a claim of nuisance." Id. at *4; see also id. (rejecting as minimal harm plaintiffs' claims that excessive light made it difficult to sleep, read, work, or concentrate inside their home and that exhaust fumes made it difficult to plant flowers and socialize outside).

A court would likely find that Mr. Lambert experiences only minimal harm, not pervasive interference, from the disruption to his seasonal backyard entertaining. In both Mackenzie and Wilke, where the courts found significant harm, noise from the defendants' businesses prevented the plaintiffs from using and enjoying both the outside and the inside of their homes, much if not all of the time—five days a week in Mackenzie, 174 N.W. at 163, and seven days a week in Wilke, 2007 WL 1828788, at *4. Here, the noise from Mr. Hendricks's business only affects Mr. Lambert's backyard entertaining, only on weekends, and only during warm weather—which, in southeastern Michigan, is limited to half the year or less. In Childs, where the court found no significant harm, there was insufficient evidence that ordinary vehicular noise prevented the complaining family members from using and enjoying their property. 2001 WL 1199901, at *4. Similarly, there is insufficient evidence that the noise from Mr. Hendricks's business prevents Mr. Lambert from using and enjoying his property, too, especially because no other neighbors have complained that the noise prevents them from using their backyards. See Radziewicz, 2009 WL 2974733, at *3 (finding no significant harm where single property owner complained). Altogether, a court is likely to find that the interference with Mr. Lambert's backyard entertaining represents, at most, a diminution in the enjoyment of his property, not anything more significant.

For all of these reasons, a court would probably conclude that the noise from Mr. Hendricks's motorcycle repair business does not cause significant harm.

II. Unreasonable Interference

The second key element of the test for private nuisance is whether the defendant's conduct unreasonably interferes with the plaintiff's use and enjoyment of the property. Adkins, 487 N.W.2d at 720. Where an alleged nuisance involves noise, the courts consider the residential make-up of the neighborhood; the nature and volume, the frequency and duration, and the time of day of the noise; and the necessity and value of the conduct responsible for the noise. See, e.g., Smith, 158 N.W.2d at 468 (citing Borsvold, 81 N.W.2d at 382); Waier v. Peerless Oil Co., 251 N.W. 552, 553 (Mich. 1933); Adams, 602 N.W.2d at 219. Here, a court would likely conclude, on balance, that the noise from Mr. Hendricks's motorcycle repair business does not represent an unreasonable interference. The neighborhood may be primarily residential and the noise loud, but the noise comes in short spurts, intermittently, and at times of the day when most adults are awake and other ambient noise, including vehicular noise, fills the air. In addition, a business cannot repair motorcycles without running them occasionally, and Mr. Hendricks's business contributes to the social and economic well-being of his neighborhood.

A. Character of the Neighborhood

One factor courts evaluate when deciding if noise creates an unreasonable interference is the character of the neighborhood in which the noise occurs. Smith, 158 N.W.2d at 468 (citing Borsvold, 81 N.W.2d at 382). Here, a court would likely find that Mr. Hendricks's neighborhood is residential and that Mr. Hendricks is therefore subject to stricter standards regarding the production of noise. Nevertheless, a court would probably conclude that the noise from Mr. Hendricks's business does not create an unreasonable interference within the neighborhood because the noise itself is not unreasonable.

The courts are likely to find that a neighborhood is residential even if some businesses are interspersed among the dwellings. Mackenzie, 174 N.W. at 162-63. The court in Mackenzie found that a large urban district was generally residential, although various small shops, stores, and other businesses were scattered throughout it and, in some portions of the district, the property owners used their lots for a combination of residential and business purposes. Id. In contrast, the court in Moore v. Johnson, 222 N.W. 120, 121-22 (Mich. 1928), found that a neighborhood was "at least a semibusiness district" because of its proximity to the central business district of the town, its location near several main streets and railroad tracks, and the business character of nearby properties. Id. The court in Capital Properties Group agreed that a neighborhood zoned and primarily used for business purposes was not residential at all, even if it included a building with apartment units next door to a nightclub. 770 N.W.2d at 112-13.

The more residential the neighborhood, the more strictly will the courts evaluate the noise that may be permissible in it. See Smith, 158 N.W.2d at 468; Restatement (Second) of Torts § 821F cmt. e. ("The location, character and habits of the particular community are to be taken into account in determining what is offensive or annoying to a normal individual living in it.") In O'Connor, where the neighborhood was highly residential, the court found that nighttime noise from a creamery was impermissible because it disturbed the residents' peace and comfort in their homes. 248 N.W. at 558-59. Although the neighborhood was not restricted against business use, it was densely populated; the creamery was the only business in the immediate vicinity; its property directly abutted the property of one of the residents; and multiple residents were subjected throughout the night to noise from the truck drivers' shouting and from the starting, stopping, loading, and unloading of the trucks. Id. at 557-58. The court concluded that the owner's right to conduct the business could not "justify the invasion of a residential district" and resulting disturbance to the inhabitants. Id. at 558-59. Conversely, in Moore, where the complaining homeowner lived in a "semibusiness" district, the court found that both daytime and nighttime noise from an adjacent automobile garage was permissible. 22 N.W. at 121-22. "[T]he plaintiff cannot claim for her property the same protection from the encroachment of business activities that she might claim were it . . . in a strictly residential district." Id. at 122. Moreover, in Capital Properties Group, where the neighborhood was zoned for business, the court found that late-night noise from a nightclub was not unreasonable. 770 N.W.2d at 112-13. The noise was only to be expected, and the landlord was aware of it when he built the apartments next door. Id. at 112. Similarly, in Waier, where the district was industrial, the court found that homeowners must tolerate noise from an oil refinery across the road that would be intolerable in a residential neighborhood. 251 N.W. at 553.

Ultimately, however, the courts find that noise in a residential neighborhood creates an unreasonable interference only if the noise itself, i.e., the second factor the courts assess, is unreasonable. In O'Connor, the court found that families living in a highly residential neighborhood successfully established that noise from a local creamery was unacceptable, where the drivers and delivery trucks created loud noise throughout the night. 248 N.W. at 557-59. But in Childs, the court found that a family living in a primarily residential neighborhood failed to establish unreasonable interference by a Super K-Mart store across the street, where the noise from vehicles and pedestrians in the parking lot was just "ordinary." 2001 WL 1199901, at *4. Likewise, in Cunningham v. City of Grosse Pointe Woods, No. 212642, 2001 WL 716882, at *4 (Mich. Ct. App. Mar. 13, 2001) (per curiam), the court found that families living in a residential neighborhood failed to establish unreasonable interference from the noise at the local high school's evening football games, where the loudest noises were infrequent.

Here, a court would likely find that North Ypsilanti, where Mr. Hendricks and Mr. Lambert live, is a residential neighborhood. It consists of homes inhabited by families, working people, and college students. The nearest stores are located on two main streets, a half-mile away, unlike the commercial district within two or three blocks of the plaintiffs' homes in Moore, which helped give the neighborhood a "semibusiness" character, 222 N.W. at 121-22. Even the recent proliferation of home businesses has not altered North Ypsilanti's residential character. The presence of scattered stores, shops, and other businesses, including some home businesses, did not alter the generally residential character of the urban locale in Mackenzie. 174 N.W. at 162-63. We do not know the exact nature of the other home businesses in North Ypsilanti, but their presence would not likely change a court's view that the neighborhood is generally residential, too.

Accordingly, a court would probably apply a stricter standard for evaluating permissible noise where Mr. Hendricks and Mr. Lambert live. Even more than the neighborhood in O'Connor, in which the private residents greatly outnumbered the single business establishment, 248 N.W. at 557-58, the North Ypsilanti neighborhood has no commercial businesses at all within its borders, only the small, home businesses that have expanded in number since the recent recession began. A court, therefore, would be ready to protect the inhabitants from any "invasion" and unreasonable disturbance from Mr. Hendricks's home business. See id. at 558-59.

Nevertheless, a court would probably find that Mr. Hendricks's business does not create an unreasonable interference within the residential, North Ypsilanti neighborhood because a court would probably find that the noise from the business is not unreasonable. In O'Connor, the court found that noise from a creamery was unacceptable both because it occurred in a highly residential neighborhood and because it was loud and lasted through the night. 248 N.W. at 557-59. In Childs, however, the court found that noise from a Super K-Mart store was not unreasonable, even though it occurred in a residential neighborhood, because the noise was "ordinary." 2001 WL 1199901, at *4. Likewise, in Cunningham, the court found that noise from high school football games was not unreasonable, even though it occurred in a residential neighborhood, because the noise was infrequent. 2001 WL 716882, at *4. Here, a court would probably conclude that noise from Mr. Hendricks's motorcycle business does not unreasonably interfere with the Lambert household because—as the next subsection illustrates—the character of the noise is not, on balance, unreasonable.

B. Character of the Noise

A second factor courts evaluate when deciding if noise creates an unreasonable interference is the character of the noise itself. Smith, 158 N.W.2d at 468 (citing Borsvold, 81 N.W.2d at 382). The courts balance several considerations: the nature and volume of the noise, its frequency and duration, and the time of day when it occurs. Id. Here, a court would likely find that the motorcycle noise from Mr. Hendricks's business, although loud, is produced only intermittently, does not last long, and occurs when adult neighbors are awake and can hear other suburban noise.

Courts find greater evidence of unreasonable interference the higher the volume of a noise and the more abrasive its sound. See Smith, 158 N.W.2d at 468 (citing Borsvold, 81 N.W.2d at 382). In Smith, the court agreed that explosive noises from a gun shooting range could unreasonably interfere with the neighbors' peace and quiet if the noises exceeded 88-1/4 decibels at one-quarter-mile distance. See id. at 472 (enjoining noise in excess of that level). Similarly, in Cunningham, the court agreed that bursts of noise from football game spectators could unreasonably interfere with the neighbors' peace and quiet where the noise measured 80 or 90 decibels, which "would be like being . . . behind a power lawn mower." 2001 WL 716882, at *4 n.5. In Wilke, the court found that rock-crushing noise at a cement plant did unreasonably interfere with the neighbors' peace and quiet, in part because it exceeded 100 decibels and sounded like a jet engine from 200 feet away. 2007 WL 1828788, at *4. In Mackenzie, the court found that noise from a saw at a lumberyard unreasonably interfered with the neighbors' peace and quiet where it produced a "high-pitched, screeching, whistling" sound. 174 N.W. at 163.

On the other hand, courts find less evidence of unreasonable interference as the frequency and duration of the noise decrease, and they tend to give frequency and duration greater weight than the sheer volume and abrasiveness of the noise. See Smith, 158 N.W.2d at 471. For example, in Smith, the court found that noise from a gun shooting range was not unreasonable, "especially considering" that the noise happened very infrequently, during approximately ten competitive meets each year. Id. Similarly, in Cunningham, the court found that spectator noise at high-school football games fell "short of constituting an unreasonable burden," with only three or four home games each season and between eleven and twenty-four loud bursts of noise during each game. 2001 WL 716882, at *4. In Radziewicz, the court found that noise from a paddlewheel boat's whistle was not unreasonable where the boat made seven or fewer tours a day, the whistle sounded only several times each tour, and the whistle blasts lasted no more than six seconds. 2009 WL 297433, at *2-3. Notably, in both Smith and Cunningham, the courts found the infrequency of the interference more important than its volume: both noises exceeded 80 decibels, Smith, 158 N.W.2d at 469-70; Cunningham, 2001 WL 716882, at *4, and the court in Cunningham characterized the loudest noises as "extreme eruptions of sound," which would "disturb[] . . . a reasonable person," 2001 WL 716882, at *4. The courts in both cases found the interference was not unreasonable because the loud noises did not occur often enough. Smith, 158 N.W.2d at 471; Cunningham, 2001 WL 716882, at *4.

In addition, courts find less evidence of unreasonable interference the more the noise is confined to adults' waking hours and times when other, ordinary noise occurs. See Smith, 158 N.W.2d at 468 (citing Borsvold, 81 N.W.2d 378). Whereas the court in O'Connor found that loud noise from delivery trucks at a creamery was unreasonable in part because it continued throughout the night, 248 N.W. at 558 (enjoining creamery's operation from 11:00 p.m. until 6:30 a.m.), the court in Radziewicz found that noise from a paddlewheel boat's whistle was not unreasonable in part because the boat stopped operating by 9:00 p.m., 2009 WL 2974733, at *2. As these decisions suggest, the courts appear to equate the time when noise may become unreasonable with the time when adults go to bed. See supra pp. 7-8. Although "unreasonable noise may be enjoined whenever it occurs[,]" Smith, 158 N.W.2d at 469; see, e.g., Mackenzie, 174 N.W. at 166 (enjoining use of lumberyard's loudest saws throughout workday), the courts also consider the other noises occurring at or around the same time before deciding whether one particular noise is unreasonable. For example, in

Smith, the court found that noise from a gun shooting range was not unreasonable, in part because it was masked by the sounds of birds and cars in the background. 158 N.W.2d at 470; see also Borsvold, 81 N.W.2d at 382 ("No one is entitled to absolute quiet in the enjoyment of his property; he may only insist upon a degree of quietness consistent with the standard of comfort prevailing in the locality in which he dwells."). If a noise is reasonable according to other factors the courts consider, the courts do not find it unreasonable simply because it continues into the night. Childs, 2001 WL 1199901, at *4. In Childs, the court found that ordinary vehicular noise from a Super K-Mart parking lot did not cause unreasonable interference, even though the store operated twenty-four hours a day. Id.

Here, a court would almost certainly find some evidence of unreasonable interference because the motorcycle noise from Mr. Hendricks's business is loud and potentially disruptive. We do not know the decibel level of the noise, but the volume is probably at least as great as that of a power lawn mower, if not quite as great as that from a jet engine—both of which the courts have said might produce unreasonable interference. Wilke, 2007 WL 1828788, at *4 (jet engine); Cunningham, 2001 WL 717882, at *4 n.5 (power mower). We do know that the motorcycle engines produce bursts of explosive noise, as if combining the disruptive features of the gun shot sounds in Smith, 158 N.W.2d at 472, and the crowd noise in Cunningham, 2001 WL 717882, at *4 n.5. A court would very likely regard these characteristics as evidence of unreasonable interference.

Conversely, a court would probably find no evidence of unreasonable interference in the infrequency and short duration of the motorcycle noise, and those characteristics would tend to outweigh the volume and abrasiveness of the noise. We do not know exactly how often Mr. Hendricks tests the engines he repairs or how long he runs them. Judging from the limited number of customers he has, however—five or six from the immediate neighborhood and some others from surrounding areas—

Mr. Hendricks may not be fully occupied at work even when he is open for business. When he does have work, he must spend more time disassembling the engines, identifying what needs to be fixed, obtaining or repairing the parts, and reassembling the engines than he does running the engines to diagnose them at the start of a job or to test them when he has finished. Moreover, not every motorcycle Mr. Hendricks accepts to work on requires engine repair; for those jobs, it may not be necessary to run the engines at all. Thus, a court would likely find the noise from Mr. Hendricks's business is more analogous to the bursts of noise from the football spectators in Cunningham, 2001 WL 716882, at *3, loud but infrequent and brief, than it is to the loud and continuous noise from the lumberyard machinery in Mackenzie, 174 N.W. at 166, or from the stone-crushing machinery at the cement plant in Wilke, 2007 WL 1828788, at *4. As such, the noise would not unreasonably interfere with Mr. Lambert's household activities.

Nor would a court be likely to find evidence of unreasonable interference in Mr. Hendricks's evening and weekend hours of operation. First, the noise ends before most adults go to bed. Mr. Hendricks stops work in the evenings by 10:00 p.m. or 11:00 p.m., an hour or two later than 9:00 p.m., the last time each day when the paddlewheel boat blew its whistle in Radziewicz, which the court found reasonable, 2009 WL 2974733, at *3. He stops work no later than 11:00 p.m., the time when the court in O'Connor deemed it necessary to enjoin noise from the creamery so it would not disturb the neighbors, 248 N.W. at 558. The court in Radziewicz did not have to decide whether noises later than 9:00 p.m. might disturb the neighbors, see 2009 WL 2974733, at *2-3, whereas the court in O'Connor did address the question and found that 11:00 p.m. was the time when interference from noise in the neighborhood could become unreasonable, 248 N.W. at 558. Implicit in O'Connor's reasoning is the assumption that most adults do not go to bed earlier than 11:00 p.m.; the creamery's noise became unreasonable only when adults went to bed. Id. Mr. Hendricks stops working before most adults in his neighborhood go to bed. A court would likely find no evidence that his hours of operation lead to unreasonable interference.

Second, other noises fill the neighborhood at the same times when Mr. Hendricks runs his motorcycles. The court in Smith found that in a given location, ambient noise of various kinds can minimize the interference from one particular source of noise. 158 N.W.2d at 470. In North Ypsilanti, residents are subject to ordinary, suburban noise from multiple sources during the evenings and on the weekends, such as music from the college students living in the area, voices from other neighbors' outdoor entertaining, and the sound of motorcycle owners in the neighborhood—probably more than just the five or six who are Mr. Hendricks's customers—starting and driving their machines. A court would likely find that the motorcycle noise is no more unreasonable than any other ordinary aural interference to which Mr. Lambert is subject before 11:00 p.m. and on weekends.

On balance, a court would probably find that the character of the noise from Mr. Hendricks's business provides little evidence of unreasonable interference.

C. Necessity and Value of the Conduct

A third factor courts evaluate when deciding if noise creates an unreasonable interference is the necessity and value of the conduct responsible for the noise, compared to the harms of which the plaintiff complains. Waier, 251 N.W. at 553; Adams, 602 N.W.2d at 219, 222-23. A court would probably find that noise is necessary to a motorcycle repair business and that the social and economic value of Mr. Hendricks's business outweighs Mr. Lambert's complaints about the noise it produces.

The necessity or unavoidability of creating noise during an activity tends to lessen the unreasonableness of any disturbance the noise causes. Waier, 251 N.W at 553. In Waier, ordinary noise from moving and loading railroad tank cars and trucks at an oil refinery was unavoidable and gave neighboring residents no cause to complain. Id. at 552-53. But "unnecessary" noise produced when the workers permitted the iron tank covers "to drop and strike the . . . tanks with a loud clang" made that noise unreasonable. Id. (also finding employees' loud talking unnecessary and easily avoidable). In Radziewicz, whistle soundings necessary to the safe and lawful operation of a paddlewheel boat gave a riverside property owner no cause to complain, 2009 WL 2974733, at *3, whereas in Borsvold, early-morning noise from milk trucks leaving a dairy company's parking lot was a nuisance to nearby homeowners—in part, the court suggested, because the company failed to implement "alternate plans" that could have reduced or eliminated the noise, see 81 N.W.2d at 382. Noise may be unreasonable "even though it arises from the operation of a factory, industrial plant, or other lawful business or occupation." Id. Noise becomes more reasonable, however, when it is both inherent in the nature of a business and no greater than necessary for the "prudent operation" of the business. Radziewicz, 2009 WL 2974733, at *2 (citing Louisville & N.R. Co. v. Commonwealth, 166 S.W. 237, 237-38 (Ky. Ct. App. 1914)); see also Childs, 2001 WL 1199901, at *4 (finding residents failed to prove that objectionable noise from cars, trucks, and pedestrians resulted from anything other than "ordinary operation" of retail superstore).

Similarly, the social benefits of noise-producing activity tend to lessen the overall unreasonableness of any disturbance the noise causes. Adams, 602 N.W.2d at 219 & n.10, 223 (noting doctrine of nuisance requires "public-policy assessment of [the] overall value" of defendant's conduct). In Cunningham, "the benefit that [high school] students, parents, faculty and the community derived from" Friday evening football games outweighed the disturbance certain neighbors experienced from the spectators' noise. 2001 WL 716882, at *4. Among other things, the games fostered a stronger sense of community, provided Friday evening activities for students, and permitted lacrosse, soccer, and track events to be scheduled on other, early-weekday evenings when more parents could attend them. Id. In Childs, the benefits of constructing a Super K-Mart store in place of a crime-filled lot in Detroit outweighed the "noise pollution" the store allegedly created for a nearby family. 2001 WL 1199901, at *3-4. The store reduced neighborhood crime, increased commerce in the area, and was likely to increase local property values. Id. at *4. In Radziewicz, the benefits of whistle soundings from a paddlewheel boat outweighed the disturbance one riverside property owner experienced from the noise. 2009 WL 2974733, at *3. Not only did the soundings ensure the safe operation of the boat and other watercraft using the river, but they also facilitated a tourist business of economic value to the community at large. Id. at *2-3. Conversely, in Wilke, the benefits of a concrete plant were outweighed by the extremely loud and continuous rock-crushing noise it produced, even though the plant was "undoubtedly valuable to the surrounding community." 2007 WL 1828788, at *4.

A court would likely find that the necessity of noise to a motorcycle repair business lessens the unreasonableness of the disturbances Mr. Lambert experiences. Mr. Hendricks knows that his business creates noise, so he tries to limit the number of startups each day. Nevertheless, some noise is unavoidable; it would be impossible to conduct a motorcycle repair business without creating noise. In Childs, the court found that noise emanating from the ordinary operation of a Super K-Mart store was not unreasonable absent any zoning restrictions. 2001 WL 1199901, at *4. Here, a court would probably find that noise produced by the ordinary operation of Mr. Hendricks's business is not unreasonable, either—and that there are no zoning restrictions on the use of North Ypsilanti residential properties for home businesses. Further, just as the courts in Waier and Radziewicz distinguished the permissible noise of a business operated in a "careful and prudent manner" from the unacceptable noise of a business operated recklessly, carelessly, or negligently, Waier, 251 N.W. at 553; Radziewicz, 2009 WL 2974733, at *2 (quoting Louisville & N.R. Co., 166 S.W. at 238), a court would recognize that Mr. Hendricks deliberately limits the startups to those that are absolutely necessary. The necessity of the noise, and Mr. Hendricks's considerate management of the noise, would probably lessen the unreasonableness of the disturbance his noise causes to Mr. Lambert.

A court would also probably find that the social benefits of Mr. Hendricks's motorcycle repair business outweigh the harmful effects of the noise from its operation. Mr. Hendricks's business promotes public safety. His repairs ensure that his customers are driving properly functioning motorcycles. A number of the customers reside in North Ypsilanti. Mr. Hendricks's work contributes both to their safety and the safety of the community at large, just as the whistle soundings in Radziewicz contributed to the safety of the paddlewheel boat's customers and others on and around the river, 2009 WL 2974733, at *3. In addition, Mr. Hendricks's business contributes to his own and his community's economic well-being. The business provides him with supplemental income in a tough economy, so he can make ends meet and avoid losing his home. Maintaining his home also helps support the property values in North Ypsilanti—which have already suffered from foreclosures elsewhere in the neighborhood—a benefit comparable to that in Childs, where the presence of a Super K-Mart store was likely to increase the value of nearby residential properties, 2001 WL 1199901, at *4. Overall, a court would probably find the social utility of Mr. Hendricks's motorcycle repair business outweighs its harmful effects on Mr. Lambert.

For all of these reasons, a court would probably conclude that the noise from Mr. Hendricks's business does not constitute an unreasonable interference.

CONCLUSION

A Michigan court would probably determine that the noise produced by Mr. Hendricks's motorcycle repair business is not a private nuisance. Neither key element of the test for private nuisance is present. The noise does not create significant harm because Mr. Lambert's migraines and his children's interrupted sleep do not represent actual physical discomfort to ordinary persons, and the interference with his backyard entertaining represents only minimal harm. Nor does the noise create an unreasonable interference. The noise is loud and the neighborhood is residential, but the sound is a type of ordinary street noise that is sporadic, brief, and limited to adults' waking hours. Moreover, the social utility of Mr. Hendricks's business far outweighs the interference with Mr. Lambert's rights.

MEMORANDUM

TO: Senior Attorney
FROM: Junior Attorney
DATE: January 25, 2010
RE: Law Firm Disqualification in the Eastern District of Michigan

---

INTRODUCTION

One of our new associates, John Gillespie, split his 2009 summer between our firm and opposing counsel in the Minton Mobile litigation, Torin & Conover. While at Torin, Mr. Gillespie did some legal work for Defendant Clark Monroe on a matter involved in the case. Mr. Gillespie is personally disqualified from working on the case for us, and today, on his first day or work, we notified the Eastern District that we have screened him from any involvement in the case. Nevertheless, the Torin firm may move to disqualify us from continuing to represent Minton Mobile in the lawsuit.

You have asked me to determine how stringently the Eastern District courts apply the screening and notification requirements of Michigan Rule of Professional Conduct 1.10(b) to law firms subject to a motion to disqualify counsel.

SUMMARY

In general, the Eastern District courts strictly construe both requirements. The courts require "timely" screening, which obliges the hiring firm to implement effective screening measures at least as soon as the firm becomes aware of the potential conflict. Similarly, the courts insist on written notice; oral notice will not do. The courts require notice prompt enough to allow them to oversee the proper screening of the infected attorney, but in an exceptional case, they may overlook a delayed notice if the screening was timely and effective and the delay was not very long.

DISCUSSION

The Michigan Rules of Professional Conduct (MRPC) apply in the Eastern District of Michigan. E.D. Mich. LR 83.22(b). Rule 1.10(b) governs the imputed disqualification of a hiring law firm when a new attorney at the firm would be personally disqualified from representing a client with interests adverse to those of the attorney's old client. MPRC 1.10(a).

> (b) When a lawyer becomes associated with a firm, the firm may not knowingly represent a person in the same or a substantially related matter in which that lawyer, or a firm with which the lawyer was associated, is disqualified under Rule 1.9(b), unless:
>
> (1) the disqualified lawyer is screened from any participation in the matter and is apportioned no part of the fee therefrom; and
>
> (2) written notice is promptly given to the appropriate tribunal to enable it to ascertain compliance with the provisions of this rule.

Id. 1.10(b). The rule allows the hiring firm to avoid disqualification if it screens the infected attorney from all participation in and compensation from the matter from which the attorney is disqualified, id. 1.10(b)(1), and if the firm "promptly" gives written notice of its compliance with the rule to the court adjudicating the litigation, id. 1.10(b)(2).

A. The Screening Requirement: Rule 1.10(b)(1)

Eastern District of Michigan courts require timely and comprehensive screening of an infected attorney.

Timely screening. Although the language of Rule 1.10(b)(1) is silent as to timing, the Eastern District courts construe it to require "timely" screening, consistent with the Rule's objective of protecting client confidences. Cobb Publ'g, Inc. v. Hearst Corp. (Cobb I), 907 F. Supp. 1038, 1048-49 (E.D. Mich. 1995). In Cobb I, the leading Eastern District decision on law firm disqualification, the court found that a hiring firm's screening measures were not timely when they began eleven days after an infected attorney had joined the firm. Id. at 1049. The firm's failure to implement a timely screen created the risk that confidential information about the attorney's old client could have been disclosed to his new firm—a risk "that the provisions of M.R.P.C. 1.10(b) were intended to eliminate." Id. at 1050 n.9. As the court put it in a later opinion in the same case, "time is of the essence for the 'infected' firm to establish the necessary protective devices," to guard the confidences of the former client and to demonstrate to the client and the public "that the legal profession is responsive to the confidences of the clients that it serves." Cobb Publ'g, Inc. v. Hearst Corp. (Cobb II), 891 F. Supp. 388, 393 (E.D. Mich. 1995) (denying hiring firm's motion for reconsideration).

Relation to disqualifying event. To ensure that screening measures are timely, the Eastern District courts require a hiring firm to implement them no later than the time when the "potentially disqualifying event occur[s], either when the attorney first join[s] the firm or when the firm accept[s] a case presenting an ethical problem." Cobb I, 907 F. Supp. at 1047 (quoting LaSalle Nat'l Bank v. Cty. of Lake, 703 F.2d 252, 259 (7th Cir. 1983)). In Cobb I, the hiring firm violated the timely screening requirement by failing to implement a screen on the date the new attorney joined the firm, by accepting its offer of employment, or on the date he started work, a week later. Id. at 1049. The attorney had informed the firm's recruitment coordinator of the conflict when they scheduled his job interviews, a month before he accepted the firm's offer. Id. at 1040. But the firm failed to act on that knowledge before the disqualifying event—the attorney's joining the firm—occurred. Id. at 1047. Conversely, in Faith Baptist Church v. Waterford Township., No. 08-11028, 2009 WL 3756891, at *2 (E.D. Mich. Nov. 6, 2009), a hiring firm complied with the timely screening requirement by implementing a screen as soon as the new attorney's employment began. (The firm was disqualified, however, because it failed to provide written notice of the employment to the court. Id.) In Walker v. Sweet Cravings, Inc., No. 89-CV-73084-DT, 1990 WL 300284, at *4 (E.D. Mich. Sept. 6, 1990), a law firm complied with the timely screening requirement where the potentially disqualifying event involved a new case presenting an ethical problem, rather than the employment of a new attorney with a conflict of interest. The firm implemented a screen as soon as it discovered that one partner had named as a defendant in a lawsuit he was handling a company that another partner had previously represented in a small, unrelated matter. Id.

Risk of confidence sharing. In weighing a firm's response to a potentially disqualifying event, the Eastern District courts apply the timely screening requirement more stringently where the risk of confidence sharing is high. In the Cobb litigation, the court found that the hiring firm violated the timely screening requirement in part because the facts indicated a "significant potential" for violating the former client's confidences. Cobb II, 891 F. Supp. at 392. The new, infected attorney had played a major role in the case at his old firm; he worked more than 300 hours on it and had extensive contact with the client. Id. at 389 n.2. When he joined the hiring firm, he brought part of his old case file with him, and he could have uploaded the former client's confidential information to the hiring firm's computer file on the case, to which he had access. Id. at 392. Moreover, the hiring firm did not implement a screen until after the infected attorney's old firm moved to disqualify his new one—confirming that the hiring firm was not "sensitive to the potential for conflict." Id. The court readily found that the hiring firm violated the timely screening requirement. Id. at 394. In Guaranty Residential v. Homestead Mortgage LLC, No. 04-74842, 2007 U.S. Dist. Lexis 35275, at *3-4, (E.D. Mich. May 15, 2007), however, the court found no evidence that the hiring firm violated the timely screening requirement where the risk of disclosing client confidences was very low.

The new, infected attorney had minimal involvement in the case at his old firm; he wrote only a single, short memo about it; he did not remove his case files when he left the firm; and the hiring firm screened him from any contact with the case as soon as it employed him. Id. at *3.

Comprehensive screening. Given the omnipresent risk of confidence sharing when conflicts exist, the Eastern District courts require the hiring firm to "persuasively demonstrate to [the] judicial arbiter" that the firm's screening measures are "truly impenetrable." Cobb I, 907 F. Supp. at 1048. In American Sigma, Inc. v. QED Environmental Systems, Inc., No. 87-CV-70070-DT, 1989 U.S. Dist. Lexis 10358, at *5-6 (E.D. Mich. Nov. 7, 1989), cited with approval in Cobb I, 907 F. Supp. at 1048, a hiring firm satisfied the court that its measures for screening two new, infected attorneys and their support staff were effective in preventing any disclosures. The firm segregated the infected attorneys and staff from any participation or access to the files in the matter, required their written acknowledgement of the segregation, prohibited all firm personnel from discussing the matter in their presence, and, by virtue of the two attorneys' specific employment arrangements, prevented them from receiving any fees derived from the matter. Id. at 6-8 & 8 nn.5-6. In Guaranty Residential, the hiring firm, much smaller than the one in American Sigma, also satisfied the court that its measures for screening an infected attorney were effective. 2007 U.S. Dist. Lexis 35275, at *4. The firm segregated the attorney from any participation in and any verbal or physical contact regarding the case, instructed the entire staff to comply with the segregation, and paid the attorney, an associate, no compensation based on the fees from the case. Id. at *3-4. But in Cobb, the hiring firm, comparable in size to the firm in American Sigma, could not demonstrate that it had implemented any of these protections during the infected attorney's first eleven days at work, and the court duly disqualified it. Cobb I, 907 F. Supp. at 1049-50.

B. The Notice Requirement: Rule 1.10(b)(2)

The Eastern District courts insist upon receiving written notice of a potential conflict promptly enough for them to oversee the hiring firm's screening measures, but in limited circumstances they may overlook a short delay.

Written notice. In general, the Eastern District courts construe the "written notice" language strictly: oral notice is not acceptable. In the Cobb litigation, the court disqualified the hiring firm on the partial ground that it failed to provide written notice to the court when it employed the infected attorney. Cobb I, 907 F. Supp. at 1049. In Faith Baptist Church, the court disqualified the hiring firm on the sole ground that it failed to provide written notice when it hired the opposing client's primary attorney—even though the firm had screened him as soon as he started work. 2009 WL 3756891, at *2. The attorney's timely motion to withdraw as plaintiff's counsel did not disclose his new employer, and although he had notified a magistrate judge in the case of his new employment at a motion hearing on the day before, "he did not do so in writing, as required by the rule." Id. at *1-2; see also Nat'l Union Fire Ins. Co. of Pittsburgh, Pa. v. Alticor, Inc., 472 F.3d 436, (6th Cir. 2007) (holding, in case arising in Western District, that hiring firm's failure to provide court with written notice of infected attorney's employment required firm's disqualification).

Prompt notice. Nevertheless, the Eastern District courts may construe the prompt written notice requirement more leniently in an exceptional case, where the hiring firm fully complied with the screening requirement and its delay in providing written notice was only slight. In Guaranty Residential, the court found that the hiring firm "effectively complied" with the requirements of Rule 1.10(b) by screening the infected attorney from the start of his employment, even though the firm did not provide written notice to the court until eight days after the firm entered an appearance in the case. U.S. Dist. Lexis 35275, at *4-5. At an evidentiary hearing on the motion to disqualify, the court assured itself that "extensive protections" had been and still were in place and that the hiring firm and the infected attorney were committed to honoring them. Id. Based on those protections, the court decided that the eight-day delay was "not a fatal flaw." Id. at *5. Conversely, in Faith Baptist Church, the court found that the hiring firm failed to comply with the requirements of Rule 1.10(b) where the firm properly screened the infected attorney from the start of his employment but took more than three months to provide written notice to the court. See 2009 WL 3756891, at *1-2. Such a long delay was a fatal flaw. See id. In the Cobb litigation, where the hiring firm blatantly disregarded its screening obligations under Rule 1.10(b), the court was not willing to overlook a delay in providing written notice that was shorter than three months but longer than eight days. 907 F. Supp. at 1049. The firm provided notice "23 days after the 'infected' attorney joined the firm, 16 days after he began work there and 15 days after [the firm] had appeared before the Court on a matter involving that very same case." In the circumstances, the delay was also a fatal flaw. Id.

Woodside-Parker Noncompetition Agreement

Junior Attorney jattorney@newmanbenedetti.com Fri. Mar. 13, 2015 at 2:31 PM

To: dbenedetti@newmanbenedetti.com

Dean:

As you requested, I have drafted a noncompetition agreement between our client, Woodside Review, and Charlene Parker, the seller's CEO in Woodside's acquisition of the assets of Steeplechase Test Preparation. Parker's execution of the agreement is a condition to Woodside's obligation to close, and Woodside has instructed us to draft the agreement to incorporate the maximum restrictions on Parker's post-closing activities that a Michigan court will enforce. This e-mail summarizes the major provisions I have included in my draft.

Model agreement

My draft is based on a publicly available noncompetition agreement used in the acquisition of the assets of another educational services company, which, like the Woodside-Steeplechase transaction, primarily involved the transfer of proprietary intellectual property. Although both that transaction and the noncompetition agreement were governed by New York law, I have edited the provisions in my draft to conform to Michigan statutory and decisional law. For your convenience, I am attaching clean and marked-up copies of the draft agreement. The specific noncompetition restrictions are included in Section 1.

Michigan law on noncompetition agreements

Michigan permits the use of noncompetition agreements to protect a company's reasonable competitive business interests, provided that the restrictions are reasonable as to duration, geographical area, and type of employment or line of business. Mich. Comp. Laws Ann. § 445.774a(1) (West, Westlaw through P.A. 2015 No. 6) (limited to employment context); Bristol Window & Door v. Hoogenstyn, 650 N.W.2d 670, 680 (Mich. Ct. App. 2002) (clarifying that Michigan courts apply statute to both employment and non-employment contexts). Courts more readily enforce noncompetition agreements entered into during the sale of a business than those signed in ordinary employment relationships. M. Scott McDonald & Jacqueline C. Johnson, Drafting and Enforcing Covenants Not to Compete § 3.II(A), at 49 (2014), Bloomberg Law.

Key provisions

- **Recitals: Competitive business interests.** The Recitals identify several of Woodside's competitive business interests in the underlying transaction:

- to purchase the goodwill and proprietary, confidential intellectual property associated with the successful Steeplechase test preparation methods and materials;
- to incorporate those methods and materials into Woodside's own operations and then to expand its operations nationally; and
- to protect its investment by requiring Parker, who created the intellectual property and made the Steeplechase business successful, not to compete with Woodside while the agreement is in force.

Courts recognize that these kinds of interests are reasonable to protect by means of a noncompetition agreement. See, e.g., Perceptron, Inc. v. Sensor Adaptive Machs., Inc., 221 F.3d 913, 920 (6th Cir. 2000) (applying Michigan law).

- § **1: Noncompetition (duration).** The agreement would remain in force for four years. In M&A transactions, courts find that durations as long as five years can be reasonable, e.g., to enable the purchaser "to establish itself as a full-fledged market participant." Id. (finding five-year duration reasonable in asset purchase transaction); see also Spradlin v. Lakestates Workplace Solutions, Inc. (In re Spradlin), 282 B.R. 830, 836 (E.D. Mich. 2002) (same). Woodside has advised us that it intends to complete its business plan of expansion within four years after the acquisition. A four-year duration should be reasonable, since it is no longer than necessary.

- § **1: Noncompetition (geographic scope).** The agreement would apply throughout the U.S. In both business and employment contexts, courts find that a very broad geographic restriction can be reasonable if the company's interests are sufficiently national or international in scope. See, e.g., Lowry Computer Prods. v. Head, 984 F. Supp. 1111, 1116 (E.D. Mich. 1997) (finding unlimited scope reasonable where employer had accounts in 48 states and various foreign countries). The academic admission tests are standardized across the country, and the test preparation business operates nationally, especially with the proliferation of online instructional platforms. Woodside has a reasonable interest in preventing Parker from working for another test prep company—or starting a new one—in a state where Woodside does not yet operate but from which she could compete with Woodside in the states where it does, or will soon, operate.

- § **1: Noncompetition (type of employment).** The agreement would prevent Parker from competing with Woodside in the academic admission test preparation business by "creating, designing, producing, manufacturing, publishing, distributing, or conducting individual or group instruction using test preparation strategies or materials based on the intellectual property rights" she sold to Woodside. Courts recognize that key personnel with knowledge of a company's trade secrets and confidential information can make unfair use of that knowledge if they later compete with the company. See, e.g., Kelly Servs. v. Eidnes, 530 F. Supp. 2d 940, 952 (E.D. Mich. 2008) (enjoining owner of temporary legal services business, acquired by national corporation, from using her extensive knowledge of the business at direct competitor). Parker created the intellectual property she sold to Woodside, and so Woodside has a reasonable interest in preventing her from using her knowledge of it at a competing academic test prep company.

- § **2: Nondisclosure.** The agreement would also prevent Parker from disclosing any portion of the intellectual property she sold to Woodside, either during or after the four-year term of the agreement. A separate nondisclosure clause enables the enforcing company to prevent dissemination of its confidential information without having to prove that the restricted individual made noncompetitive use of it. See McDonald & Johnson, supra, § 4.I(B), at 113-14. Any disclosure by Parker of the intellectual property she sold to Woodside, even if she were not personally involved in using it, would dilute the value of Woodside's purchase and frustrate its business objectives.

Other provisions

The agreement contains certain other provisions, common in noncompetition agreements, that also protect Woodside's interests, including:

- **§ 3: Specific performance**, to ensure that Woodside can enforce the agreement should Parker breach or threaten to breach any of the restrictions in sections 1 or 2;
- **§ 4: Severability**, to ensure that the rest of the agreement remains in force should a court deem any provision unenforceable;
- **§ 7: Governing law**, to ensure that the agreement is subject to Michigan law, without regard to its choice of law provisions; and
- **§ 8: Consent to jurisdiction and venue**, to ensure that Woodside and Parker bring any claim under the agreement in a state or federal court in Michigan, without objections as to jurisdiction or venue.

Please let me know if you have any questions. I would be happy to meet with you at your convenience to discuss them.

Junior

Index